P9-BIN-043

THE PURSUIT OF HAPPINESS

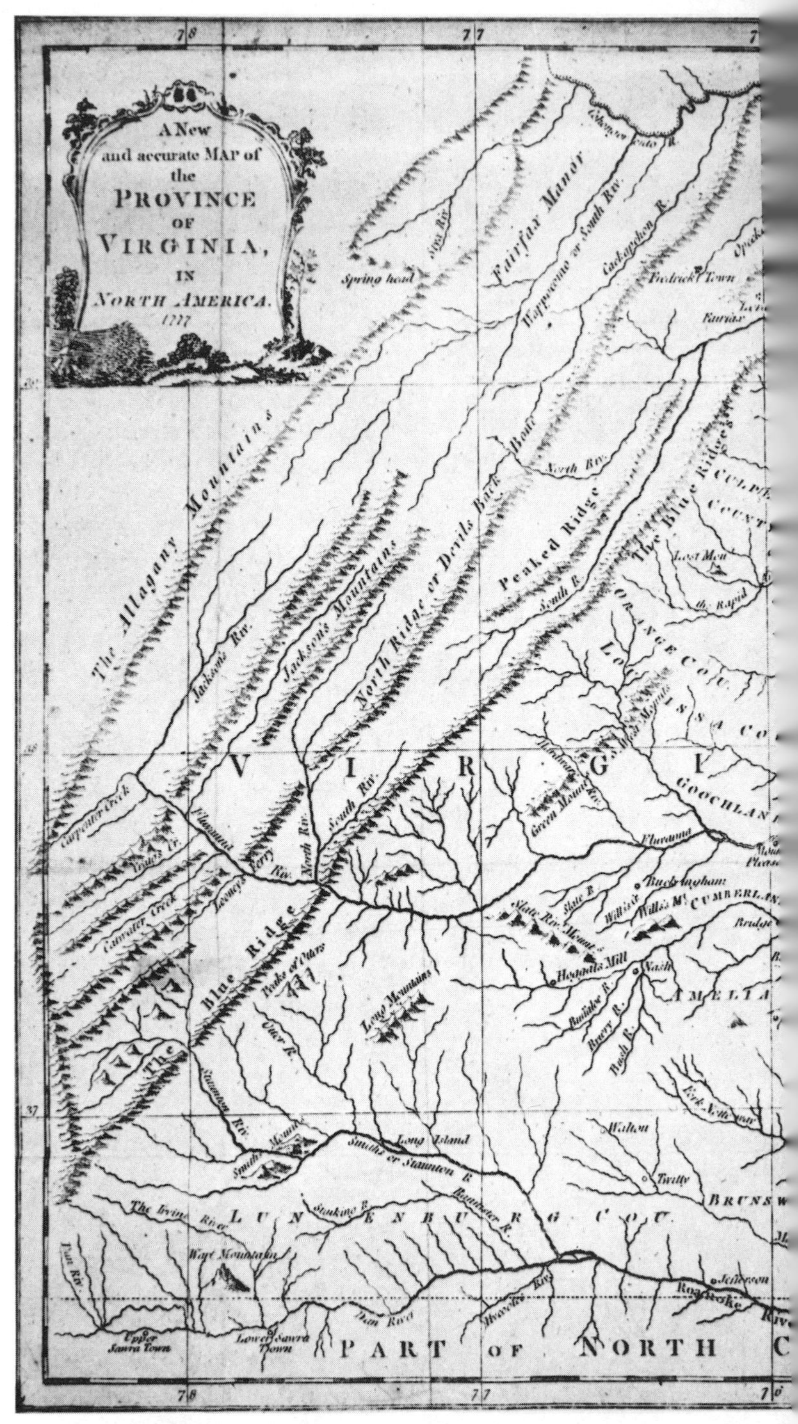

Virginia, 1777. (The Newberry Library.)

PART OF MARYLAND
Chester
Chester Riv.
Queen's Town
Annapolis
London
Severn R.
Colchester
Charles Town
Oxford
Bolingbroke
Poplar I.
Patowmack
Port Royal
Blackstones I.
St. Marys
Pt. Lookout
Somerset
Boundary Line of Virginia & Maryland in 1668
Accomac C.
Northampton County
Teachers I.
Parramore I.
Revels I.
Matchapungo I.
Rack I. Inlet
Moken I.
Smiths I.
C. Charles
Cape Henry
Hampton
York
Williamsburg
Newcastle
Walkerton
Delawar
Glocester
York River
James River
James City Co.
Henrico Cou.
Charles City Co.
Richmond
Cumberland
Urbanna
Windmill Pt.
Isle of Wight Co.
Suffolk
Norfolk
Portsmouth
Princes Ann Cou.
Nandsemond Cou.
South Hampton Cou.
Nottoway Riv.
the Black Water
Long I.
Cedar I.
Curratuck Inlet
Hermitage I.
Curratuck Sound
LINA
74 West from London

The pursuit of happiness

Family and values in Jefferson's Virginia

JAN LEWIS

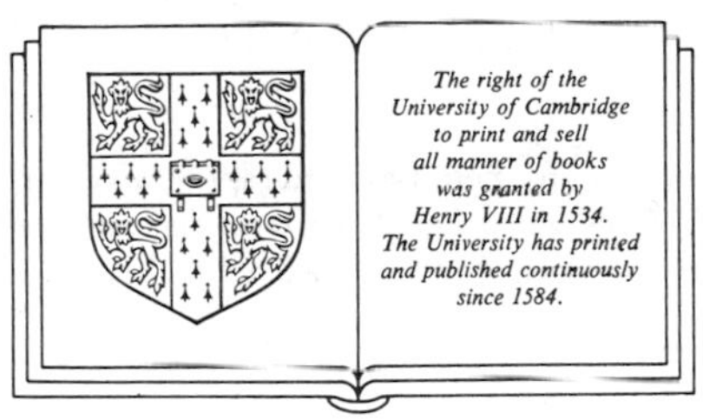
The right of the University of Cambridge to print and sell all manner of books was granted by Henry VIII in 1534. The University has printed and published continuously since 1584.

CAMBRIDGE UNIVERSITY PRESS

Cambridge

London New York New Rochelle

Melbourne Sydney

Published by the Press Syndicate of the University of Cambridge
The Pitt Building, Trumpington Street, Cambridge CB2 1RP
32 East 57th Street, New York, NY 10022, USA
296 Beaconsfield Parade, Middle Park, Melbourne 3206, Australia

First published 1983
Reprinted 1983 , 1984

Printed in the United States of America

Library of Congress Cataloging in Publication Data

Lewis, Jan, 1949-
The pursuit of happiness.

Bibliography: p.

Includes index.

1. Family - Virginia - History - 18th century.
2. Virginia - Gentry - History - 18th century.
3. Social values - History - 18th century.
4. Happiness - History - 18th century. I. Title.
HQ535.L44 1983 306.8'5'09755 83-1786
ISBN 0 521 25306 3

I thank the publisher for permission to reprint an excerpt from "Men Made Out of Words" from *The Collected Poems of Wallace Stevens*, by Wallace Stevens, © 1954 by Alfred A. Knopf, Inc.

FOR

JOHN TAYLOR LEWIS

1952–1978

Contents

List of plates xi

Preface xiii

Acknowledgments xvii

1 *"My peaceable scheme"*
The world of the pre-Revolutionary gentry
page 1

2 *"The real use of religion"*
Religion
page 40

3 *"Weep for yourselves"*
Death
page 69

4 *"Little ambitions"*
Success
page 106

5 *"Earthly connexions"*
Love
page 169

Contents

6 *"The best feelings of our nature"*
Conclusion
page 209

List of abbreviations used in notes 231

Notes 232

Bibliographical essay 272

A note on the sources 279

Selected bibliography 282

Index 285

Plates

Virginia, 1777		*frontispiece*
1.	The first floor of Tuckahoe	7
2.	William Byrd II	13
3.	Westover	14
4.	The first floor of Westover	16
5.	The old landscape and the new	33
6.	The first floor of Sabine Hall	34
7.	Ellen Wayles Randolph Coolidge	42
8.	Frances Bland Randolph	73
9.	John Hartwell Cocke	87
10.	Bremo	88
11.	The first floor of Bremo	90
12.	Temperance temple at Bremo	92
13.	Ege-Galt family	100
14.	Nicholas P. Trist	146
15.	The west front and garden of Monticello	148
16.	Virginia Randolph Cary	194
17.	Eliza Parke Custis	197
18.	The Washington family	206
19.	Woman reading in garden	218

Preface

NO ONE knows precisely what Jefferson had in mind when he asserted "the pursuit of happiness" as one of mankind's unalienable rights. The phrase is in some measure a substitution for Locke's "property," but most historians agree that Jefferson intended something more inclusive and dynamic both. No member of the Virginia gentry would discount the importance, economic or political, of property, but Jefferson seemed to be moving from a cold acceptance of self-interest to a more hopeful notion of social felicity, a secular substitution for the eternal reward. According to the most recent student of the Declaration of Independence, "When Jefferson spoke of pursuing happiness, he had nothing vague or private in mind. He meant a public happiness which is measurable. . . ."[1]

Half a century later, Jefferson's grandson clearly had something other than property or public felicity in mind when he spoke of happiness. Although his grandfather venerated property in the abstract, his devotion to the public good had made him careless with his own quantity of that basic right. As a consequence, it fell to Thomas Jefferson Randolph to save Monticello from his grandfather's creditors. He relied upon his wife to cheer him along his route. "For godsake keep up your spirits," he implored her. "Without you all events will be alike a blank to me. With you only I have known happiness. Your arms have been the haven of all my passions, hopes, & fears."[2] By happiness Randolph surely meant something private, but it was not property. Indeed, it was the pursuit of property that drove him to seek solace in his wife's arms. Happiness for him was domestic and emotional; his pursuit took him home.

During Thomas Jefferson's long life, Virginians came to define happiness in a new way, to pursue it in new arenas. Religion, property, public affairs – all of these shrank in importance for the Jefferson family and for all Virginians, whereas the family became the focus of men's and women's deepest longings. The family signified, and it sanctified as well; "without you," a man told his wife, "all events will be alike a blank to me." At home men and women sought their salvation, and they looked for it in emotions, passions, hopes, fears. No eighteenth-century person would have so inflated the importance of the family or willingly bared his passions. How such a change in feeling about the family – and, indeed, in feeling about feeling itself – took place is the subject of this work.

This study is based upon the letters and diaries, the personal writings, of Virginians from the early eighteenth century to 1830. Admittedly, such sources impose a limitation upon the researcher. People conveyed their feelings through words; they used words to shape their feelings. We do not, two centuries later, experience anger or despair as it was felt at a time in the past. Instead, we read a report of a particular feeling. We are distanced from that emotion, for a man or a woman used words to impose an order upon, to refine, or to elevate the feeling he or she had. There is a further complication: When a woman, for example, reports that she was despondent, how are we to know that she was truly in despair, and not writing what she thought her correspondent would like to hear? And what of the suitor who testifies to his love for a young woman? Or the son who is filled with gratitude to the most loving of parents? Are all of them to be believed, particularly when we know that certain roles would create just as certain expectations?

In analyzing such writings, we have to be attentive to this matter of convention; it can profitably be addressed in several ways. First, that conventions themselves changed is of no little significance. One may well ask, were people unhappy, or was it merely fashionable to be distressed? But are those not in truth variations on the same theme, despondency? Did children love their parents, or did they merely profess to? Either possibility speaks to the hope and expectation that children would love their parents. In addition, in analyzing the writings of individuals who lived long ago, the historian usually comes to know his sources; one becomes familiar with the personalities of those whose letters and diaries are read. One thus may observe how an individual uses and responds to the conventions of the age.

Because it is based upon personal writings from a time and place in which not all men and women were literate,[3] this study is necessarily restricted to a select group, the gentry. Historians use the term *gentry* to designate those few families in each county who "dominated civil, ecclesiastical, and military affairs."[4] They were also a cultural elite, with their own values and style, which gave them the education and the inclination to write.

Several other comments about the method and scope of this work are in order. Changes in family values – in the value accorded the family and the values the family taught – took place in Virginia sometime after (but not necessarily because of) the American Revolution. Such changes, which occurred in people's minds and hearts, took place slowly and affected different people in different ways. As a result, it is not possible to date them precisely, only to show that they first appeared just after the Revolution and were fully realized by 1830, the arbitrary date that historians give to the beginning of the antebellum era and that I give to the conclusion of my study. Further, not all Virginians swam in the currents of their time any more than any individual ever shares all the views and feelings of his culture. In discussing widely shared sentiments and emotions, there is necessarily some imprecision.

Finally, this is a historical work; the methods are primarily those of the historian. Nonetheless, it is informed by the sociological theory of Peter L. Berger, whose rich work proceeds from the assumptions that people are "congenitally compelled to impose a meaningful order upon reality" and that such order is socially created.[5] If the insights and methods of social science are recognized, so also are those of literary criticism. The words of men and women may be examined as closely as if they were written by luminaries, for, as Wallace Stevens observed, "The whole race is a poet that writes down/ The eccentric propositions of its fate."[6]

Acknowledgments

THIS STUDY would not have been possible were it not for the men and women who long ago wrote letters and diaries and for the archives and archivists who have preserved those documents. I wish to thank the staffs of the Manuscripts Division, Library of Congress; the William L. Clements Library, The University of Michigan; the Southern Historical Collection, University of North Carolina Library, Chapel Hill; the Perkins Library, Duke University; the Manuscripts Department, University of Virginia Library; the Earl Gregg Swem Library, College of William and Mary; and the Colonial Williamsburg Foundation, Research Archives. I especially appreciate the University of Virginia Library's loan of microfilmed materials, and permission to quote from material at the University of Virginia and the Colonial Williamsburg Foundation. I am also grateful to several archivists who took an interest in my work and were remarkably helpful: Nancy Merz of Colonial Williamsburg, Margaret Cook and Pamela Boll of William and Mary, and John Dann of the Clements Library.

For help in locating illustrations, I am indebted to James A. Bear, Jr., of the Thomas Jefferson Memorial Foundation. Frank Smith is an editor with more virtues than I have been told any author has a right to expect. I thank him and his assistant Leslie Deutsch and the staff of Cambridge for all they have done.

Acknowledgments

Travel to the South is a wonderful but costly experience. For financial support, I am grateful to The Colonial Williamsburg Foundation for a grant-in-aid for research; the Horace H. Rackham School of Graduate Studies of The University of Michigan for a Rackham Dissertation Grant and a Rackham Predoctoral Fellowship; to the Department of History of The University of Michigan for an Edward S. Beck Fellowship; to Dean David Hosford for a grant from Newark College of Arts and Sciences, Rutgers University; and to the Research Council of Rutgers University for a council grant. A Rutgers University Junior Faculty Research Grant provided a semester's leave.

In its first incarnation, this book was a doctoral dissertation at The University of Michigan, where it was directed by Kenneth Lockridge and Leslie Owens. Les Owens urged me to go South; his love of manuscript research has proved infectious. Ken Lockridge encouraged me to trust what I found. Some read this work so long ago that they may barely recognize it now. Others will find that their comments were so good that I have incorporated them word for word. Others, I hope, will see how important their influence has been. To all I am grateful: W. Andrew Achenbaum, Barry Bienstock, Russell Blake, Paul Clemens, Norman Dain, Erik Grimmelmann, Randall Jimerson, Shaw Livermore, Jr., Drew McCoy, Ellen Mastromonaco, John Shy, Carl Siracusa, and J. Mills Thornton III. Two fine teachers, John Higham and William Freehling, taught me something about the moral and aesthetic dimensions of writing history. I thank Michael Zuckerman for particular suggestions and general encouragement and Rhys Isaac for reading and criticizing the entire manuscript twice and serving as unofficial mentor.

Acknowledgments

My good and true friends Andy, Carl, Barry, and Beth have never asked for thanks, but they get them nonetheless. Barry's keen interest has increased my pleasure in writing this book immeasurably. I am fortunate in having a mother who early taught me to enjoy reading and a father to love history. I thank my son, Jamie, for his cheerful obliviousness to this project, living proof that it has overwhelmed neither his life nor mine.

1
"My peaceable scheme"

THE WORLD OF THE PRE-REVOLUTIONARY GENTRY

THE WORLD Thomas Jefferson departed in 1826 was very different from the one into which he had been born more than eighty years earlier. The state, indeed it was now a state and not a colony, had experienced important alterations in its political, economic, and religious structures, but these changes were encompassed by a different, more important change. Virginians' mental world, their collected hopes and fears, perceptions and values, predispositions and preconceptions, was different from what it once had been. This transformation in the tone of life is, perhaps, nowhere better illlustrated than in the changing fortunes of the Jefferson family itself.

The founder of the Jefferson family in Virginia is unknown. Thomas Jefferson's great-grandfather was a farmer; his grandfather pulled himself up into the gentry and, at his death, left his son Peter some land, several horses, and two slaves. Of Peter Jefferson, Thomas Jefferson's biographer has written: "He cannot be described as a completely self-made man, but the enhancement of his fortunes, like the improvement of his mind, must be chiefly attributed to his own exertions." This "man of deeds, not words" improved his fortune more than his mind, and when he died at the age of forty in 1757, he owned perhaps 7,500 acres and sixty slaves.[1] Thomas Jefferson, born in 1743, was a man of words more than deeds. The fortunes he inherited and married were dissipated by a combination of neglect, conscience, and debts to the British. Thomas Jefferson was a man of many accomplishments; making money was not one of them. His son-in-law, Thomas Mann Randolph, proved no more successful a planter. It was said of him that he took great pleasure in agricultural innovation and that his crops were always the best in the neighborhood; but once the abundant harvest had been gathered and put into the barn, there it rotted, for Randolph found no enjoyment in marketing his crops.[2] The necessity of supporting a huge family in declining circumstances fell to his son, Thomas Jefferson Randolph; he assumed responsibility not only for his wife and twelve children but also for his mother, two unmarried sisters, and five younger siblings. Although Randolph longed for a career in public service like his father and grandfather, his wife convinced him that his duties were at home. Randolph was hard-working, devoted to his wife, a man of neither words nor deeds, who – according to his sister – had an "aversion to music."[3] Four of Randolph's sisters – Ellen, Virginia, Cornelia, and Mary – inherited their grandfather's intellect and talents, yet they also were bequeathed a world in which such traits could not as advantageously be displayed. Prevented by their social position and their sex from struggling with the world as their brother did, they relied upon their brother and their husbands and turned increasingly to religion and to each other.

Although no individual perfectly symbolizes an era, each succeeding generation of Jeffersons was in some measure typical of its age. It took three generations to build the Jefferson fortune and name, three generations to give Thomas

Jefferson the position and the leisure to become a man of words. Yet for all his words, Jefferson rarely wrote about his emotions; he has thus remained curiously obscure, in some ways as remote as his own ancestors. Jefferson's brilliance crippled his son-in-law, who never could rise above his conviction of his own inadequacy; although he wrote little about himself, what he said is often revealing. Because his grandfather was brilliant and his father erratic, Thomas Jefferson Randolph was left to put together the pieces of a broken fortune. Yet he was, in a sense, broken before he started, torn by a desire to live on the scale of his ancestors and by the realization that such a life was no longer possible in Virginia, a state the grandson of the author of the *Notes on the State of Virginia* ruefully dubbed "the last of Nature's works."[4] Like his great-grandfather, his fortune, if it were to be made, would be created by his own exertions, but the world no longer seemed to invite such endeavors as it once had. It is, perhaps, little wonder that Randolph turned to his wife for comfort and that she, in turn, looked toward religion. Their attempts to come to terms with this new world are revealed in letters that are hauntingly transparent.

True, Virginia was different, but the change was not so much in the lives people led as in their thoughts and feelings. Like Thomas Jefferson Randolph, we like to think that our ancestors lived in simpler times, that the world of one's great-grandfather was both more stable and more hospitable to individual effort, as if the one did not exclude the other. But the world has never stood still, especially not for Americans. As Henry James noted just over a century ago, Europe was anchored by its ancient institutions. America, in contrast, had "No State. . . . No sovereign, no court, no personal loyalty, no aristocracy, no church, no clergy . . . no castles nor manors . . . no literature, no novels."[5] America lacked those products of culture that could seem to make time stand still, but even that was part illusion, for even Europe, as we now know, would be shaken by the tides of time. America's New England would be planted by the Puritan church, an institution in the obverse image of the mother country's established church, which, although succumbing to the American environment, would for centuries thereafter be mourned by its divines and despised by its detractors. But Virginia for nearly its first century was a vessel with neither destination nor anchor. Not even its population moored it, for in the first decades the mortality rate was so high that the population could not even reproduce itself. It was not until the late seventeenth century that births outstripped deaths, white immigration was surpassed by black, and the population became increasingly native-born.[6] And it was not until that time that Virginia developed local institutions and communities and, more important, a sense among its people that Virginia was a home, a destination. Then the more prosperous began building brick homes instead of the temporary wooden shelters they had erected earlier, when they had expected to end their days either in England or, all too shortly, a shallow Virginia grave. Virginia had been founded in 1607, but it was not settled until nearly a century later.

It would be a mistake, however, to suggest that eighteenth-century Virginia had achieved stability, a fixity in time. To be sure, order and an approximation of the social structure of England were goals of the men who came to power in Virginia in the years after Bacon's Rebellion. But

Virginia was pulled also by another powerful tide, one that Virginians themselves would have called *independence*, and that was nothing less than the egotism and daring of Drake, Ralegh, Captain John Smith, and a host of lesser schemers, scramblers, and grabbers slowly transforming themselves into the individualism of nineteenth-century America. Virginia in its first decades had been a boom society, rewarding the adept move with the quick dollar. Those clever enough to corner a market or corner less nimble men into planting tobacco for them reaped the rewards such a society has to offer. By the end of the century African slaves had largely replaced white immigrants as a source of labor, and because they, as a despised race, could lay no claim to the hereditary rights of Englishmen, Virginia had found a comparatively secure base. Yet the basis for this arrangement was exploitation backed by force. A century and a half of pro-slavery apologetics would never obscure the fact that the black slave was no villein, bound to his lord. As the blacks were being enslaved, the poorer whites were enfranchised and promised the right to prosper. Even if they did not thrive as did the gentry, even if they deferred to their betters in matters of politics, there was a bond between poor and rich. At the very least, it was the tie of race; at most, a common devotion to independence, the basis for an emerging republican ideology founded upon individual prosperity and minimal responsibility for one's neighbor. This was one of the forces that shaped Virginia: the drive of the individual to make his mark or his fortune, unhindered by his fellow man.

In the nineteenth century this right to fall or succeed on one's own would be idealized as individualism, the birthright of common folk as well as bigger-than-life heroes and thieves. But early in the eighteenth century it was an anomaly with no sanction in custom or creed. And so, as the big men began to feel secure in their fortunes, when after Bacon's Rebellion they no longer feared a white insurrection and knew how to protect themselves from a black one, they tried to mask their origins and create a society as much as possible like the one existing in England. This is the other tide that pulled Virginia, not merely the tendency of a boom society to settle down, but more a conscious, perhaps desperate attempt on the part of its settlers to make it conform to an imported image. We can feel the poignancy in a successful planter's instructions to his young sons, whom he had sent to England in 1748 for an education befitting a gentleman. "Many Children capable of Learning," Richard Ambler lectured Neddy and Johnny, "are condemn'd to the necessity of Labouring hard, for want of ability in their Parents to give 'em an Education. You cannot therefore sufficiently adore the Divine Providence who has placed your Parents above the lower Class and thereby enabled them to be at the expense of giving you such an Education (which if not now neglected by you) will preserve you in the same Class & Rank among mankind." Ambler several times

Plate 1. The first floor of Tuckahoe. Built by Thomas Randolph about 1690, this home is really two frame farmhouses connected by a large hall. As a planter increased his wealth, he could add wings to what once had been a one- or two-room house. It was not until the eighteenth century that more massive and formal brick structures were erected. This is the home in which Thomas Jefferson spent his youth. (From *The Great Georgian Houses of America*, vol. 2 [New York: Dover, 1970], 69.)

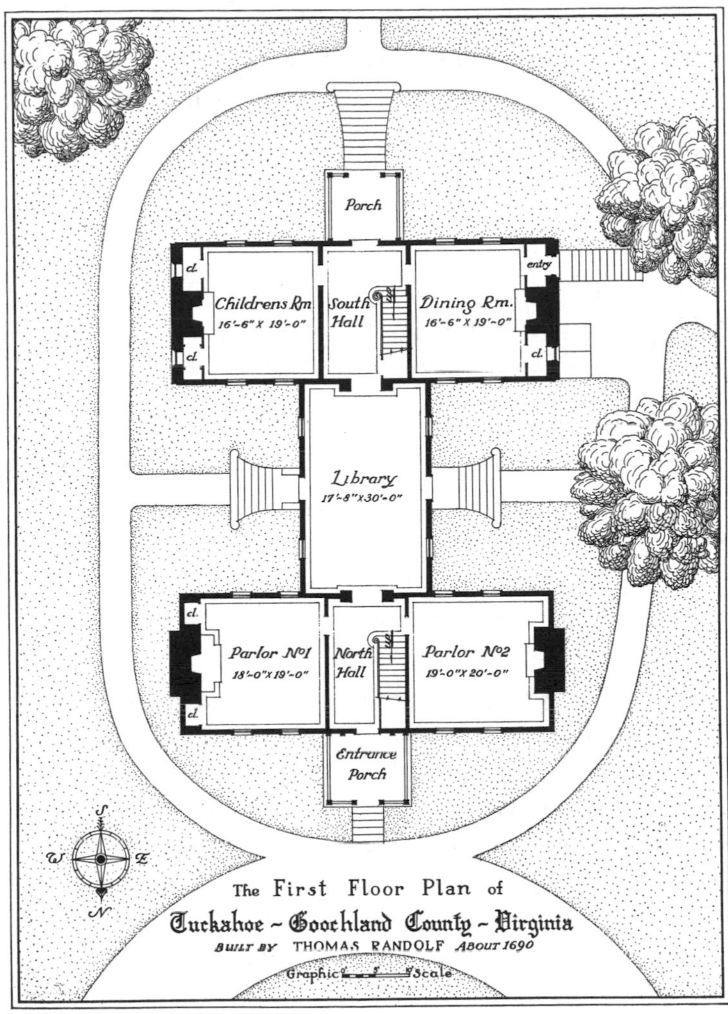
Porch
cl.
Childrens Rm
16'-6" X 19'-0"
South Hall
Dining Rm.
16'-6" X 19'-0"
entry
cl.
Library
17'-8" X 30'-0"
cl.
Parlor No1
18'-0" X 19'-0"
North Hall
Parlor No2
19'-0" X 20'-0"
Entrance Porch
S
W
E
N
The First Floor Plan of
Tuckahoe ~ Goochland County ~ Virginia
Built by THOMAS RANDOLF About 1690
Graphic Scale

reminded his sons that they were the first in their family to enjoy such an opportunity. "You have at present an advantage wch was never in the power of my Father or Self[.] I have often heard Him lament his want of Learning," he reminisced.[7] Whether thanks to God or their father's hard work, the Ambler boys were able to enter Virginia's upper class and acquire its trappings. Here we see, certainly, Virginia aping Europe, but we also must note the confusion and concerns that will characterize the American arriviste: Status comes from some combination of income and breeding; if it can be achieved, it can also be lost. Ambler and his countrymen were creating both order and process, stability and flux.

So, of course, the attempt of Virginia's great men to make themselves lords of the manor would be in vain. America was not England, slaves were not serfs nor poor whites yeomen, and the gentry themselves could never achieve that union of social, economic, and political power held by England's aristocracy, for ultimate political power lay not in Virginia but across the sea. Eventually Virginia's gentry would embrace an ideology of independence, and in this they would be joined, perhaps partly pushed, by the poorer whites who, for obvious reasons of their own, found it appealing. But before this resolution in a Revolution led by the sons of Virginia, that colony was pulled by two powerful, opposing tides, one toward the stability represented by the old world and one toward the opportunity and openness of the new. Perhaps we have nothing more than the philosopher's irresoluble dilemma of freedom versus order, but in Virginia in the eighteenth century, these concepts would mean particular things to particular men, and in the structure and beliefs of that society we can see those conflicting forces at work, two powerful tides pulling in different ways.

Two and a half centuries later, we can see those opposing forces and the way they shaped a society, but the Virginians of the time, or more precisely, the ones who had the leisure to contemplate such matters, could not. Rather, they established certain ideals – such as moderation and independence, balance and reciprocity – to which they clung hopefully, tenaciously, defiantly, as the situation or the times might require. How clearly these ideals might be articulated and what meaning they might carry are exposed by a Fairfax County planter's reaction to the sudden and unexpected arrival of his middle-aged brother. Although Catesby Cocke had heard that his only brother, William, was frequently melancholy and excessively reluctant to discuss his affairs, Cocke in 1751 welcomed him to his home, inviting him to stay. Unfortunately, however, in the words of Catesby Cocke, "The poor man had entertained the notion that I was possest of a very large Estate, and my children provided for, whereupon, he equipt himself in order to pass the rest of his Days accordingly." Having a saddle, bridle, and weapon himself, William asked of his brother only "a Negro and Horse, together with that necessary Article, Cash," in none of which Catesby Cocke claimed to abound. Thus "equipt," William commenced to "ramble about the country," draw upon his brother's credit, and "spunge" upon neighbors and kin. When reprimanded, William loudly and widely denounced his brother's "Cruelty."

Catesby Cocke ultimately wrote his brother two letters, castigating his outrageous behavior and indicating both how that behavior had disrupted the planter's life and what demeanor would be acceptable in a brother. "You were heartily welcome to the best accommodations my house afforded," Cocke assured his brother, "and should always have been so, if you could have been contented." William's financial "Extravagancies," however, were more than Cocke could support. "As my only Study in life is to make my Self and every one about me easy," he lectured further, "your manners . . . are a bar to my peaceable Scheme." He instructed his fifty-year-old brother, "Compose your Self, preserve sobriety, forbear being troublesome, particularly borrowing. Stay quietly at your home, wherever you make it, and resolve to spend no faster than it comes in."[8]

In this small familial drama we see two visions of gentry life, one expressed dramatically by William Cocke, rambling around the countryside, spending freely, and drawing, just as freely, from neighbors and kin. Display, extravagance, excess, egotism – cutting a figure and impressing the neighborhood – might establish William Cocke as a man of importance and, at the same time, undermine his brother's position. Here we see articulated the fear of the gentry: Spend too much and the family fortune is gone. Impose too much upon the neighbors, and one's welcome is worn. Disrupt the family, and unleash a pack of emotions that are best kept in chains.[9] Better to erect barriers between the family and want, between the family and neighbors, between brother and brother even, than to acknowledge the egotism that had created the family's independence and, hence, to sanction a force that might just as readily thwart a planter's peaceable scheme.[10]

In Catesby Cocke's letter to his brother, we see a mode and a mood characteristic of mid-eighteenth-century Virginia: One must exercise restraint, one must be contented. A man could ramble around the countryside, but he should stay at home; he could be drunk, but sobriety was preferable; he could run into debt, but better to avoid it. The individual, unrestrained, might wreak havoc upon himself, his family, his community in innumerable ways, but he ought not. The gentry were acutely aware that men had tendencies toward disorder or, to use the words common to the day, passion and vice, but far preferable was the opposite: virtue. Much has been written about the eighteenth-century political American's glorification of virtue – strength, courage, self-sacrifice, disinterestedness – the character necessary for a citizen of a republic.[11] And the Revolutionaries would claim that the Americans were a particularly virtuous people, but was that not a convenient fiction used to mask, to blunt the aggression and extravagance of a William Cocke or a founder of a family fortune? Drives and passions were to be restrained, retreated from. The canon of moderation erected barriers between an individual and his baser instincts, whereas the canon of independence raised barriers between individuals. In the writings of Virginians one feels the restraint, the withdrawal – from the colony's boisterous past, from its still raw present, and even from certain sorts of emotional engagements, with others and with the self.[12]

That retreat is especially evident in the writings of the

prominent planter William Byrd of Westover, who envisaged the plantation as a self-sufficient enclave. "Like one of the patriarchs, I have my flocks and my herds, my bondmen and bond-women, and every soart of trade amongst my own servants, so that I live in a kind of independence on every one but Providence," Byrd boasted to the Earl of Orrery. Byrd, however, found such a life "attended with a great deal of trouble. I must take care to keep all my people to their duty, to set all the springs in motion and to make every one draw his equal share to carry the machine forward. But then 'tis an amusement in this silent country and a continual exercise of our patience and economy."[13] By peopling his vast property only with dependents, primarily Negro slaves, Byrd sought to free himself from compromising relationships with equals and superiors. Byrd misled both his correspondent and himself, for he spent perhaps the greater part of his existence rambling around the countryside, almost frenetic in his activity, needing somehow the contact, yet eschewing any dependence. The deception with his slaves is perhaps clearer still. His income, his very independence, derived from the forced labor of others.[14] Yet Byrd, writing from the relative peace of his plantation, could describe himself as a demigod, his plantation's first cause and prime mover.

Such a conceit and its source, the ability to sever oneself from neighbors, were available to lesser Virginians as well. Peter Fontaine, a successful but not prominent planter, shared an ideal similar to Byrd's. "I look upon a small estate, which will, with a man's industry, maintain himself and his family, and set him above the necessity of submitting to the humors and vices of others," Fontaine wrote his brother,

Plate 2. William Byrd II. "Like one of the patriarchs, I have my flocks and my herds," William Byrd II boasted to an English correspondent. Yet when his portrait was painted in England, he appeared, at the age of thirty, as an English gentleman, in a periwig and a coat of blue velvet, trimmed in gold, rather than as a planter. The ship in the background is the only suggestion of an America 3,000 miles away. (From the painting by Sir Godfrey Kneller, c. 1704. Library of Congress.)

The pursuit of happiness

"the most happy state this life affords. One thousand acres of land," he explained, "will keep troublesome neighbors at a distance, and a few slaves to make corn and tobacco, and a few other necessaries are sufficient. This," he exulted, "God hath enabled me to leave to each of my younger children. . . ."[15] Peter Fontaine spoke as a proud Virginian, one who had purchased the right not to be troubled. Independence, then, had psychological as well as political and material implications: Happiness is freedom from the humors and vices of others.

Perhaps the peaceable scheme of the Cockes, the Byrds, and the Fontaines, which seeks to limit the claims of others, is an impossible one in any age; we shall see later how this ideal would affect the family and the individual. Certainly for the society there is something disingenuous in the Virginians' claim to have established a new Eden. Consider Byrd's boast, with language borrowed from Micah, to the Earl of Orrery that in Virginia "we sit securely under our vines and our fig trees without any danger to our property."[16] Life in a region barely removed from the frontier, on the one hand, and basing its prosperity on the 40 percent of its population that was black, on the other, was never so idyllic. The society could be crude and brutal. The physical violence that was an accepted part of Virginia life shocked a young man from New Jersey who was tutor in a prominent Northern Neck household. Philip Fithian feared that one of two slaves who had fought might well "lose one

Plate 3. Westover. The home of William Byrd II, built on the James River in the 1730s, believed by some to be the most beautiful of all Georgian homes in America. Formal and massive, such houses were less a personal statement than a reflection of the owner's pride and position. (Library of Congress.)

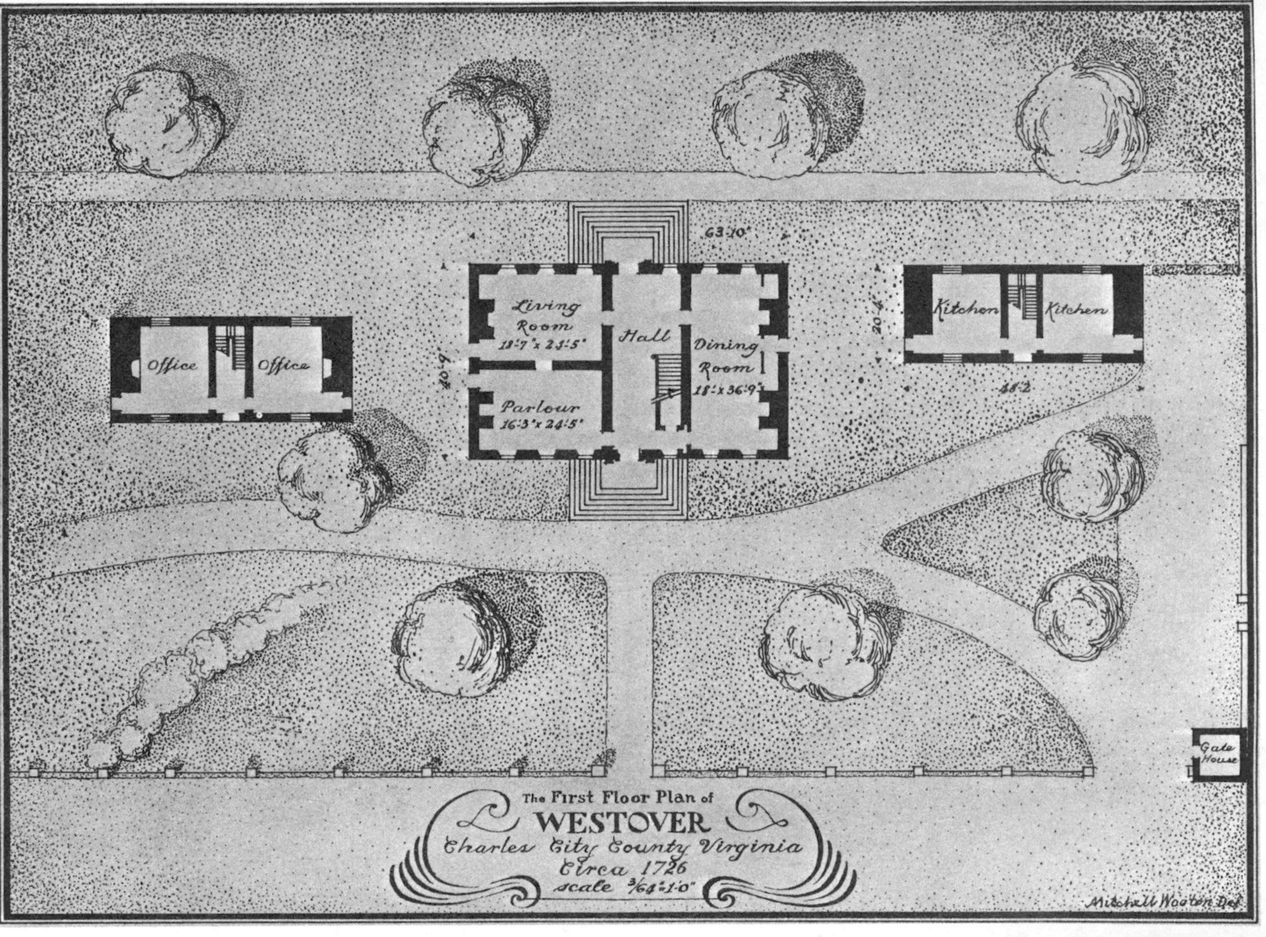

Plate 4. The first

of his Eyes by that Diabolical Custom of gouging which is the common practise among those who fight here." Fighting was a popular amusement for both whites and blacks. Fithian learned that four young men had arranged to brawl. "The Cause of the battles I have not yet known; I suppose either that they are lovers, & one has in Jest or reality supplanted the other; or has in a merry hour call'd him a *Lubber*, or a *thick-skull*, or a *Buckskin*, or a *Scotchman*, or perhaps one has mislaid the other's hat, or knocked a peach out of his hand, or offered him a dram without wiping the mouth of the Bottle; all . . . are thought & accepted as just Causes of immediate Quarrels, in which every diabolical Stratagem for Mastery is allowed & practised, of Bruising, Kicking, Scratching, Pinching, Biting, Butting, Tripping, Throtling, Gouging, Cursing, Dismembering, Howling, &c. This spectacle (so loathsome & horrible!) generally is attended with a crowd of People!!"[17] Such violence, repugnant to a northerner, was so customary in Virginia that a man who had lost an ear in a fight would have that loss recorded by the county court to distinguish him from criminals, whose ears were officially cropped as punishment for felony.[18]

Cruelty and disorder were inherent in eighteenth-century Virginia life, and Virginia society attempted to control this disorder. On the plantation, a self-styled patriarch might bring some peace by controlling the behavior of dependents, whether brothers, children, or slaves, and local government served as a means to bring order to the wider society.[19] In fact, even in the processes of county government we can see Virginians trying to shape a world in which their ideals – moderation, restraint, independence – could be realized. The goal was a peaceable life, but their environment was anything but placid. In fact, the very punishments dispensed by the county courts would seem to give evidence of the violence of the age. Actions as varied as fornicating, giving birth to an illegitimate child (who might become a ward of the county), running away (if an indentured servant), and swearing were punished by whipping.[20] More serious crimes received unique punishments. In 1737, for example, Peter, a slave convicted of murdering his master, was hanged, and by order of the county court, his head was cut off and put "on a pole near the court house to deter others from doing the like." Several years later, the same court found the slave Eve guilty of poisoning her master and had her hauled to a rock, where she was burned at the stake.[21] Punishments such as whipping, cropping ears, and execution appear harsh, but they were not levied indiscriminately; they were reserved for the least successful members of the society – vagrants, impoverished whites, women without protectors, and slaves. Those lawbreakers, however, who commanded money or property or the patronage of someone with those resources were treated with comparative leniency. Thus, those swearers, fornicators, mothers of illegitimate children, and other miscreants who could pay fines or post bonds for their good behavior were released only with the admonition that they mend their behavior.[22]

That violent or erratic behavior by a property holder might be disregarded is well illustrated by the story of Mr. and Mrs. John King. In 1739 Mrs. King came to the Orange County Court "and complained that her husband had left her and had made over all he had to his father." The court duly ordered that "no Deed or Mortgage from the said King to any one person whatsoever be recorded til his said wife be heard." A month later, a grand jury presentment was made against King "for putting his wife away and going armed as a rebel." The next day in court, when the subsheriff reported that John King "will not be taken . . . but stands in opposition with arms, etc.," the justices ordered "that the Sheriff of this County raise the power of the County to take the said King and him in safe custody keep till he enter into Recognizance to our Sovereign Lord the King in ye sum of one hundred pounds sterling each for his good behavior during a twelve month and a Day and for his appearance at the next Court." King did appear at the next court, and all charges against him were dismissed.[23] King's behavior was so erratic that the "power of the County" was required to subdue him; yet once he and two others could post considerable sums to ensure his subsequent actions, the charges were dismissed. There was no punishment for the prior actions, only an effort to ensure his future conformity.

Unlike Massachusetts during the same period, Virginia did not seek to enforce a moral code.[24] Adulterers, fornicators, fighters, and even those who abandoned their wives and went "armed as a rebel" were excused after paying fines or posting bonds. Virginians saw neither duty nor pleasure in regulating the morality of their neighbors. They only hoped to keep disruption of the peace at a minimum. Virginia's peaceable scheme was essentially a private one. Peace would be maintained on the plantation; crime, vice, and immorality were disturbing only when they could not be kept at bay. Here again we see the mode common to Virginians: Vice, crime, and violence are endemic, expected. One will keep his own house in order and try to isolate himself from anyone or anything troublesome. The mode is restraint and avoidance. We also see another tendency characteristic of the pre-Revolutionary culture: a focus upon the externals of behavior rather than internal compliance. Thus, orderly behavior was extracted from the disorderly by threatening – by fine or by bond – the lawbreaker's property.

Like William Byrd, Virginians dreamed of freedom from "danger to our property," and threatening an offender's possessions seemed the most effective way to enforce order. In a colony in which land ownership was widespread, the great majority of white people, perhaps as many as 80 or 90 percent, either had sufficient property of their own or could claim protection from a propertied friend or relation to avoid harsh punishment for infraction of the law.[25] Very poor and dependent whites, along with blacks, – who after the 1730s comprised 40 to 50 percent of Virginia's population[26] – might, however, suffer punishments that were both harsh and unusual. More than half of Virginia's population was without the power, represented by property, to protect itself from physical punishment for breaking the legal or moral code. Those with this power, however, were free to do almost as they pleased, provided they were willing to support their behavior with their money. In a significant way these Virginians possessed William Byrd's vaunted independence, the means to set themselves, in Peter Fontaine's words, "above the necessity of submitting to the humors and vices of others."

By way of contrast, the eighteenth-century Massachusetts "peaceable kingdom" was based upon an ideal of community concord founded in individual internalization of the moral necessity of harmony. Conflict was discouraged not only by the law but also by the social and moral forces of the society. Breaches of the law such as fighting and vice were considered moral as well as civil lapses.[27] Virginia's peaceable scheme was a more private and less communal endeavor. In Virginia vice and violence were widespread, but of concern primarily when they could not be circumscribed. A Virginian craved quiet under his "vines and fig trees," and simply did not want to be troubled with the vices of others.

In a certain respect, Virginia was a two-class society. True, the gentry emulated their counterparts in England and hoped to create a society of hierarchy and deference on this side of the Atlantic, but there was another tide washing the colony, increasing the liberty of those with property while diminishing that of those without. Those whose property gave them some measure of independence owned the luxury of doing very much as they pleased, whereas the other half of the society, consisting primarily of enslaved blacks but also including destitute and powerless whites, was subject to the rule and the whim of the more fortunate class. The one class was as free from external control as the other was subject to it.[28]

Through their court system, Virginians, almost as if enacting the philosophy of John Locke, united to preserve an environment in which each might enjoy the peace of his own home. Public action sought private peace, as if each citizen had promised his neighbor to leave him alone in return for being left alone; they would act together only to secure this end. This unspoken reciprocal pledge was a basis of Virginia society, both public and private. Magnetlike, Virginians both repelled and attracted one another. They sought to keep everyone at a distance, yet their private peace could be maintained only by extracting reciprocal pledges from each other. Social expectations were elaborate and almost formal, much more rigorous than they would be in the nineteenth century; but each obligation was paired with a reciprocal expectation, so that no one might feel taken advantage of, imposed upon, or troubled.[29]

In the language and practice of reciprocity we see the Virginians expressing, indeed enacting, their ideal of restraint, their preference for the external. One restrains, one moderates one's demands of others, expecting that others will behave likewise. Thus, one planter suggested that his wife, in journeying home, avoid staying with an acquaintance, for "she may think your Company an[d] Horses too great a Burthen, and I had rather be at the expense than to trouble any body." Conversely, another planter, after a week of entertaining various friends and neighbors – all of whom he mentioned by name in his diary – noted that so much company was "rather troublesome at this time."[30] Other people could be troublesome, yet in this rural society, with relatively few social institutions, visiting neighbors and relatives was by far the most common form of recreation. Especially on Saturdays and after church on Sundays, but also during the week, men and women would journey to nearby farms and plantations to relieve the loneliness of plantation life, giving rise to the legend of southern hospitality.[31] True, Virginians feted and were feted, but in the colonial period, at least, they kept a careful record of whom they visited and who visited them. In fact, eighteenth-century diaries were often little more than social account books in which Virginians calculated their social debts and credits. Theodorick Bland was speaking more than figuratively when he told a kinsman and close friend, "I have a large Ballance of Visits to settle with my *Formal* Friends, but between you and me no books are kept on that score; But all is *free* and *easy.*"[32] And once again, the goal is freedom and ease, circumscribed by a certain restraint: With you, my friend, the books are closed.

This principle of a balanced and reciprocal social life was usually, however, unspoken. Its force was noted most often in its breach, as when Robert Wormeley Carter attended his friends' wedding. He recorded in his diary that "Col° F. Lightfoot Lee was married this day to Miss Rebecca Tayloe. . . . I received a very slight Invitation; but went that I might give no Offence to the Bride & Bridegroom[.] Drank no wine, because I was expressly within the Statute made by Mrs Tayloe; who said at her Table that She wondered how Persons who were paying Interest for money & kept no wine of their own; could come to her House & to [illeg.] it in such a manner as they did; that for the future it should not be so."[33] Carter was torn by two conflicting social obligations: to attend a wedding and not to accept hospitality he could not reciprocate. He achieved an awkward compromise by going to the wedding yet quaffing no wine. Beneath an appearance of easy hospitality and gracious manners lay careful attention to who owed whom what.

Some Virginians computed social accounts literally to the penny. By the 1770s, a new custom of subscription barbecues had developed. Individuals would commit a sum of money to be used to purchase food and drink. Landon

Carter, a planter who generally assumed that advantage was being taken of him, found such arrangements inequitable. He observed that some subscribers might bring four or five extra "eaters" along with them "so that they all eat at about the price of 15d a head, when others paid at least 7/ for themselves alone. . . ." Carter believed that "the old method of every family carrying its own dish was both cheaper and better because then nobody intruded. . . ."[34] Such subscription parties later became almost like social clubs in which everyone was assessed dues, but some still feared that this new means of ensuring equal contributions to hospitality was not as fair as the older way.[35]

Virginians only pretended to ease and grace abroad; nor did they drop that mask at home. There, neither affection nor self-expression was an unqualified value; both were to be managed and restrained in the service of a higher good, domestic tranquillity. That was the assumption Frederick Jones took with him when he visited his North Carolina kin in 1757, and that was the assumption he maintained after he fell in love with his cousin and married her. He made his home with his wife's folks, and several years later reflected that except for his separation from his own family, "in every other circumstance of life, I have the greatest reason to be vastly happy & thankful to the wise disposer of all things & upon the whole submit & agree . . . that whatever is is right."[36] Like many members of the gentry, Jones struck a posture of complacency, as if a mask of composure might pass for the real thing; his studied self-satisfaction hid an abiding bitterness that he was unwilling to reveal.

When the young man fell in love with his cousin, Jane Swann, their parents entered into the negotiations that regularly preceded gentry marriages.[37] The girl's mother approvingly observed that the couple "had enough to Enable them on their first coming together to set out in the world in a way to live comfortably, and Provide for a Family," so that neither set of parents was under the immediate necessity of contributing more. Although the children were free to live with them until her husband could "set them out in the world," Mrs. Swann hoped that her Virginia cousins could help, for "young people . . . are impatiently fond of having something separate of their own to improve & manage." Samuel Swann's letter to Jones's father was more explicit. He could give his daughter no dowry, for he had suffered from a bad harvest and a failed investment and had heavy current expenses, including the costs of educating his only other child, a son, in England. At Samuel's death, however, Jane would receive a share equal to her brother's, "which will be sufficient to make [the couple's] circumstances Easy in the world." Swann made it clear that he expected young Jones to receive an equal share with his brothers and sisters in his father's estate.[38]

Such negotiations reveal widely shared expectations about family relationships. Prospering parents felt an unquestioned obligation to "launch" their children "out into some happy subsistence in the world." So well understood was this responsibility that one planter could invoke it in cutting off trade with a London merchant who refused to extend further credit: "You must know that I have a large family, & that the chiefest of my estates entailed on a few of my children so that I [am?] under a necessity of purchasing lands for the others which I can now do to advantage under the present condition of our country."[39] Premarital negotiations thus consisted in actualizing and making specific the general obligation. Typically, Henry Fitzhugh advised Francis Thornton that he was "well pleased with your son and what you have given him. . . . I will give them three hundred and seventy five pounds curren[cy], the one half of which I oblige myself to pay this market as soon as my Rents can be collected and disposed [of] and the other half to be paid next year, also three slaves."[40] Children, knowing what they might receive from their parents, accepted these commitments as their due.

How such expectations could shape family relations is well illustrated by Frederick Jones. He and his cousin were married in North Carolina and early the next summer were making plans to return to Virginia. The young husband wrote to his father (who, unknown to his son, had recently died), requesting a pole chair; his wife's pregnancy made it impossible for her to ride horseback. "Was there any such thing to be had here, my Father in Law would not allow me giving you this Trouble," Frederick explained. A chair ordered from England could not arrive in time; "besides I would choose to avoid it; indeed I think it is more than I expect from him, as he has acted so generously by me, since my Marriage as well as before." His father-in-law hoped to sell land for Virginia currency so that Frederick could buy slaves when he returned to Virginia. Frederick implored his father for the chair, asking that its value be deducted from his inheritance and promising that he would be accountable for it to his brothers and sisters. "Your complying," he suggested, "will be a particular Instance of yours and my Mother[']s Love and Affection to me, as it will be advancing so much for me toward my Share or Part, which I have no reason to expect 'till your Death to share with the rest." Young Jones asked no more than his due. Two months later, thinking that his brothers and sisters might be anxious, he explained to one brother why he preferred not to ask the chair of Samuel Swann: "I should choose to avoid being under obligations of this Nature, so soon to my Father in Law, tho' his unbounded Generosity & Goodness has already layn me under greater obligation, I doubt I shall ever be able to compensate."[41]

Frederick Jones used the language of an almost mechanical reciprocity in explaining his dilemma. As a son, he felt entitled to a share of his parents' estate. He was reluctant to accept such aid from his wife's father, knowing that he would ultimately be called on to balance the accounts in some way. The young man, however, never received the pole chair from his parents, and so he and his wife remained in North Carolina, no doubt increasing their already large debt of gratitude to Samuel Swann. The Swanns must have been delighted with the arrangement, for Mrs. Swann had borne only two children and dreaded an empty house; as his daughter's family began to grow, Samuel Swann boasted that she was "likely to make up for the deficits of her Mother." Frederick Jones might still have preferred to live in his native Virginia. When informed of his mother's death and the plans for the disposition of her estate, he did not hide his bitterness from his brother. The estate was to be apportioned among the four brothers and four sisters. "Had my father thought proper to have divided [his estate] between his four Sons," Jones complained, "it might have been the means of our spending our days happily near each other, and have afforded pretty Settlements, – but as he ordered it otherwise, it deprives us from ever hoping to have so great a blessing."[42]

His brothers and sisters established their families in Virginia, and Frederick Jones remained in North Carolina. A number of years later, Frederick's brother Thomas explained that he would not be able to pay the debt he owed Frederick resulting from the sale of their parents' estate. Frederick was "in much pain to be informed your Circumstances are not so easy and clear as I very sincerely wish they were," but he could not forgive the debt, for "the present Situation of my affairs, undoubtedly calls very pressingly for it; & it is no small disappointment & obstacle to my advancing & improving my Estate and increasing family, as I might otherwise do."[43] Jones had a young family; providing for them was his greatest obligation, a responsibility he had assumed the moment he married. He would demonstrate his love and affection for his children by establishing them in the world. He knew from experience that a father who defaulted would surrender his claim to companionship and affection from his offspring.

Parents, then, owed their children a settlement. The obligation was both material and measurable. More striking than the formal style of Frederick Jones's letter to his parents is that he demanded, and then intended to provide for his own children, something tangible as "a particular Instance of . . . Love and Affection." Emotions were presented formally; the manner of expression in a young man's letter to his parents was appropriate to the sentiment: The style was precise, restrained, mannered; the emotion clear, explicit, external. When Jones later spoke of his vast happiness, his thankfulness to God, and his conviction that whatever is is right, these sentiments covered his feelings of disappointment in his parents and antagonism toward his siblings. Clearly, the manner of expression and the emotional style sought to check and control human feelings.

That the aim was restraint emerges in the correspondence of other Virginians in the pre-Revolutionary period. Several examples, once again from the Jones family but typical of the gentry, should serve to make the point. After the death of their father, Thomas Jones became guardian of his younger brother Walter. When the latter went to Edinburgh to study medicine, he came to depend on his brother as a son on a father. Anxious at not having received funds from home for over a year, he reasoned that "some unexpected event has obliged you to withhold the Testimonies of that Kindness & affection, which I have always Experienced & which Love & gratitude have as constantly prompted me to deserve."[44] This is the language of Frederick Jones: Reciprocating love was the right of a dutiful and loving son, and parental affection should be demonstrated materially. How did a young man acquire such a mechanical and external notion of love? Consider that seven years earlier, when Walter Jones in a letter had misspelled "write" as "right," his older brother had lectured him: "This is the Consequence of being thoughtless, and Passionate, which follies , I hope you will endeavour for the Future to Conquer." If such a trifle could seem so heinous, surely passion was feared. Consider also the proud letter Thomas Jones drafted to his brother in 1770 when he received his medical degree: "It caused such an emotion in me that obliges me to leave the room, I can imagine you have no conception of the feeling & know not what I mean. . . . [H]owever let it suffice that I love you."[45]

In the final copy, Jones omitted that last clause: an explicit declaration of love was not appropriate.

Strong emotions, even of love, were thus to be blunted and curbed. To be sure, this restraint was partly a matter of style, but it was more than that when an earlier Thomas Jones (in fact mourning the death of his horse) proclaimed, "It is my opinion we ought not to have any immoderate concern for any thing that happens to us in this world."[46] And the style became the substance when young men schooled in emotional restraint were able to think of family relationships as formal contracts.

Several historians have viewed the eighteenth-century Virginia gentry family as particularly affectionate, shaped by that "surge of sentiment" that would distinguish so-called modern families from their more traditional European antecedents.[47] Surely, if a young man could and did demand from his family "testimonies of . . . kindness and affection," love was one of the bases of family life; yet pre-Revolutionary gentry relationships lacked – or, more precisely, stifled – emotional intensity. Put another way, love was important, but it was not central.[48] Both within and without the family, other ideals – such as peace and moderation – prevailed, creating the context within which emotion might safely be displayed.

If parents had clear material obligations to their children, so also had children duties to their parents. They showed their love by their deportment. Even when grown, they were expected to be cheerful and obedient – in the language of the time, a "comfort" to their parents in their old age.[49] Thus, when the planter William Fitzhugh heard that his mother had experienced misfortune, he released money to his brother in England to aid her. "I . . . do think it both our dutys . . . not to suffer one to want, who gave us our being, nor suffer her to struggle to live, who (under God) gave us life here," he explained. "Nature, duty, the Laws of God and Man . . . command . . . to give the utmost help to a distressed Parent." Fitzhugh was doing no more than adopting for himself a standard he held for others. The sentiment and language were similarly stilted when Fitzhugh hoped that a cousin's son would as "he grows in years . . . grow in grace to serve his God, & then without question you his Parents will find him abound with all dutiful observance, & due Obedience."[50] Literally repaying a parent was one way of discharging the child's debt, but men and women whose parents were materially secure could lighten the burdens of old age and discharge their debts in other ways. When he completed his college education, John Clopton hoped he would "cease to be so expensive" to his father. He appreciated the older man's "paternal kindness . . . for which may I ever retain a grateful Sense, study to be an Honour to your old Age by diffusing thro' the world the Fruits of that liberal Education you have been so careful to give me."[51] The language is mannered, but, significantly, Fitzhugh and Clopton felt that by sending money or a noble sentiment they were playing the part of the dutiful son.

The language was stilted because the role was scripted and most children learned their lines. In the wider world the gentry were bound to assert themselves, prove their prowess, leave their mark. They were trained to act with more restraint and less individuality at home: The goal was a family life that was at once simple and affectionate.[52] So long as a son or daughter was obedient and appreciative, most parents felt amply repaid for the expense and care of rearing them. When expectations were thus clear and simple, children could be confident that they had discharged their duties. An exception that helps prove the rule of reciprocity comes from the agitated domestic experiences of Landon Carter, an unusually bitter and bad-humored man, who found his children a continual disappointment. Carter contrasted their disobedience to his devotion to his own father. When his father was declining, Carter used to sleep at his head, to comfort and divert him. "I did it with both duty and pleasure," Carter boasted to his diary; "but I fancy not a child of mine but would refuse even their duty." In fact, Carter kept the diary in the hope that his offspring would one day read it and recall how they had failed him; in it he recorded his frequent quarrels with his children, one daughter-in-law, and his son-in-law.[53]

The most serious confrontations were with his eldest son, Robert Wormeley Carter, who lived with his wife and children in his father's home. The younger Carter, a notorious gambler, was as relaxed as his father was rigid, and the great difference in temperaments made arguments inevitable. The two men could not refrain from goading one another; their disputes revealed deep tensions. During an afternoon tea, Landon remarked "in a joke" that his son probably thought they should drink tea, an expensive commodity, only once a week. As the father told the story, his son's "replye was neither ought you to use it any more than we." The father retorted, "What Sir, can't I spend my own money[?]" Robert answered, "By God You will have none to spend soon. I replyed I might owe about £1000. [He] answered . . . that [he] would not pay it. I then indeed grew

Plate 5. The old landscape and the new. In the 1730s, an Englishman laid out Landon Carter's formal garden at Sabine Hall, beyond which stretches the tidewater of Virginia. (Library of Congress.)

outrageous and said it was a damned infamous lie etc. For which I do suppose Mr. Carter leaves the house. . . . Indeed he said abundance more and I replyed as tauntingly . . . he had been my dayly curse." When he cooled, the son told the father that although it would be inappropriate to instruct a stranger how to spend his money, a man might take such a liberty with his father, for the son would be obliged to pay the debts the father left at death. The elder Carter concluded that "Sons are determined against the least indulgence to the Grey hour of a Parent."[54]

Landon Carter was extremely proud of the skill with which he had worked his plantation, established all his

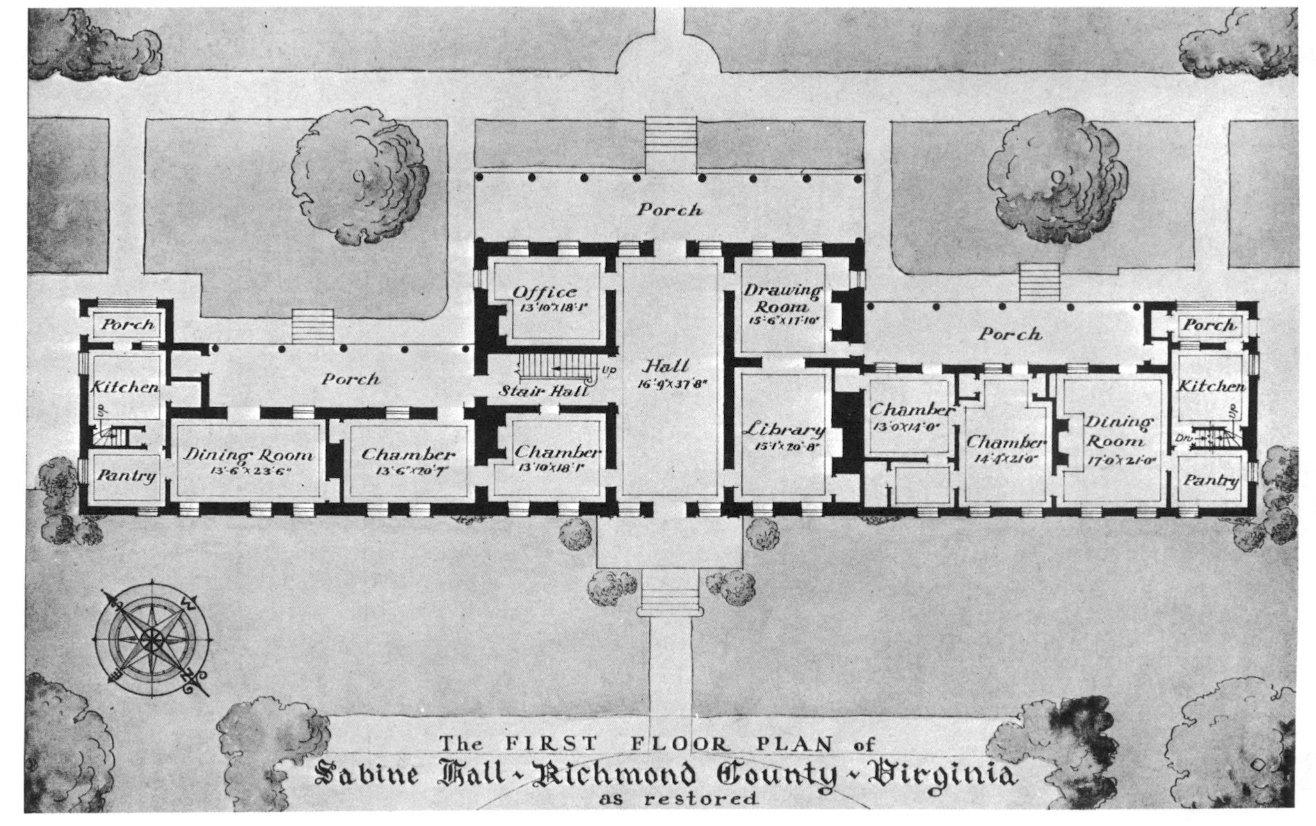

Plate 6. The first floor of Sabine Hall. Again, note the prominent central hall. Here the rooms open onto each other;

children, and, contrary to his gibe, avoided debt. He was outraged that Robert could not so manage his share as to make money rather than draw from his father. The estate he had given his son was worth £300 a year if directed properly. "I have tried every way to be better treated, but cannot even Purchase it of him; many are the Pounds that I have paid out of my Pocket for him; but nothing will do."[55] Carter would never understand why the obedience he believed he had bought from his son was not forthcoming; after all, he had paid his own father what he owed him.

Robert thought his father's demands were excessive, and with good reason, for Landon was a self-styled patriarch in whose home a subservient role was difficult, especially for a son whose temperament was so different. After Landon disrupted one of Robert's card parties, removing the table and cards, the father and son argued. The father recorded, "I was told by the 40 year old man he was not a child to be controuled; but 40 ought to hear reasons." A month after the outburst over the tea, ten years before the interrupted card game, Robert had determined to move from the house in order "to avoid the frequent quar[rels between?] Father and me." He changed his plans when he learned that such an action would cause his father to "take away the maids that tended my Children, & that he would not aid me but distress me." This threat made the son "bid adieu to all Satisfaction, being compelled to live with him who told me I was his daily curse; & who [imp]uted to me his Negroes running away. . . . [But] he is still my Father & I must [torn] bear with every thing from him; in order [to lead a?] quiet life." To protect his own children's interests, Robert resolved to remain in his father's house, to refrain from criticizing his management, to renounce all interest in "domestic affairs," and to endure insult and humiliation. All this he attempted for twelve years, until Landon died.[56] Despite the acrimony, he was constrained both by his sense of obligation to his own children and by his belief that sons ought to be obedient and domestic life quiet.

It is a commonplace of southern history that the family was of overriding importance, that the family line took precedence over the individual.[57] True, family obligations were taken seriously, but it is easy to oversimplify, for notions of family responsibility were neither vague nor overarching. More important was a particular vision of domestic happiness. The premium was placed not on honor (as those who emphasize the traditional nature of southern culture would expect), nor on affection (as those impressed by its modernity believe), but on peace.

As a result, Virginians of the gentry class were neither introspective nor self-critical. They masked and moderated their feelings; consequently, they did not expect or demand intimacy with others. Thus, in 1769 one man could inform a good friend of his recent marriage in these words: "Last Tuesday Miss Kendall gave me her hand, and I am happy in having all the reason in the world to believe that her heart also gave me the preference to every other person."[58] To be sure, the language is in some measure conventional, but the convention itself is revealing, for it dissociates the heart from the hand; and once again, behavior – here, the act of marrying – serves as a sufficient index of love. Edmund Randolph voiced the belief on which the convention was based. At the time of his wedding, he did not believe that marital happiness "depended upon an exclusive preference being given to [the husband] before all other men, and I desired nothing more than that she should sincerely persuade herself, that she could be happy with me." If he did not expect his bride to know and love him deeply, neither did he stare into her soul. Writing three and a half decades after his marriage, Randolph noted that he had not at that time "reflected much upon that range of qualities which I afterwards found to be constituents of marital happiness."[59] Virginians did not like to reflect upon matters of feeling.

Emotional intensity between husband and wife, as between parent and child, was avoided. Landon Carter, for example, found a Mrs. Foy "more fond of her husband Perhaps than the politeness of the day allows of."[60] There is a suggestion that good manners or even happiness required the curbing of instinct and its expression. Thus, one young bride, pregnant for the first time and distressed by her husband's sudden departure on an extended business trip, thought she could "bear the disap[p]ointment better at any time than this as I expect within these two months to stand in need of some such a comforter as you but I will not make you uneasy with complaints & will summon all my small stock of philosophy to wait with patience till that mercifull director of all things . . . Shall think fitt to bless me with meeting you again."[61] The only acceptable way in which Margaret Parker could reveal her anxiety was by saying that she would hide her true feelings for fear of disturbing her husband's peace: In baring her emotions, she feared she did wrong.

The gentry adopted a philosophy appropriate to their tastes. Disciples of a "moderate enlightenment," students of the English Augustans, the Virginians scorned extremity and advocated moderation in all things. As one man rhymed:

> Thus you, great Sage, that wisest course each Day,
> (not both Extreams by turns) pursue;
> But smoothly steer the Middle happy Way,
> Your well chose Motto sets to view.[62]

Fits of temper and tears, grief and euphoria, love and complaint: All were to be avoided, or so Virginians told themselves and each other. Happy was the man or woman who, like William Byrd II, could note in his diary the passing of a satisfying day: "I said my prayers and had good health, good thoughts, and good humor, thank God Almighty."[63] Yet these words came, and came often, from a man whose rambling around the countryside would have put William Cocke to shame, who stormed and fumed and argued violently with his wife, who routinely whipped both black and white dependents, who once made a slave drink a pint of his own urine to cure him of bed wetting, and who after a particularly unsettling period in his life dug up the grave of his long-deceased father to see what of the old gentleman remained. Inescapably, between Byrd's wish and his deed, there is some measure of disconnection, disengagement, and denial.[64]

The Virginians' peaceable scheme included restraint, moderation, and balance, yet the men and women who voiced those ideals never achieved the tranquillity to which they aspired. In trying to blunt, to curb, to pull back their feelings, the gentry were not able to withdraw into a calm. At most, they might circumscribe, check, or impose an order upon the feelings and tendencies they found threatening. Life and relationships were made, as much as possible, contractual, explicit, and external. As a result, there was a certain openness to the culture. Having wrested a society out of the wilderness, Virginians had no desire to explore the recesses of the human heart. Life in the Virginia of Thomas Jefferson's youth was lived, in many senses, in the open, out of doors. In the years to come, Virginians would close some of the doors between themselves and their world and, if not retreat from the outer world, at least section off an inner space of home and of self, removed from the tumult their ancestors had known. And in so doing they would open other doors, to interior rooms, there to explore a world their ancestors had only dimly imagined.

2
"The real use of religion"

RELIGION

ELLEN COOLIDGE had been raised a Deist. Her grandfather Thomas Jefferson, and her parents, Martha and Thomas Mann Randolph, had taught her to shun "mummery & intolerance" and displays of religious enthusiasm, and she and her sisters mocked their evangelical neighbors and kin. But by 1825 Ellen Coolidge's beloved grandfather was slowly dying, leaving (upon her brother) an enormous burden of debt – over $100,000 – and the responsibility for the support of a huge family. Ellen told her mother of Boston's "nabobs, one of whose incomes, taken separately, would restore tranquility to my dearest friends, & brighten the hopes of so many loved ones." She found herself lamenting such unequal distribution of wealth until she remembered "that these very persons have made themselves what they are & risen superior to all the obstacles which poverty & obscurity & original insignificance would accumulate in their paths." That reflection gave her hope "that the younger branches of my family may one day achieve the fortunes to which they were born." As for herself, her mother, her sisters, her grandfather, "for those who from sex or age are condemned to a passive endurance of whatever may happen, I cannot help hoping that brighter days are in store . . . for I feel a stronger confidence in the doctrine of an immediate providence, & greater trust in its interference with the affairs of men th[a]n I think I used to feel."[1]

In the lament of this reflective and articulate woman are condensed the elements of change in post-Revolutionary Virginia. Times are hard, and the old families are falling while nobodies rise. Call it democracy, and Ellen Coolidge accepts its imperatives, if reluctantly. She, however, as a woman may not achieve, but must remain passive; men and women exist in different spheres, one sex in the world, the other at home. Accept for the moment that this separation of the worlds of men and women is a concomitant of the spread of democratic values.[2] Consider, also, that at the same time Americans, including Virginians and the grandchildren of Thomas Jefferson, were discovering or concluding that their fortunes were their own to make, they also turned to a religion more sentimental and more evangelical than the one their ancestors had known. When a granddaughter of Thomas Jefferson expresses "a confidence in the doctrine of immediate providence," more has changed in Virginia than the fortunes of a particular family.

If anything distinguishes Ellen Coolidge from her fellow Virginians, it is the tentativeness of her confession of faith: Reflective and intelligent, she is aware of the incongruity of a Jefferson's turning evangelical. Thus she equivocates, and God's immanence, his active presence in the world, is termed formally "the doctrine of an immediate providence & . . . its interference with the affairs of men." She cannot use the name God, nor can she say firmly and fervently "I believe," merely that she has more faith "than I think I used to feel." In the decades following the American Revolution,

Plate 7. Ellen Wayles Randolph Coolidge. Thomas Jefferson's favorite granddaughter resembled him more in appearance than thought. She looked to God for help in reversing her family's decline: "For those who from sex or age are condemned to a passive endurance of whatever may happen, I cannot help hoping that brighter days are in store . . . I feel a stronger confidence in the doctrine of an immediate providence." (Collection of Mrs. Charles B. Eddy, Jr.)

genteel Virginians would abandon the religious style of their ancestors with less self-consciousness than did Ellen Coolidge. Not only would men and women openly avow their faith in God and Christ, but they would do so in a certain manner: They accepted Christ into their hearts. A devotion to God and to Christ and, more especially, a particular way of expressing that devotion and thinking and feeling about matters of faith became socially preferable and personally necessary even to the offspring of Deists.

It is not so much that Virginians in the early nineteenth century became profoundly religious as that they became religious in a different way. To be sure, Virginia before the Revolution is not conventionally thought of as a religious society. Our conflicting images of early Virginia come to mind: one rough-and-tumble, brash, acquisitive, and the other genteel, elegant, cultivated. Neither picture seems to jibe with a standard sense of *religious*: God-fearing, pious, righteous. Virginia was never Puritan New England in style or in substance, yet until the disestablishment of the Anglican Church in 1785 and 1787,[3] that church at the very least served an important social function in Virginia. The Church was the legally established religion of the colony, and regular attendance at services was required by law.[4] Until the mid-eighteenth century, except for small pockets of dissenters, Virginians were all Anglicans.[5] The Church, because it was the only church, united the entire population. Thus, when several Virginia women, following the lead of their Philadelphia sisters, wanted to raise money for the patriot troops during the Revolution, they decided to make the collection in the parish churches. In Philadelphia and other towns to the North, the solicitation was door-to-door, but in rural Virginia an appeal at church seemed the most effective means of reaching the entire population.[6] The Virginia women realized what a young man from New Jersey would notice at church on an Easter Sunday: "All the Parish seem'd to meet together. High, low black white all come out – "[7]

The Church brought the entire community together for worship and also for "giving & receiving letters of business, reading advertisements, & consulting about the price of tobacco, Grain &c. & settling either the lineage, Age or qualities of favourite Horses." Put simply, the parish church was an institution whose local importance transcended its "prayrs read over in haste, a Sermon seldom under & never over twenty minutes, but allways made up of sound morality, or deep studied Metaphysicks."[8] The Church united the society and, by the very brevity and unexceptionableness of its services, justified that society and sanctified its internal order. It told its parishioners, "This is the way the world is, and this is the way it ought to be," and in so doing, it was performing one of the primary functions of any religion.[9]

The seeming unobtrusiveness of the Anglican Church was a measure of both its success and its failure. For many years, as one historian has noted, "A good many Virginians simply took the Church for granted as a familiar source of comfort and instruction, with words and actions appropriate to the daily rounds of life and also to its great emergencies." Celebrating and comforting, with rituals for each occasion, the Church participated in the lives of its members. It preached a "rational piety . . . a golden mean between" man's utter depravity and powerlessness before

God and his ability to achieve his own salvation. "God was sovereign, but he could not violate his own goodness or forget his promises." Such a creed, which held forth order, moderation, decency, and a reasoned optimism, discouraged "too much speculation about predestination and eternal punishment."[10] Virginians were taught that an all-wise dispenser planned things for the best. Belief in a divine order would mitigate anxiety about the unknown and despair over the uncontrollable.

Virginians, especially the more prosperous ones, accepted the doctrines of their Church, and their personal writings reflected its teachings. Landon Carter, for example, believed God to be both all-powerful, and hence not subject to man's will or wish, and just, and thus inclined to favor the man who was good and faithful. Such questions about God's nature, which have perplexed theologians for centuries, go to the heart of religion: Is God all-powerful? May he destroy a Job if he wishes, or is he just? But is not the very concept of *justice* a human artifact, a constraint upon God's will? Carter found it best not to trouble himself about such matters. "I see it is a good thing," he reflected, "to have some business to keep our thoughts employed for the man who cannot divert the present moment falls naturally into a disponding way and makes even the common cares of life a very heavy weight upon himself." Finding himself slipping into such a mood, Carter "shook myself and roused into a religeous mood of doing all I could."[11] Religion, then, lay in self-exertion more than self-examination. Reflection itself was to be avoided, and Virginians simply tried not to think too hard about perplexing matters. Man's duty was to do his best and trust in God. Religion thus was part of the dominant mode, external and active. It aided Virginians in their search for tranquillity.

This formula worked rather well for the Virginia gentry, and again and again they thanked the Lord for his mercies, prayed for his dispensations, accepted his decrees. Planters whose crops had been saved by rain would be "thankful to our Great God," whereas those less fortunate would "know no other remedy than Patience and resignation to the Decrees of Providence. . . . our duty is to do the best we can in our different Stations, and this done we have the permanent Satisfaction of having Discharged our Duty." To be sure, eighteenth-century life could be grim, but many planters were remarkably complacent. Reflecting upon his separation from his brother, Frederick Jones noted that "in every other circumstance of life, I have the greatest reason to be vastly happy & thankful to the wise disposer of all things & upon the whole submit & agree with you that whatever is is right."[12] Comfortable in this world and sanguine about the next, such Virginians were inclined to accept rather than to question, and in this their Church guided them.

Such a religion was well suited to the gentry, active by temperament and successful in their world. Religion would not expose the contradictions in their thought and their lives; rather, it would justify their world and discourage contemplation. In fact, by the time of the Revolution, enlightened Virginia gentlemen were espousing an optimistic Deism, a "natural religion" of rationalism and order.[13] But such doctrines – the moderate Anglicanism and the even more complacent Deism – had a limited appeal to the less successful or powerful members of the society. Women's role limited their activity; women simply could not charge about the countryside or amass a fortune as men could. They were expected to be pious, modest, resigned to God's will and their lot.[14] Skepticism was considered a masculine province, and although young Edmund Randolph flirted with Deism, his bride "never permitted to herself, nor heard without abhorence from others . . . the questioning of sacred truths." In fact, when George Wythe and Thomas Jefferson, Virginia's reigning Deists, came to play chess with her husband, Betsey Randolph refused to appear in the room. Gentlemen such as Edmund Randolph expected their women to be more "religious" than they, that is, to engage in the rituals more faithfully and to take matters of faith more seriously. "A woman," intoned Randolph, "in the present state of our society without religion is a monster." Perhaps such men realized that women were less able to embrace a cosmic optimism than they, or perhaps they were dimly aware that they themselves, as later Virginians would claim, had laid their own security upon a foundation of sand.[15]

Once again, we see the disjunction characteristic of pre-Revolutionary Virginians: Religion is necessary for women, dispensable for men. Once again, there is the refusal to examine or explore: If religion is more than manners or decorum, how could it be more appropriate for one sex than the other? Does the truth of a doctrine depend upon the sex of its advocate?

The contradictions in the gentry's religion, and indeed in its whole structure of faith and values, would not be exposed by the women. Rather, changes in religious belief and practice seemed to originate in the lower orders, if not the poorest members of the society, at least those for whom a religion of order and optimism, moderation and calm seemed inappropriate. Distrusting passion, the Virginia gentry had adopted a religion that also shunned emotional display. Perhaps not unsurprisingly, Virginians with less commitment to the prevailing ways would look for a religion of more intense feeling. That such a search might disrupt a precarious balance was for them not a fear; in fact, it became a goal.[16]

Both the challenge of the evangelicals – as those who believed in an immediate and vital religion, based upon a new birth and understood more by the heart than the head, are called – and the response to them are part of our story. The signs of change in Virginia appeared first in its religion. That change began slowly and spontaneously, and it grew out of dissatisfaction with the established religion. In the late 1730s, one Samuel Morris and several of his Hanover County friends began reading religious books together. As others heard of these meetings, attendance grew, and soon a meeting house was needed. Still others heard of the great interest in religion in Hanover County, and more reading groups were formed, eventually sapping attendance at parish churches. Public officials then took notice, arresting and fining several of the leaders for absenting themselves from church. In their defense, these newborn Christians invoked the English Act of Toleration, which protected Protestant dissenters. Asked to name their sect, they called themselves Lutherans, for they had read and admired Martin Luther's *Commentary on Galatians.* Not until 1743, when they were addressed by a Presbyterian revivalist, did these Virginians decide that they were in truth themselves Presbyterians. Thus began the Great Awakening in Virginia.[17]

So long as the dissenters practiced their more "vital religion" "in a peaceable manner" they were tolerated, although there was some fear that, in the words of Peyton Randolph, they would seduce away Anglicans and "sow dissention and confusion among the people." Here is the fear of the gentry: that a new and different religion would disrupt the peace. That fear was met with the appearance of the Baptists in the 1760s. Perhaps because they were at first largely lower class; perhaps because their worship sometimes caused their members to cry, bark like dogs, tremble, jerk, and fall to the ground; perhaps because they openly disdained the established religion and gentry mores; and perhaps because, as one Virginian charged, "they cannot meet a man on the road but they must ram a text of Scripture down his throat," the Baptists were reviled. They were seen as troublesome, and they were met with violence. Baptist preachers were regularly imprisoned, not as violators of the Toleration Act but as "disturbers of the peace," and in prison, attempts were often made on their lives.[18] The Baptists grew in number, and their threat to the establishment and the local peace was blunted only by the fervor of the Revolution.

During the Revolution and the decades immediately following, Presbyterians, Baptists, and the recently formed Methodist groups converted thousands of Virginians. These denominations' popular strength, combined with the Revolutionary ideology and an antipathy to things British, eventually secured the disestablishment of the Anglican

Church in 1785 and 1787.[19] All religions in Virginia now had equal standing. No Virginian was compelled to support by his opinions, his presence, or his taxes either the Episcopal or any other church. Churches became voluntary organizations that, in a democratic society, had to compete with one another for membership and support.

The result of a half century's religious revivals was religious liberty, which one historian has rightly concluded was "the most amenable solution for civic life."[20] Freed from the debilitating religious battles that had convulsed the West for two centuries, America's citizens and Virginia's might now devote themselves to the pursuit of happiness as it might be attained in a secular world. Religion became a matter of choice; one might select a church or a creed much as he chose a political candidate, a new costume, or a line of work. Religion was made subordinate to democratic principles, in the widest sense, and in fact democratic principles infused religion, as faith became a matter of personal choice and individual feeling. Position, breeding, learning counted for naught; worse, they might make a man complacent, insensible of the precarious state of his immortal soul. Yet complacency had been the stock-in-trade of Virginia's Anglicanism; the gentry had tried very hard not to be troubled, but now they met trouble from all sides. The very style of their religion was challenged, and so were the circumstances that had made such a stance possible. When religious liberty became a fact in Virginia, the gentry not only had to surrender dominance in the unifying institution of the Church but also had to give up the comfort that derived from having their creed, their notions of life and death, truth and right serve as the standard interpretations of all matters temporal and eternal. In short, the gentry lost the cosmos, and they lost the world.[21]

When they could no longer run it and dictate to its other inhabitants, their world would no longer seem so benign a place to the gentry. The evangelicals' notion of a forbidding, grief-stricken world would seem increasingly plausible. Life for the disestablished gentry seemed much as the evangelicals described it. Thus, in the decades after the Revolution, members of the Virginia gentry would find themselves drawn to a religious style that was in many ways responsible for undermining the security they had known.

The shattering of the pre-Revolutionary religious world was irreversible. Neither unity nor moderation would be restored. Whereas eighteenth-century religion had guarded against strong emotions, later Virginians embraced them, bounding from one to another. The Awakening had encouraged feelings of unworthiness and depravity as a precondition for the delights of salvation. Virginians were forced to plumb their feelings, to savor the depths and the heights. Religion encouraged emotion, and in the end was almost reduced to emotion, for knowledge of one's damnation or salvation was grounded in a personal feeling. Religion based upon sentiment, personal experience, and one's own feelings was a legacy of the Awakening.

Fifty years of religious upheaval shattered Virginia's religious unity and balance. The changes in religious life fragmented social unity, forced individuals to select a meaning for the universe, and made that choice a matter of sentiment, something that could not be given or explained but had to be felt. Paradoxically, religion became more important as it embraced less, for Virginians had to seek and ponder and discover individually what once was shared by all.

Perhaps because religion was so acute a concern, open disbelief became socially unacceptable. Thus, in 1789 one young man implored his father to "let me alone ab[ou]t . . . Voltaire, Rousseau and your Frederick the II King of Prussia's opinion on Religion . . . it by no manner of means, becomes such Reptiles, as these must be in the Sight of God, to Set up an opinion in opposition to the Declared & Established will of God handed down to us by the prophets & Apostles . . . [which] people of my *blind way of thinking* . . . [hold] Sacred." If his father were not "a Heretick or rather an *Athiest*," he might pray for his daughter-in-law to be safely delivered of her child.[22] Enlightenment skepticism, once popular among the well educated, had become threatening. Former Deists such as Edmund Randolph recanted, and those who had not been reborn became defensive. The measure of the change is that even the unbelieving now used the language of the evangelicals in discussing matters of faith. C. H. Harrison, for example, gently put off a solicitous sister by assuring her that he had been thinking much about religion recently, even attending church: "Altho' my mind has been somewhat busy in religious inquiry, my heart has not accompanied it with that degree of fervour which seems necessary to a useful result. . . . the heart . . . grows more & more obdurate as we advance in life." Susanna Harrison perhaps failed to convert her brother to her creed, yet her religion shaped the way he understood and expressed himself: Is this not in some sense a triumph for that religion? The change in Virginia's religious style is epitomized in Edmund Ruffin, later to fire the first shot upon Fort Sumter. Years earlier, in 1827, Ruffin admitted in a letter to a friend, "The most that I have ever obtained from [religious] reading is to unsettle belief – to awaken doubts – to produce a strong desire & earnest prayers to become a Christian. . . . I must confess, with regret, that I am now far more distant from that state, than years ago, when a strong sense of misery drove me to seek consolation in religion." Yet Ruffin tried to hide his unbelief, fearing to "furnish to any member of my family an example of infidelity. . . . I [am] . . . very far from boasting of that which (even I fully believe) is one of the greatest misfortunes of my life. Pray throw this into the fire as soon as you have read it."[23] Not believing in God had become cause for shame.

Thus, again we see the seeming triumph of sentimental religion, but the preachers of the Great Awakening sought more than a change in religious sensibility; they challenged the doctrine of justification by works alone, especially if those works were wholly secular. Evangelicals who contended that "true religion is an inward thing, a thing of the heart" implicitly and explicitly warned that too much outward display and accumulation created a false sense of security; worldly success could not procure eternal happiness.[24] Under attack, thus, was both the gentry's stunning material success and the social dominance and individual pride to which that success gave rise. By the nineteenth century this potentially revolutionary threat to the standing order had been blunted, as even the society's most successful members spoke piously. John Cocke, a wealthy planter prominent in both the temperance and colonization movements, enrolled sixty of his slaves in the "Fork Union Temperance Society for Color'd Persons." Yet this evangelical Christian was well known for his ability to drive a hard bargain.[25]

Sentimental religion posed no threat to Virginians' patterns of getting and spending, for piety was a personal and private matter, separated from the business of life. The point is well illustrated by the advice given and accepted by the Clopton family. John Bacon Clopton received a great deal of parental advice about taking care of both his soul and his family's interests. The elder John Clopton, a Jeffersonian representative to Congress, rejoiced in his son's "predilection for a profession of grace. . . . I . . . earnestly entreat you to look up and fervently solicit the fountain of grace and of all good to pour out that blessing upon you." He urged his son to study diligently "so that you may arrive under God's blessing to great eminence in life." John Bacon was also told to implore "his divine assistance and grace to enable us so to devote ourselves to him." He was not expected, however, to devote himself to God alone, for his parents also relied heavily upon him to conduct family business. Waiting to hear if his son had executed a particular transaction "almost distracts me," John Clopton moaned. "I am rendered almost unfit for any business – I have a heavy pain in my head. . . ." Sarah Clopton was more direct in reminding her son to "take all the cear that you can of the interest of the family for money is all in all in this world." John Clopton instructed his son precisely about how to secure the family's "all in all." He told the young man "to go to the Bank and try the note I left. . . . To prevent any difficulty you might alter the date of the note by changing the 5 into a 4 as it is in the figures, so as to make it the 24th, that being the date of Friday-week, the discount day." The younger Clopton was assured, "I think you can do it so as for it not to be noticed. If you can, you may do it. . . . In turning the 5 into a 4 to make it as little blacker than the other figure as possible."[26] With no sense of contradiction, John Clopton told his son that in this world a Christian should follow the maxim "if you can, you may."

John Bacon Clopton, who as a Virginia jurist rose to the eminence his father had desired, was well taught by his parents to serve both God and Mammon. In subsequent years he struggled against both temptation and his family (engaging in a bitter fight over an inheritance). One night Clopton sat at his desk and penned a long resolution. He began with philosophical premises, as befitted a lawyer. "Feeling that as a rational and moral agent I am accountable to the precious author of my being for all my actions," he reasoned that he could best serve God by "persevering efforts" toward that "moral and intellectual improvement . . . best calculated to advance the highest interests of man as a mortal." Clopton's mission, then, was in this world, improving himself, thereby to advance the welfare of his fellow mortals. Clopton believed that apparently innocent amusements might deflect him from his course; thus, he resolved and pledged "to myself my own feelings as a firm man and my own respect for myself as a consistent man, that I will not henceforth play backgammon at all at home – for the space of *Ten years*." Now in the wee hours of the next morning, Clopton concluded with a prayer for God's assistance and "mercy on me, a sinner, for the sake of the only saviour the adorable *Jesus*, – Amen:"[27] Clopton's concern was not that his sins might jeopardize his reward in the world to come, but rather that they might impede his progress on earth. Clopton was using his religion to enhance just those (masculine) traits of character best "calculated" to ensure worldly success: perseverance, improvement, firmness, consistency. As for his father, religion was intended to advance success; more than damnation, failure was the fear. Religion had to be confined to the narrowly personal if it were to shape a character suited for success.

For women, for whom worldly success was rarely an issue, religion might just as well be restricted to personal piety. Consider the religious thoughts of eighteen-year-old Louisiana Hubard. She first felt the consolations of religion after the sudden death of her mother. "This was the first affliction I had ever known. . . . The world was then stripped of all its gayety, all its beauty." Several years later, prayer and Bible reading led her to a "blessed season of delightful peace and [I] was almost constrained to shout." Thus far, we see a typical account of a conversion: feelings of desolation replaced by those of joy. Typical also is the backsliding into pride and anger, and Louisiana Hubard still felt "great inward conflicts . . . for my heart is so prone to the love of the world. . . . My temper is so passionate and fretful that I am constantly sinning." She resolved "to restrain my passionate, fretful disposition and . . . live *peaceably* with *all* and live in Charity." Perhaps the resolution was difficult to keep, for in late September 1831, Louisiana confessed "how thoughtless have I been of a future state . . . yesterday I felt so full of the spirit of the world and so great an anxiety for its honours and pleasures." But that day she had been shocked by the news of the Nat Turner rebellion, and she thanked God, "who mercifully . . . has saved us . . . tho we were continually sinning . . . I humbly pray . . . I may be more diligent in the service of my God." Although she helped organize a society to educate preachers, two weeks later she chided herself for backsliding, for entering "again into the world and its pleasures. . . . In the last 2 days I have been wearing my earrings. . . . I believe that they are merely ornaments . . . sinful only as they induce a person to spend money unnecessarily – ." Louisiana Hubard later confessed "the love of dress I find a besetting sin. . . . So much levity and folly draws my heart away from my Savior."[28] Earrings and backgammon: The good Christian would forgo such self-indulgences, signs of weakness that would provoke God's wrath. To control oneself was to control one's destiny, not directly but through God's mediation. Thus reasoned the young woman who associated America's greatest slave rebellion with her own vanity in an almost magical, childish way.

That so extreme a personalization, in fact an isolation, of religion should have been the outcome of Virginia's half-century of religious revivals is ironic, for earlier evangelicals had found both joy and meaning, support and strength in the community of fellow believers.[29] Yet a religion based upon sentiment made emotion the test of conversion and the individual necessarily the best earthly judge of his or her own heart. At the very least, the evangelical sects would be pulled by the tension between the individual and the community, but in a society committed to personal profit and the institution of slavery, as those sects developed into populous and stable denominations they not surprisingly accommodated to the economic and social order, essentially by isolating religion from that order.[30]

Isolating religion from the world seems to have been at

least partially the intent. Clearly, women, not only in Virginia but throughout the new nation, were encouraged to maintain the home as a sanctuary from the amoral public world.[31] After the death of her nine-year-old daughter, Virginia Cary found consolation in her religion. Her husband, Wilson Jefferson Cary, a Jeffersonian politician and pillar of the Episcopal Church, encouraged her interest in religion. "You have acquired in Religion, a support which will be effectual to uphold you in your earthly trials," he congratulated her. Wilson Cary was delighted that his wife had found the means both to relieve her grief and cheer her spirits and to make their home a haven from business, politics, and his mounting debts. "Experience has long satisfied me, my dear Wife," Cary later wrote, "that we have not much else to look to, besides ourselves and children in this World of selfishness."[32] The home was a sanctuary from the world's corruptions. Home was where the heart, and consequently – in an age of sentimental religion – piety was.

There is, it must be noted, something disingenuous about Wilson Cary: Clearly, he enjoyed his life in politics and away from home. Yet his language, extolling hearth and home and contrasting it to "this world of selfishness," was typical of that of Virginians at the time. Another measure of the triumph of evangelicalism is the pervasiveness of its grim image of this world. The world might easily be described as one of "troble and deceit," a "theatre of *vice & wickedness*," "a howling wilderness of woe." It was personal immorality – the fact that "People in this World are not to be trusted" – that distinguished "the vast dreary wilderness of the World" from home and family, where gentler values prevailed.[33] Although other forces were at work fashioning a domestic paradise, it was evangelical religion that defined the world as a wilderness from which such a refuge would be necessary. Is it possible, however, that such language was merely convention, written without depth or sincerity? Yet how the image of the world had changed since the more cheerful – perhaps defiantly cheerful – days before the Revolution, and how much stranger for Virginians to describe their world as a barren wilderness if that view did not contain at least a kernel of emotional truth.

Evangelical religion presented a stark vision of the world and then told men and women how to live in such a dreary place. True, it helped them to accommodate to their world without challenging its economic or social arrangements, but it told them that such a world was a howling wilderness of woe. We find, then, religion in post-Revolutionary Virginia placing a great burden upon the individual: He or she must choose what and if to believe. The individual, in turn, asks a great deal of religion, for it must console him or her for having to face so great a task. Little wonder, perhaps, that a grim view of the world had a certain appeal.

Little wonder, too, that men and women found their crosses difficult to bear. Such was the case with the Nicholas family. Sarah Nicholas blamed herself for her inability to nurse an ailing relative back to health. Perhaps one more death should not have been too hard to bear, but since her father's sudden death eight years previously (hastened, people said, by enormous debt), the family had had so much to endure. Two brothers had gone to Louisiana to recoup the family's fortunes, and one had already died there; the third was at sea. Sarah's beloved sisters were dispersed throughout Virginia and Maryland, and their husbands were in debt. Sarah was reminded by her sister Jane Randolph that "the reflection, that 'the Lord loveth those whom he chasteneth' is the only comfort left for our family, & Oh! what I would not give to have this, *such* a comfort to me, as I know it is to you. . . . I can say with all the fervour of faith & truth 'Oh Lord! have mercy upon us,' but I cannot, Oh! I cannot say 'thy will be done.'"[34] Jane envied her sister's source of consolation but could not find that peace herself.

The Anglican faith had required a stoic resignation,[35] yet evangelical religion seemed to demand more. Jane Randolph believed peace would come only when she accepted her family's suffering as proof of God's love. Similarly, a woman nursing both her sister and niece feared that the responsibility "called for the exercise of more fortitude & holy submission, than my poor heart possesses. I feel that I cannot kiss the rod, though it be in the hands of a Father." Like Jane Randolph, she could not say "thy will be done." It was not sufficient to bend to the rod that chastened; one also must kiss it. Virginians felt that they must actively acquiesce in God's dispensations. They thus tried to limit the randomness and impersonality of suffering. If the Lord loved those he afflicted, then calamities were a sign of divine favor. If a person kissed the chastening rod, not only did he prove his worthiness of God's love, but also he seemed to gain some measure of control over that suffering, as if he had willed it himself.[36] (Once again, we see Virginians using religion as an indirect means of controlling their destinies.) Such a task, however, might add to the burden of pain, rather than lifting it. Those who sought peace often found anguish instead. A lonely woman, far from her family, meditated, "Fortitude and submission to the will of Heaven must be my support. But . . . I think of how often I've looked for peace and found bitterness of Soul. . . ."[37]

Although some might turn tragedy into triumph, many found acquiescing in their own affliction too difficult a task. Rather, they found themselves questioning God's mysterious ways. Evangelical religion in the nineteenth century required men and women to accept Christ into their hearts; as is perhaps appropriate to a democratic age, eternal salvation was an option available to all. Nonetheless, such a choice often proved difficult to make, and a language of doubt, of "repining" and "murmuring," infrequently used in the eighteenth century, became common in the nineteenth. Thus typically, a man falling into debt in his old age considered it "the will of Providence, which it is sinful to repine at and our duty to submit to. . . ." And a young mother so grieved for her dead son that she was "almost tempted to wish him back such is the weakness of human nature, yet I know I ought not to . . . murmur at the allwise dispensations of Heaven. . . ." Distressed and discontented Virginians flagellated themselves for their inability to accept the decrees of a loving God. Once again, their religion proved both a burden and a comfort, for Virginians believed their afflictions, for which they needed consolation, to be the proof of God's affection. Thus, Sally Faulcon consoled her brother on the death of his wife: "Religion my Brother is the only thing that can give you comfort." She also, as so often happened, reflected upon her own numerous misfortunes and her endeavor "to be resigned to the will of the Almighty – tho I find my dear Brother that resignation is a hard task to learn."[38]

Resignation was indeed a difficult lesson, and even the

most pious individual occasionally repined or murmured. Accepting misfortune was a test of faith, and so men and women tried desperately to stifle their discontent, but their inability and indeed the very existence of doubt indicated the waning power of religion to explain the universe, to spread a sacred canopy of meaning over life and death. Voluntary and sentimental, nineteenth-century evangelical religion necessarily spread doubt and despondency, yet disquiet itself might ultimately lead to tranquillity. Sally Faulcon later received comfort from a minister's words that "It is a sure mark that the true grace, by Jesus Christ is conceived in the heart, when the cry of the soul is for more grace." Only those who suffered could crave relief. When John Cocke feared he had not fortitude enough to bear the loss of his wife, an elderly aunt counseled, "Your doubt . . . I consider as the surest Rock to build on . . . for none are so apt to [fall] as the presumptious self opiniated mortal, who thinks he is too perfect, to swerve from the line of rectitude."[39] Salvation – in both this world and the next – was open only to the weak, the suffering, the doubtful. If evangelical religion increased doubt and heightened pain, it also reassured that those feelings were marks of grace.

Feelings of insufficiency and the precariousness of life, the pain of separation and loss, the conviction of sin: These were the first steps on the road to rebirth, for men and women knew there could be no true joy without such suffering. "My dear sister," John Dabney admitted, using the language of evangelical Christians, "I have plainly perceived . . . the insecurity of my situation; that I am an offender in the sight of my creator . . . tho' dependent on his fatherly protection and care in every respect, yet I am a self sufficient, presumptious, poor mortal and that the hardness and depravity of my heart is greater than [I] have words to express." The young medical student agreed with his sister "that he who builds his hopes of happiness and peace of mind . . . on the things of this world, will be sadly disappointed in the end." The self-reliant man would find that "tho he may succeed to the utmost – if he wishes . . . his persuits have been in vain, and that his mind is quite unsatisfied." As we have seen, nineteenth-century religion accommodated Virginians to their world; this was the case with John Bacon Clopton and Louisiana Hubard, and apparently also with John Dabney, who believed that he could "succeed to the utmost – if he wishes." Nonetheless, their religion exacted a price, for in styling men and women for success, it told them at the same time that the rewards of this world were for naught, that the self-reliance so necessary for success was nothing less than the sin of pride. Thus, Mildred Lewis discovered that "I was never happy tho possessed of the most affectionate & devoted husband & kind friends & all the things which are necessary to happiness if it could be acquired without religion." She had, apparently, all that a woman could want; she was even, to all appearances, a model Christian, "but I depended on self two much . . . & of course invariably failed." It was eight years before her "Rebellious heart would come as a little child to the foot of the cross. . . . We must become as little children before we can be born again."[40] Worldly success, loving family, good friends: None of these could bring true happiness. Nor was peace to be found within oneself or by one's own exertions; to rely upon the self was rebellion and delusion.

Self-reliance brought not peace of mind, but terror. The

proud individual "to day flushed with Health and Prosperity – will tomorrow droop under the smallest reverse of Fortune or situation and confess . . . that all within him is a dark and dreary void into which he cannot look without horror."[41] This, then, was the terror: The human heart was empty, and nothing could fill that dreary void. As men and women studied their world, their lives, and their hearts, they found only a wilderness. They confronted the possibility that life and their own lives were utterly without meaning or joy. It is no wonder that they felt insecurity and dissatisfaction, "bitterness of Soul," and horror.

Changes in the structure of Virginia's religious life and the nature of sentimental religion itself may have reinforced genteel Virginians' growing despair. As Anglican unity had been shattered, as religious life and belief itself became voluntary, and as religion became a matter of personal experience and feeling, men and women began to seek salvation separately. Religion had become personalized; it began not with shared rituals but with self-scrutiny and adjustment to one's own afflictions. Perhaps to give meaning to suffering and to gain some control over it, men and women required themselves to acquiesce actively and personally in their own afflictions. As religion was personalized and individualized,[42] however, men and women in some degree rejected their increasing isolation. They found the world a dreary wilderness, filled with hardened and self-serving individuals. They saw the signs of hardness and self-sufficiency in themselves also. Changing religious patterns had forced Virginians to rely increasingly upon themselves in matters of religion, and they found in this only bitter isolation and horror. This world afforded little peace or comfort. It was ugly, as ugly as the human heart.

The veneer of eighteenth-century moderation had been cracked. No longer were life's real pleasures and pains accepted equally as God's decrees. Nineteenth-century men and women mistrusted earthly joy, whether backgammon or earrings, love or success, for all were delusions or snares, lulling one into a false sense of security. Pleasure was divested of its pleasing qualities, and thus Virginians could not look to earthly happiness for an antidote to earthly pain. Instead, they slipped into despondency. Landon Carter had known that "the man who cannot divert the present moment falls naturally into a desponding way and makes even the common cares of life a very heavy weight upon himself,"[43] but his descendants shouldered those weights, afraid to dispel the gloom. Virginians who found nothing but suffering in this world could anticipate happiness only in another world beyond the grave. There, in a world free from suffering, sickness, and death, the sorrows of this world would be erased. Heaven was "a peaceful abode, where all tears are wiped from our eyes; where sorrow & affliction is unknown." It was a place "where there is no more parting" (according to a woman who had moved to Missouri), a place "free from disease and all the distress of this transitory life."[44]

Early-nineteenth-century existence was grim; to speak of life as a journey through sickness and separation, pain and death was to use an apt metaphor. Life, however, had always been harsh, but now men and women were thrown back upon themselves to explain "all the evils of this unstable & painful life." They were cast upon the world entirely dependent upon their own exertions, and they sought release from that responsibility in religion. Many became "more convinced, that religion is the one thing needful . . . only that can smooth the rugged path of life. . . ." Indeed, "How delightful it is to rest our hopes on him who holds the destinies of Mankind – what a load of anxiety is removed – " And how easy to lift that load, for despite the bleak view of this world these Virginians, unlike their Anglican ancestors, believed that God was not merely good, but more, that grace was theirs for the asking. All one had to do was "examine himself thoroughly, & be convinced of his need of this divine assistance . . . [to receive] spiritual strength. . . ." As one man strikingly put it, " . . . the assured hope of a blessed immortality [is] given freely in the Gospel, and daily offered to us, without Money and without price."[45] The use of economic language is significant, for it suggests pointedly why the next world would be a very different and much more pleasant place.

Rarely did Virginians express fear of hell or eternal punishment. Life itself seemed damnation enough. Men and women dreaded most the possibility that life's suffering would go unredeemed. Thus, religion smoothed the rugged path by reassuring men and women that the transitory pleasures of this life would be eclipsed and its haunting sorrows erased by "that happiness which the world cannot bestow." "Our inheritance is laid up in a better, & more permanent world." We will "be repaid with richer harvest than this world affords."[46] Men and women tried to numb the pain of this world by fixing their gaze upon the next, by conceiving of the world beyond the grave as a reverse image of the one in which they were living. The next world would compensate them for the ordeal of life.

If this mechanism worked by holding out a better world to come, it of course also depended, as has been suggested, upon the belief that life's joys were illusory or insufficient. As a result, eternal happiness depended upon forsaking the seeming delights of this world. So reasoned Elizabeth Carr. She had lost her parents, her brother, and a young child, but she then gave birth to a son. "I had long wished for a son, and when I saw how fine and promising he was, and how much his father was delighted with him, I had nothing more to wish for." She lost him, too. "My affections were too much set on him, and I was too much attached to this world; such a stroke was necessary to wean me from it. . . . I thank my God I can now say 'it is good for me that I have been afflicted.' Religion is the only consolation that can support us under such trials." By reminding her of the better world to come, even the worst calamity could prove "to the real Christian, blessings in disguise."[47]

Religion's offer of a better, happier, more real world after death protected an individual from his unstable and painful life. With the assertion that suffering was divinely ordained and cosmically significant, religion placed a psychological buffer, a comfort, between a person and this world. A dissatisfied man could be reassured "that nothing of a terrestrial nature can gratify an immortal Soul." Virginians used religion as a shield. Thus, a woman whose husband had received public criticism might be counseled that "the opinions of mere men are of very little account," for God is the ultimate judge. And "this my dear Jane is the real use of religion, it reconciles us to the injuries, ingratitude,

& selfishness which we must expect to meet with in this world." Similarly, a young woman whose mother was dangerously ill was advised to profit from her trial and seek strength through religion, "which I firmly believe places us out of the reach of many troubles in this world –."[48] Religion was a suit of armor and a fortress, a means to protect and isolate the individual from the cruelty of others and of life itself. Men and women would cling to religion and embrace the detachment it offered. Thus, after an illness convinced her that her heart had been "fixed . . . too much upon earth," a woman "fervently prayed that . . . I might be more and more weaned from time and sense, and have my supreme affections fix'd upon God my Savior."[49] Pious Virginians dressed themselves in detachment from the world, from time, and from sense. There is some irony here, for sentimental religion commenced by heightening the senses; its foundation was the individual's intense experience of his own sinfulness. Yet the only escape from that pain was to deaden the very senses that had been aroused. The equilibrium of the previous century had been shattered, as Virginians were left reeling and staggering from one emotion to the next. Unlike their ancestors, nineteenth-century genteel Virginians longed for comfort and ease not in this world but in the next.

3
"Weep for yourselves"

DEATH

"THE EARTH belongs to the living, not to the dead," Thomas Jefferson told his son-in-law. This brave declaration of freedom from the past and equanimity about the future belied the pains Jefferson and his eighteenth-century fellows took to bury their grief with their dead. After the death in 1782 of his beloved wife, Martha, Jefferson noted the event laconically in his account book: "My dear wife died this day at 11:45 a.m." He retreated to his room for three weeks; he emerged, only to take to the saddle, riding incessantly. Not for two months could he return to the public life in which he had already made so great a mark.[1] Jefferson destroyed the letters he and his wife had exchanged. Neither love nor death was to be immortalized by words; neither love nor death was to be described. Jefferson wrote easily and prolifically about the widest variety of matters, but not about his emotions. Several months after his wife's death, in one of his rare mentions of that event, he told a correspondent that he had now "emerged from a 'stupor of mind' which had rendered him 'as dead to the world as she was whose loss occasioned it.'" Jefferson knew that to chronicle his wife's last days and hours, and later to turn those pages or once again to read letters traded with a wife now dead, would only prolong the "stupor." "The Creator had made the earth for the living."[2] For them to enjoy it, they must cut themselves off from the ghosts of the dead.

Only several decades later, sentimental religion would tell Virginians that the same world that Thomas Jefferson in the lonely weeks after his wife's death struggled to rejoin was but a howling wilderness of woe. Nowhere more clearly than in the changing patterns of consolation and grief can we see how profoundly Virginians had changed.

Jefferson, in truth, was a transitional figure, bridging two historical eras and two modes of mourning. In his love for his wife and his near collapse after her death, Jefferson had much in common with his descendants of the nineteenth century. But in his fierce determination to gallop over his grief and obliterate its traces, he was a child of the eighteenth. Those men and women believed that to discuss death was to invite stupor; to contemplate it, to succumb. As a result, they kept their descriptions of death and their letters of consolation brief. One young woman, for example, told a friend about the unexpected death of another young woman: "Who would have thought when last we saw Miss Brown so blooming, her Fate was so near a Crisis? but hold! we'll quit this gloomy subject." The obvious lesson, that death comes without warning, would not be drawn; rather, it would be defended against. Virginians refused to dwell upon even the deaths of those dearest to them. When his infant daughter died, one man wrote to his brother, "Providence has been pleased to handle us lately very Severely. . . . enough of that melancholy Subject." In the letter the melancholy thought occurs, but it is suppressed: Men and women told each other that death was not to be discussed, grief not to be indulged. Did men and women perhaps mourn in private, revealing to themselves more than convention let them show to the world? Here Jefferson was the model, for death was no more the subject of diaries than of letters. For example, on his tenth wedding anniversary, Robert Wormeley Carter wrote tersely: "I have now living two Sons & a Daughter my Wife has miscarried five times; brought a dead Child & lost a fine little Boy about 18 months."[3] The facts noted, no more was to be said. Consider William Byrd II's reaction to the death of his ten-month-old son: "God gives and God takes away; blessed be the name of God." He compared his stoicism favorably to his wife's grief. She "was much afflicted but I submitted to His judgment better, not withstanding I was very sensible of my loss, but God's will be done." Proud of his ability to govern his emotions, Byrd carefully scrutinized his wife, finding signs of grief, evidence of weakness, up to twelve days after their son's death.[4]

Were the gentry able to subdue the wilderness of grief as effectively as they shaped the Virginia landscape? Byrd, for example, chased disquieting thoughts out of his consciousness and then displayed himself as a model for his afflicted wife. But ghosts are not always easily laid to rest. Thus, in January 1710, the events of a particularly difficult month betrayed Byrd's attempts to master his feelings. Distemper had been spreading among the neighborhood slaves when Byrd's own daughter fell ill. Two of the planter's slaves became sick, and several on other plantations died. On the twenty-second, Byrd's daughter had a fever, and a runaway horse and coach knocked over his mother's tombstone. Although his daughter seemed to have recovered the next day, she then relapsed, so that Byrd "could not sleep all night for the disturbance my daughter gave me. . . . I had my father's grave opened to see him but he was so wasted there was not anything to be distinguished."[5] Under stress, Byrd sought comfort from the father who had left him six years before. What Byrd wanted was not his father's spirit but his flesh and bones, yet no rotted corpse could give solace or advice on an earth that granted the dead no sway. Even in moments of anxiety and despair, pre-Revolutionary Virginians looked for signs of life.

And if grief could not raise the dead, it was in vain. So Virginians consoled one another, and so William Lambert reminded a grief-stricken woman that "the most excessive grief cannot raise from the dead. . . ." Similarly, Frances Randolph was told by her brother when their sister died, leaving several young daughters: "Alas Fanny tis in vain for us to grieve at Misfortunes. . . ." That was also the message she conveyed to her sister, who shared her grief, "but as you say . . . it is of little use to dwell on Melancholy Subjects." Men and women urged reason, believing, like Thomas Jones, that thought could control feeling. Thus, Jones bluntly informed his brother that the death of their elderly mother "could not be of any great Shock to you, it being no more than you might hourly expect to hear. . . . your Grief must have ceased as soon as your reflection took place."[6] In grief, quite simply, there was no practical benefit.

As in other realms of life, pre-Revolutionary Virginians strove for balance when confronted by death. They sought moderation in grief and compensation in consolation. The bereaved were advised to count their remaining blessings, balancing them against the loss. A young woman sorrowed

Death

Plate 8. Frances Bland Randolph, 1752–88. "It is of little use to dwell on Melancholy Subjects," reflected a woman who herself would be widowed at the age of twenty-three and then, thirteen years later, would leave her second husband a widower in charge of three adolescent boys. (Library of Congress.)

when "a sweet little girl of my brother's died," but found some consolation in the reflection that "my brother & Sister Hansford will soon be blest with a pledge of their mutual affection which will in some measure compensate for the loss of their other dear little Angel."[7] It is not that such men and women were callous or indifferent, for the characterization of a baby as a "dear little Angel" certainly betokened affection, indeed a studied affection. Yet there is a belief that the loss is not irreparable: Children are in some measure interchangeable, "little Angels" every one.

The complexity of Virginians' feelings about love and death is illustrated by the letter of consolation William Ronald wrote his friends when he learned that one of their two young sons had died. Ronald was relieved that the couple had lost the infant rather than the older child. "I could not help being a good [deal] pleased at finding your loss so small in comparison to what [it might have been]. However tender the heart may be, and whatever the attachment a parent may have to his offspring, the heart can be but little affected with their loss in comparison with what we feel when deprived of those whose infant prattle and dawning reason . . . has deeply impressed their image in our breasts, and fancy long after paints to us what the little innocent would have been in their riper years had not Death untimely cut them off."[8] There is something in the thought that is detached and jarring, the juxtaposition of a sentimental view of childhood with a matter-of-fact stance toward infant mortality. Childhood was rhapsodized, but not the child.

Lest one think that men and women treasured children only after they had passed through the first perilous months, consider Peter Fontaine's thoughts about the death of his grown niece. Fontaine agreed that his "brother's loss is great in being deprived of his only daughter, in the bloom of her years." He reminded his brother and sister-in-law, however, that "your two precious lives . . . are of much more consequence towards directing and providing for the four hopeful boys under your management, who are but young, and beginning to launch out into the world."[9] Fearing grief, striving for equanimity, Virginians looked to the brighter side.

Men and women seemed to grieve most when, through death, the reciprocal bonds, the mutual expectations and material responsibilities between family members were broken. Fontaine, after all, hoped that his brother and sister-in-law would live to establish their sons in the world. An orphaned girl "labour'd under many disadvantages" because of her guardians' "incapacity for doing any essential services." A child without a protector, someone to launch him or her on life's voyage, was at a great disadvantage. Likewise, those who had neared their destination might also suffer a loss. Although consoled by the good life his daughter had led, Landon Carter considered her death a "Severe stroke indeed to a Man bereft of a Wife and in the decline of life because at such periods 'tis natural to look for such Connections that may reasonably be expected to be the support of Grey hairs and such an one I had promised myself in this child in Particular."[10]

"'Tis natural to look for . . . Connections," and when bereaved, Virginians turned their gaze not to the spirit of the departed but to the life he or she had led. Thus, men and women found no greater consolation than in the assurance that the life had been well spent; indeed, this was the consolation they offered most frequently. Men and women, even the most pious, rarely made explicit or graphic reference to an afterlife, although they generally believed in one. Nor did they describe deathbed scenes in great detail. They did, however, find great comfort in a good life, for life to them was more important than death. Mourners and consolers both noted the happiness or the virtues of the departed's life. Rebecca Aitchison wanted no "pompous" tombstone for her husband, for she trusted that "his virtues will be handed down from Children to Children."[11] A good and honorable life not only comforted the bereaved, it also enabled a dying person to leave the world with tranquillity. "Mrs. Waugh left this wourld with more composier then I could have thought any being in their sinces could [,] which she had to the last moment," a woman wrote her sister. "But this my Dear Madam I impute to good contience, I co'd not look at her without noeing the words of the Holy psalmest, let one die the Death of the righteous, and let my Latter end be like hers – ." Martha Carr similarly consoled a young woman on the death of "The Dr. old Ladie your Grand Mother. . . . she lived to be a good old age[,] spent her latter days in Comfourt & Serenity[,] was sencible of her approaching end[,] was perfectly resigned to death & has left behind her a respectable Character." The consolations of a good and respectable life were not reserved for the death of the elderly. Landon Carter found comfort in the conviction that his daughter Susannah had been "universally applauded by All who knew her and this before she could have received any of the Advantages of Education. In her therefore Pure Nature must have been pure Goodness."[12]

If the eighteenth century found consolation in a life of benevolence and the admiration of the departed's peers, the nineteenth century would not. So bright a flower did not transplant well to the shadier mood of a society watered by sentimental religion. Benevolence could be sham, admiration mere flattery, and "pure Goodness" better suited to the world to come.

As sentimental religion spread, so also did a new understanding of death. Virginians were now haunted by that "*grim monster*, who is frequently visiting the poor, helpless mortals." Such a characterization was, in truth, no exaggeration, for all Virginians – in both the eighteenth and nineteenth centuries – could expect to lose at least one, and frequently more, close relations before they reached adulthood. There is no evidence that mortality rates changed significantly after the Revolution, yet there was certainly an increased willingness to discuss death, a heightened awareness of "how uncertain . . . is Life!"[13] From the presence of death, people now drew unhappy lessons. Thus, one woman whose daughter, young as she was, had already lost three of her playmates, concluded, "Truly this World seems full of death & woes –" Once a "melancholy subject" that Virginians had tried to keep at bay, death and its sadness were now invited indoors and made part of life. Thus Louisa Cocke, in addressing a group of Sabbath school children one November, delivered a warning certain to impress her young charges. "Such is the well known uncertainty of Life," she began, "it would be more a matter of wonder – that, in the number of children & grown persons now assembled here – every one should escape through an entire Winter, than that some should fall victims to Death in the same period of time."[14] Suddenly, it was appropriate to remind a group of children that not all of them would survive the winter.

To be sure, New England's Puritans had alerted their children to the precariousness of life and the danger of dying a sinner's death. But when Louisa Cocke and other Virginians began their lessons on mortality, they did not – like Cotton Mather and Jonathan Edwards – conclude with chapters on hell's fires and eternal damnation. The Puritans had described hell so vividly in order to keep their children out of it, but the nineteenth-century evangelicals were not Puritans; they were concerned neither with predestination nor with eternal punishment. Death for them taught a different lesson. Death brought home, literally – in an age in which most people died in their own beds – the unhappiness of life; yet for nineteenth-century Virginians, death was thought to mark the end of the individual's world of misery and the beginning of his happier time to come. Sentimental religion, in emphasizing the insubstantiality of earthly pleasures, contrasted them to the joys of the future reward. Again and again mourners were told – and this was the most common consolation of the nineteenth century – that the dead had made a "happy Exchange." They had "gone to seek a better World," one "better suited" to those "pure in Spirit" or "too sensitive to be happy here." The dead, certainly, were "better off."[15] If life was "a sad and weary pilgrimmage on earth," then it followed that the dead were "beyond all the troubles of this life," and from that, men and women concluded, the departed were "much more fortunate in being spared the trials which attend every one in this life."[16] So the logic went; around and around the phrases were traded whenever consolation was required.

The examples could be multiplied almost endlessly; they appear in virtually every letter of consolation written in the first third of the nineteenth century. It had become conventional to reassure the bereaved that the dead were better off. Virginians voiced that belief so mechanically that it is tempting to view them as so under the sway of sentimental religion that they invoked its creed and pieties unthinkingly. True, the conviction that the dead had made a happy exchange depended upon a belief in the insufficiency of this world in contrast to the fulfillment of the one to come. Yet men and women spoke not by rote, but from experience; the evangelical creed corresponded to their own deepest feelings. Consider, for example, the words Agnes Cabell used in consoling her daughter upon the death of her adored son. Mrs. Cabell urged her child to subdue the "despair and agony of [your] grief. . . . [for your] dear little Paul"; she feared the effects upon her daughter's mind and health both. "I do not ask you to forget your dear child. – Oh, no! that cannot be – but try to prevail on yourself to think of him as having gone before you but out of a world of trouble to a Heaven of rest & bliss." Such a consolation followed the convention, but then the older woman spoke from the heart: "What has *he* lost by leaving the world so young – you know how seldom life is a blessing to any –." Could anyone write those bleak words and believe they would be soothing without giving them credence? So also must Lelia Tucker have spoken from conviction when she advised a friend whose nine-year-old daughter had just died. That the dead were now in heaven was not questioned. "Of her immortal & unchangeable happiness you can now have no doubt – Had she lived to experience the various trials of human life who can tell what might have been the final result. . . . who of us has not wished in bitterness of spirit, wished a thousand & a thousand times that it had pleased our heavenly Father to have taken us to his bosom in our days of childhood. . . ."[17] The belief was clear: So unhappy was life that it was better to die a child.

Surely such a consolation is extraordinary. It depended upon the shared conviction that life was no blessing. Why did genteel Virginians find life so bleak? As we have seen, sentimental religion held that this world was inferior to the one to come. As a result, the bereaved might determine that a loved one's death had been necessary "to wean our hearts from the vain world & turn them to [our Almighty Father.]" Here we see religious beliefs shaping the response to death. So also when a bereaved woman was reminded that she had lost a beloved daughter, true, but also "the magnet that drew & fixed your Soul to Earth. – How could you have wished to leave a world that contained her? . . . look to the future."[18] Religion tried to detach people from the world, and as a result, men and women increasingly saw their lives on earth as in some sense unreal. In the early nineteenth century, they began to use images of life as theater or a stage. George Blow, for example, informed a friend that ". . . the Christian alone can fearlessly meet the closing scene," and an elderly man confessed that "I look forward to a close of the scene, the dropping of the curtain."[19] The use of such language, uncommon in the years before the Revolution, suggests that Virginians could see life as a play or, more precisely, as an act. Such a vision, potentially tragic, more often for the Virginians sentimental, disassociated them from their own lives, reinforcing the religious characterization of life's actions as just so many shams.

Yet to say that men and women were inclined to see life as pretense or preparation does not directly answer the question posed: Why did life seem that way, why was it so unhappy? What, precisely, made Heaven preferable to earth? Perhaps by studying Virginians' vision of heaven, their eternal reward for their earthly pain, we may better understand that pain. Heaven, men and women said, was quite simply "a world where there is no parting." Those words were uttered again and again: Heaven was "that world where sorrow and sickness and parting are no more." After death, we would go to a "better World (*never to part again!*)." Heaven was a place "where death and sorrow shall no more prevail," "where there is neither sickness [n]or sorrow. . . ."[20] The same words, the same phrases, the same vision, stunning in its simplicity: Heaven was the world without death and without grief. Although the notion of heaven was a sacred concept, its depiction was not: Heaven was defined as a family reunion where those separated by death would be rejoined, never more to part.[21] What distinguished heaven from earth was the absence of death. Life's greatest joys were to be found within the embrace of the domestic circle, whose sanctity could at any time be violated by a visit from death. It was death, then, that made life unbearable.

If the letters and diaries of nineteenth-century genteel Virginians show that sentimental religion increasingly shaped their understanding of death, those writings also reveal the growing importance of love. Religion argued for detachment from the world, but that world was filled with people one loved. Sentimental religion awakened the emotions and those emotions allowed for both more affection and more despair than had been considered wise in the previous century. No wonder that people focused their hopes on a world to come: There, at an eternal family reunion, they could love each other to the end of time. Love could be enjoyed without risk of pain.

But on the earth that belonged to the living, men and women found that affection could bring sorrow in its train. Usually cultural change takes place slowly, almost imperceptibly; the transformation being discussed here transpired over several decades, so that its full import is most often realized when personal writings from, say, 1825 are contrasted to those of 1775. Thus, the emotional world of Thomas Jefferson's grandchildren would be noticeably different from that of their grandfather. Occasionally, however, we are able to see one person experiencing, in a brief period, a lifetime's worth of change.

John Hartwell Cocke in certain ways was typical of the early-nineteenth-century gentry. Rational and unsentimental, patriotic and devoted to "improvement," whether of his mind, his farm, or his nation, he superficially, at least, resembled his older friend, Thomas Jefferson. Like virtually all planters, he kept a farm journal in which he recorded the important events that occurred on the plantation. In it he also on occasion noted family matters, such as the birth of his fifth child in September 1816. This time, however, his wife, Nancy, failed to recover as quickly as she had in the past. For two and a half months she suffered from a "sick stomach," and her strength "manifestly diminished." Although his wife had not shown "the least depression of spirits," Cocke was becoming alarmed. "Oh God," he prayed, "If it is my destiny to lose her, grant me fortitude under this heaviest of earthly afflictions."[22] Unlike his friend Jefferson and their eighteenth-century ancestors, John Cocke was willing to permit his wife's illness and his own emotions to become the stuff of his diary. A farm journal had become a personal one, and the willingness to translate observations and feelings into words and to commit them to paper marked an important change, not only for John Cocke but for other Virginians as well.

By November 29, Nancy Cocke had realized the gravity of her illness. She told her husband that "She had been reviewing her past life, and although she saw in it many things to blame . . . yet she could not charge herself with any great or alarming judgment against her before God. She avowed her faith in the Christian doctrines and declared if it should be God's will to call her at this time from the world, she would not murmur against the decree." She told her husband that she "was convinced of the vanity of earthly things." She was especially happy that she had taken communion while in Norfolk the previous spring.[23]

A week later, sleeping fitfully, Nancy Cocke called her husband to her bed at four in the morning, "saying that her feelings were indescribably distressing." "Now for the first time," John Cocke observed, "her fortitude seemed to give way under the accumulated sufferings from her disease. She expressed herself greatly dissatisfied at her want of composure, said she had flattered herself she had been better prepared. Still . . . she could charge herself with no great offense, that all her causes of dissatisfaction were offenses of omission. . . . She expressed herself mortified . . . to find that her feelings were so much concentrated on herself. . . . I enjoined her to take consolation from the example of the meek and blessed Jesus, the only created being who ever lived without offense, and who, when he approached the awful trial of his dissolution gave utterance to expressions which manifested his dread of the event." The Cockes discussed religion and read several prayers, seeking comfort and consolation. After a while, Nancy's "spirits were evidently tranquilized."[24]

Four days later, drifting off to sleep, Nancy Cocke told her husband that she had "heard Mrs. Coalter died as easily as I am now going to sleep," and she recounted what she had heard of that woman's last moments. Nancy then remarked that "'I have been entirely unable to account for my feelings the other night when I called you to the bed to me . . . I feel not the least alarm and never have at contemplating death since my sickness but on that occasion.' I expressed to her the consolation I experienced from this declaration." She replied to her husband, "'I am mighty happy.'"[25]

John Cocke's first diary entries about his wife's illness had been included among records of other daily occurrences on the plantation, but Nancy's perilous condition had rapidly become the only subject of his diary. In his writing Cocke found solace. "I have employed myself with much consolation to my wounded spirit," he wrote, "in making out the . . . account of some of the most impressive scenes of her last days."[26] Cocke allowed himself his feelings. No longer were old affections to be burned, old anguishes to be destroyed. And so the record continued.

On December 9, Nancy Cocke believed her last day had come; she began to make arrangements for her death. She conversed with her family and "desired us to moderate our grief and submit with resignation to the Divine Will."

Although usually composed, she "gave way to tears" when discussing her family. "She did not wish to leave us. She loved us all. She had been too happy in her family, in her children, in her friends, in all the circumstances of her earthly fortune, not to look back with feelings of pleasure and gratitude to her past life." She believed she had been a dutiful daughter, but feared she had not made her husband "as happy in every respect as she ought to have done, – but, Oh God! I call Thee to witness . . . that she was to me all that I could have hoped for in a wife, or expected in a woman." She feared that she had not been as good a mother, plantation mistress, or neighbor as she might have been "but felt no dread at obeying God's summons." She prepared small gifts for her family and friends and gave her husband her wedding ring, saying, "'You must have this, it has never been off before.'" "During this heart-rending scene," her husband continued, she "was tranquil and composed, and frequently recalled our distracted minds back to a sense of duty and humble submission to the Will of God." She remembered and named "many of her beloved friends who had gone before her, and with whom she was soon to meet. . . . an angelic smile lighted up her emaciated features, and her whole manner seemed to be the result of supernatural power." In such a way did Nancy Cocke spend what she believed would be her last day.

Nancy, however, awoke the next morning and told her husband, "'It will be a pity if I am not to die now, for perhaps, I shall never again be as well prepared.'" She would lose her composure only once more, when her eldest child returned home from boarding school. When he perceived his mother's condition, "and when his tears began to flow, her fortitude and resignation, great as it was, yielded to the feelings of nature. The Saint, for a moment, gave way to the Mother, and she wept." A pious friend, however, found Nancy well prepared for her death and told Cocke, "'We have nothing to weep for but ourselves. She is already an angel.'"

Christmas Day, her fourteenth wedding anniversary, found Nancy Cocke still alive but extremely frail. That day John Cocke found his "agonizing trial . . . carried to its last excess." Only his wife's composure enabled Cocke to control his grief: "Had I beheld her, who had been the source and participator of all my joys, clinging to the world, and lamenting her untimely separation from it, where could I have found a ray of consolation? But when I saw . . . her spirit meek, submissive, resigned and participating of none of the feelings of this world save compassion, and tenderness for the beloved objects she was about to leave in it, every generous principle of human nature conspired with the dictates of devotion in prompting me to exclaim, Lord, thy will be done. Take thyself her languishing spirit!" Two days later, Nancy Cocke knew her end had come. She closed her eyes and, too weak to talk, said goodbye to her family with "gentle pressures of her enfeebled hands. Finally such was the calm and peaceful rest of her blessed spirit, that it left her mortal remains without the slightest tremour of a nerve or the agitation of a muscle."[27]

John Cocke, unlike earlier Virginians, let his emotions spill onto paper, there to be shaped by his words. Proceeding from his plantation accounts, his style seems simple and uncontrived, yet the words are chosen, the phrases arranged. They shape the feelings and comment upon them.

Plate 9. John Hartwell Cocke, a planter, a reformer, a military man, and a Christian gentleman, known by his neighbors for his ability to drive a hard bargain. (Virginia State Library.)

Plate 10. Bremo, the home of John Hartwell Cocke, completed in 1819. Like that of his friend, Thomas Jefferson, it was designed to appear more modest than it in fact was, a monument to good taste, but not ostentation. (Library of Congress.)

Consider again Cocke's description of his wife's reaction to her son's grief: "and when his tears began to flow, her fortitude and resignation, great as it was, yielded to the feelings of nature. The Saint, for a moment, gave way to the Mother, and she wept." Here we see eighteenth-century restraint giving way to Romantic expression. A son's tears untie a mother's heart; she yields to nature and cries. John Hartwell Cocke was a military man and a planter, but like the Romantic poets he knew that we would be affected most by the mingled tears of mother and son. But once that grief

– which an earlier age had been so afraid to discuss and release – was displayed, how could it be restrained, how could it be kept from sweeping all life in its tide? This was the challenge to John Cocke and his heirs.

Part of the solution lay in shaping those emotions that were unleashed. Thus, Nancy Cocke was laid to rest in the family plot at Bremo and in her husband's affecting words as well. In expressing himself, John Cocke found solace. But his greatest consolation came from his departing wife herself. It was, finally, her resignation to her approaching death that enabled John Cocke also to submit. Cocke looked not to religion but to his wife for reassurance.

Although nineteenth-century Virginians were, in their display of sentiment, more religious than their eighteenth-century counterparts, the ways in which they discussed death suggest that they were less easily reconciled to it. The common consolations that death was good and necessary for the dead and the living both were offered to quiet fears to the contrary. But it was from the dying themselves that the living sought assurance that death was not to be feared, and it was from the departing that they asked the meaning of death, and, ultimately, of life.[28] John Cocke's fears and consolation would be shared by many nineteenth-century Virginians who watched their loved ones die. So similar would other deathbed scenes be that they would almost become rituals.[29]

Not all men and women, however, were prepared to die, for they were not ready to leave their loved ones. Separation from her family, after all, had been Nancy Cocke's greatest regret about leaving the world. Sarah Nicholas wrote her sister about the death of their uncle. "His own

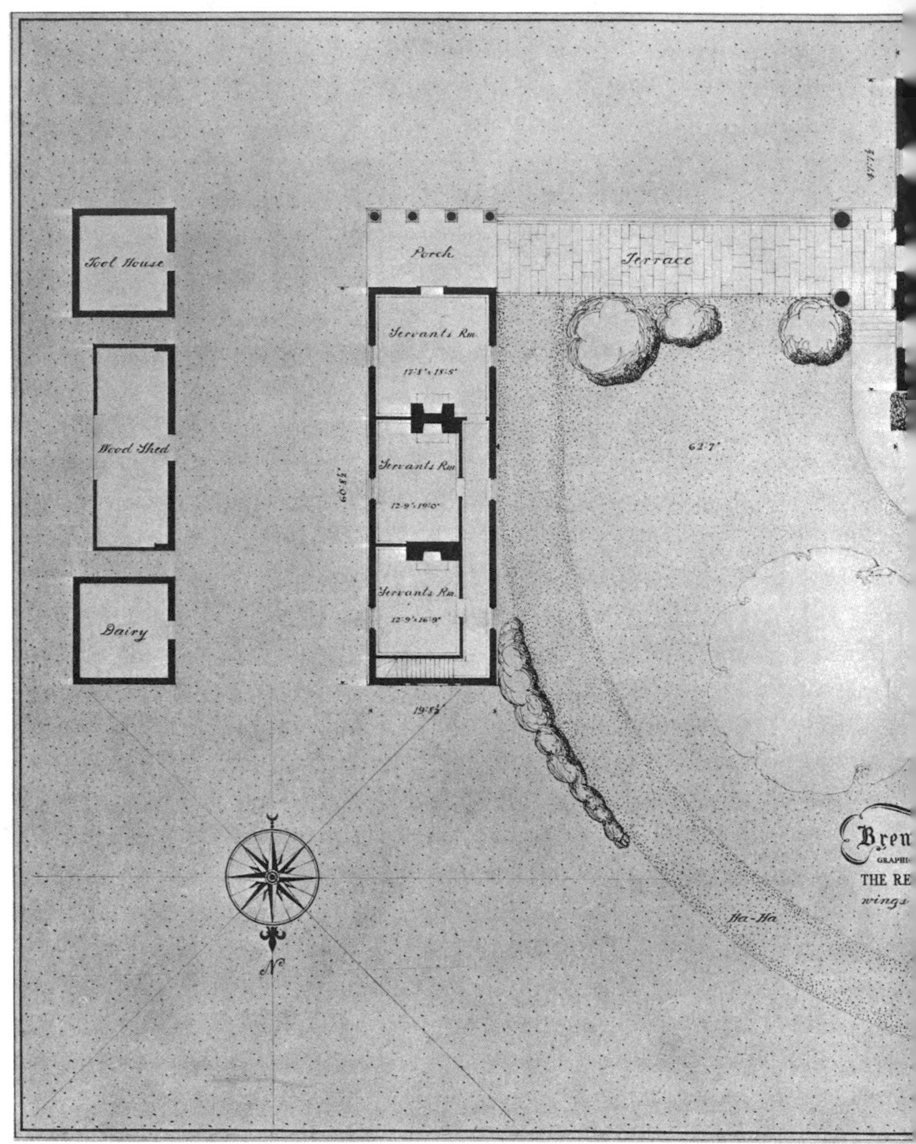

Plate 11. The first floor of Bremo. Formal still, yet an expression of Cocke's personality. (From *The Great Georgian Houses of America*, vol. 1 [New York: Dover, 1970], 97.)

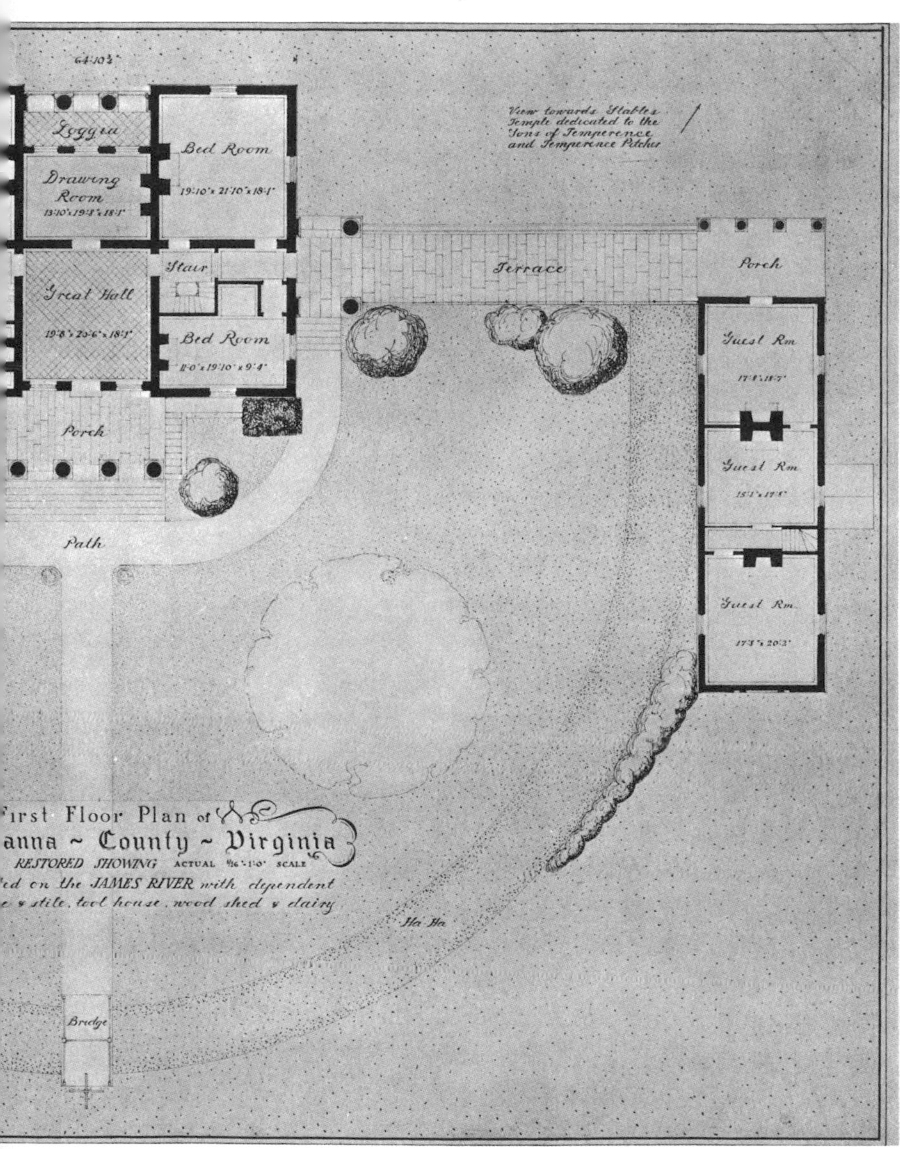
View towards Stables
Temple dedicated to the
Sons of Temperence
and Temperence Pitcher
Loggia
Bed Room
Drawing Room
Stair
Great Hall
Bed Room
Terrace
Porch
Guest Rm
Guest Rm
Guest Rm
Porch
Path
Ha Ha
Bridge
First Floor Plan of
anna ~ County ~ Virginia
RESTORED SHOWING ACTUAL SCALE
ed on the JAMES RIVER with dependent
e & stile, tool house, wood shed & dairy

Plate 12. Temperance temple at Bremo. After the death of his beloved wife, Nancy, John Hartwell Cocke dedicated himself to Christ and good causes. He built a temperance temple at which the residents of his plantation could drink pure spring water. The inscription reads: "Dedicated to the Sons of Temperance." (Library of Congress.)

agitation was very great – he told us, just as my dear Maria [a cousin who had recently died], he loved us all so much he could not bear to part with us, & kept his eyes fixed on Mary Jane [his daughter] & her hand in his all the time. . . . I think he was frightened. . . . " Others might be less fearful of death itself, such as Sallie Faulcon's sister, who "felt no fears at the thought of death. . . . she did not poor soul see her dear little children three days before her death – she would frequently mention them, & say the sight of them wou'd perhaps make her unwilling to leave this world –"[30] Whether frightened or resigned, men and women knew that death meant separation. Some might hold on to a loved one until the last minute weakened the grasp, whereas others might send their loved ones away; in either case, the last thoughts of the dying seem to have been about those they were leaving, not whom or what they might meet in a world to come.

Although descriptions of deathbed scenes suggest that those who were dying were most upset by the impending separation from those they loved, these documents show even more clearly that it was the living who were unprepared for the parting. Leaving seems to have been easier than being left. Thus, in October 1829, Louisiana Cocke Faulcon was brought to her father's home, "amaciated & broken down by disease." A month later she was completely resigned to her death and asked her very pious stepmother why she was still kept on earth. "[Louisiana] said she wondered if it should be because she was not prepared to die . . . I said, 'it was not permitted to us to know the reasons for God's dealings with us – but perhaps though prepared herself, she might be kept with us because we were not prepared to lose her yet.'"[31] God knew, it was surmised, that her family needed more preparation to relinquish her than she to surrender them.

If a man or woman or even a child could maintain fortitude in the face of death, he or she could help the family to accept the approaching separation. It was, finally, separation from their loved ones that Virginians most feared; and if, like Nancy Cocke, the departing displayed courage, so also would the bereaved. Hence, the living began to take great interest in the manner in which their loved ones died. Martha Terrell, for example, wrote her brother that their sister had died two months after giving birth. "With unexampled patience . . . she resigned her spotless soul into the hands of her God. If there can be any comfort in such a stroke, we ought to derive it from the manner of her death. Perfectly resigned to the will of her Master, she spent her last moments in endeavoring to alleviate the afflictions of her friends." Josepha Nourse "frequently entreated [her parents] not to grieve for her; oh no, she said, [do not grieve] as for those who have no hope, and spoke with complacency of our Journey home together. . . . Our tears have copiously flowed, but . . . we have often said what she frequently repeated . . . 'How good God is.'" One final example makes the same point even more succinctly. Agnes Wirt's parents took consolation from the manner of her death: "The pious, I might say *triumphant* Christian death she died seemed to rob it of its bitterest sting."[32] By their resignation, young women, taken before their time, gave their families this most important bequest.

Even those who anticipated that they might bear a loved one's death philosophically often found themselves wanting in fortitude. In discussing the resignation to death others had displayed, Philip Barraud had asked, "Where then are the Terrors of Death?" When his son John failed to recover from a debilitating disease, Barraud, however, saw his courage deserting him. "I feel a state of mind that I am ashamed to express even to you," he confessed to a close friend. "I have resisted Despair for a long Time – I must not yield to it but I fail of my accustomed Fortitude." A year and a half later, John Barraud was still alive, but declining. His father still suffered. "It is hard," he wrote, "to yield such a child to the Grave." It was only his son's fortitude that relieved Philip Barraud's despair: "Our beloved John was calm, collected, and undismayed & even cheerful to his latest Breath – . . . his address to his Parents was the most Eloquent, Dutiful & full of affection and wisdom of his whole Life and betrayed a development of his preparation for another world, that proved . . . that his change in his own Opinion (& our own) was replete with joyful Hopes & Expectations." It was the dying son who consoled the bereaved father. "The angelic conduct of my darling John seem[s] to have tranquilised my afflicted mind and disposed me to ask of Heaven forgiveness for my Despondency and Ingratitude. . . ."[33]

A good death was for nineteenth-century Virginians a great consolation. A century earlier, men and women had taken comfort from the excellence of the loved one's life. Later, it was the manner of the death that best assuaged grief. Dreading the departure of a loved one, the living were calmed by the dying's acceptance of the approaching separation. And perhaps fearing their own mortality, the living were reassured by the dying that death need not be feared. The frequent report that a man or woman accepted death peacefully implied that death was indeed dreaded, but if it could be met with resignation, with fortitude, and even with triumph and joy, where then were its terrors?[34]

It was not death, finally, that was feared. The dead,

departing with resignation, were intended for heaven, never more to be afflicted with earthly pain. Had they not made a happy exchange? Several months after his wife's death, John Cocke had spoken with a dying man: "Experienced feelings different from what I ever did before at conversing with a man who I thought hastening to the grave. They were not exactly the feelings of envy . . . but they partook in no degree of that horror with which I had hitherto regarded such an object."[35] Perhaps not envy, but also not fear.

Where, indeed, were death's terrors? Why did nineteenth-century Virginians so grieve? Sentimental religion, alas, consoled the dying better than the bereaved. The dead met their reward, whereas the survivors lived on. The death of a loved one was life's greatest trial; for the living there was simply no consolation. Thus, Eliza Prentis mourned the deaths of her mother and father: "The loss of an affectionate Parent, (is in my opinion) the greatest that can befall us."[36] Whereas Virginians had sought compensation and balance for the death of a family member, later Virginians would find such efforts unavailing. "The loss we have sustained is irreparable," Eleanor Parke Lewis wrote after the death of her father. Bathurst Jones consoled a kinsman on the death of his wife with the same words: "I truely commiserate your situation, and Feel sensibly for your Irretrievable Loss; Irreparable." The same thought, again: A young woman whose father had died was told she had "sustained an irreparable loss. . . . "[37] If each individual was unique and irreplaceable, there could be no compensation for the death of a parent, a child, or a spouse.

The bereaved were not consoled for their irreparable

losses. Rather, they were warned that even to wish the dead back from their happy exchange was mere selfishness. Thus, a woman was certain of her uncle's "happiness in another world . . . that it is selfish in me to wish him back in a world of sorrow." Another was admonished, "My dear Jane, reflect, only reflect, how much happier [your child] is now. . . . Is it not a selfish feeling, longer to lament one, in such perfect bliss?" The dead, in leaving this world for a better one, were happier than they had been here and, indeed, were happier than the family they left behind. The bereaved were asked "to congratulate the dead. . . . our departed friends still live . . . in the presence, arms, & happiness of our blessed Lord & Savior! Removed from all dangers, anxieties, cares & uncertainties incidental in a life of probation. . . . we should grieve, watch & pray for ourselves. . . . " The dead were not to be mourned, a mother was reminded: "Your grief now will be for yourself alone." The dead would not even want to be lamented; if a departed sister could "speak to us she would say, 'weep for yourselves, but not for me.'"[38]

This, then, was the consolation offered the bereaved: Weep for yourselves. Was not such a consolation really torture, robbing the bereaved of solace, offering them self-pity instead? We can observe men and women, seeking relief, only inflicting further pain. As we have seen, Virginians such as John Cocke might turn to pen and paper for com fort, trying to shape their feelings with words. Similarly, others turned to verse, no doubt hoping in art to find meaning and solace for their grief. Thus, a bereaved mother rhymed, "His felicity shant give me pain/I would not wish him in this world again." There it is, the familiar thought, now expressed in a couplet. Another mother imagined her infant speaking to her from heaven:

> Now my cries shall cease to grieve thee,
> Now my trembling heart find rest,
> Kinder arms than thine receive me,
> Softer pillow than thy breast.[39]

If the writing itself could provide relief, surely what was written must have increased the pain. What more heart-rending thought could there be for a bereft mother than that her love had not been enough?

Adrift in a sea of self-pity, Virginians inflicted further torture. If one mother had suggested that her baby found a better home with God, implying a failure on that woman's part, another woman could draw the opposite conclusion from a child's death. Lucy Smith, reflecting upon the death of a young man, his parents' only child, "felt alarmed lest he had been withdrawn from them in consequence perhaps of his being too much an idol – this led me earnestly to pray that I might not love my child more than I ought. . . ." Thomas Bolling reasoned the same way; the death of his infant daughter "proved" to him "the fact that God will not permit an Idol to remain with us."[40] God seized our loved ones if they drew our affection from him, if we became so interested in this world that we forgot the next.

Men and women believed that they often brought suffering upon themselves, not by improper or immoral actions but by their very feelings. Mothers who believed their infants happier with God must at some level have doubted their own ability to make their children happy; they must, inescapably, have doubted the quality of their own love. And parents who, on the other hand, thought that God took children who were loved too much just as inescapably found the source of their children's death and their own suffering in the quality of their affection. Again, we see the double message of the nineteenth century: To live, we must sense and we must feel, but sensation both brings and in itself is pain.

Make no mistake: These Virginians both expected and admired emotion. Virginians were counseled to weep for themselves, and they did. Consider Thomas Williamson, who, after the death of his "dear boy," was typically consoled "to know he is better off." Believing himself composed, Williamson returned to his office "when on entering the door and viewing the countenances of all my daily companions filled with sympathy for my misfortune, not one word was uttered from either side!! all silent! until forced to unman myself I retired alone to a room [to weep]." Although Williamson believed that it was unmanly to cry, the sympathy of his co-workers and, indeed, his dramatic rendering of their pity conspired to unleash his grief. Long gone are the days of William Byrd; would Thomas Williamson have confessed his breakdown to a kinswoman had he been ashamed of that display of emotion, had he not wanted to arouse her pity, too? Virginians had begun to consider emotions and feelings as both real and good; melancholy itself was valued. Sympathizing with his brother's grief at the death of his wife, Joseph Lewis could find no higher compliment, no finer consolation, than "I like you better for the grief that you feel. . . ."[41] The times favored mothers over saints, the suffering over the immune, and so to weep – like Nancy Cocke or Thomas Williamson – was expected and approved.

What else could they do? "Weep for yourselves," and

Plate 13. Four generations of the Ege-Galt family. The baby is Frederick Williamson, whose father sought consolation for his son's death in 1803 with the thought that his "dear boy . . . is better off." (Anonymous, c. 1801–3. Abby Aldrich Rockefeller Folk Art Center, Williamsburg, Va.)

they did. What else could Mary Anderson do? In July she lost her infant son. Three months later, she confessed to her brother Duncan that she still was not able to control her sorrow. "I stifle my grief because it hurts my friends but alas it preys on the vital part of my afflicted heart, & in spight of all the fortitude I can summ up I cannot regain my former feelings. I feel that I am wrong, but I know also that My

God will pitty & I Hope will soothe my sorrow to rest." Early the next summer, Mary Anderson's second infant succumbed to smallpox. Her husband took her on a voyage to "relieve her mind." A month later, however, she reported to her brother that her sorrow was "yet unsubdued. - but I am endeavoring to take the advice of my friends & to obey the dictates of reason -." In 1800, reason could no longer subdue feeling, and the bereaved mother suffered. Two weeks later, she explained that she was still "trying to overcome a useless & unavailing Sorrow & I will & I pray for the aid & assistance of my maker." She wrote her brother again, two days later, describing her thoughts and feelings: "Altho I stifle my feelings they are not subdued [,] my pillow is witness to my feelings, when every eye but mine is closed in sleep; then it is I think & weep for those whose eyes are closed in death & to me gone, gone never to return. -" Again, we see the themes of loss and separation, and again we shall see the nineteenth-century Virginian's characteristic response when, in November of the following year, Mary Anderson gave birth to another son: She feared she would lose him, too. "Oh my Duncan I have lost two! - that ought alone to teach me the vanity of placing too fondly my affections on any one subject, yet alas it rather serves to weaken when it ought to strengthen me most."[42]

With no consolation but to weep for herself, with no counsel but to limit her affection for her child, is it any wonder that two years later found Mary Anderson still grieving? Her sister observed, "Mary poor thing looks very badly, she bears her misfortunes with truly Christian fortitude, & resignation, her grief is always of the unobtrusive kind, she says little, but often you may see the big drops chace each other down her pale cheek, when she thinks she is least observed." Mary Anderson's trials were not over. Shortly after its birth, she lost another child. She prayed for her brother, "May you my beloved brother never feel the bitter pangs your poor Sister has had repeated to her. . . ."[43] We sympathize with this afflicted woman and, more significantly, so did her family. Remember the glaring contempt with which William Byrd had scrutinized his wife for signs of weakness, and contrast that to the Romantic light shed on Mary Anderson by a loving sister. Though she tried to hide her grief, the tears "chacing" down the bereaved mother's "pale cheek" were not ignored. Clearly, Mary's sister loved her for the grief that she felt.

Painfully aware of life's losses, yet suspicious of its joys, Virginians lost the balance so characteristic of the eighteenth century. Indeed, the virtues of balance and moderation themselves no longer held sway, as they had in the days when Enlightenment philosophers and enterprising planters alike sang their praises. Instead, there was an expectation that people would "yield to the feelings of nature" (as John Cocke had put it). And although men and women were saddened to see their loved ones faltering under the burden of grief, the most common consolation – that the dead were better off, that we should weep only for ourselves – could only heighten melancholy feelings.

It is no wonder, then, that Virginians such as Mary Anderson could be overwhelmed by grief; it certainly did not surprise their friends and families. Mary's husband, for example, took her on a trip to "relieve her mind," thereby acknowledging and accepting her grief in a way that William Byrd never could. In the decades after the Revolution the head fell victim to the heart, and Mary Anderson was not the only one to suffer. Frank Carr was unable to recover after the death of his wife. "Poor fellow," observed a kinsman, "His severe loss, seems to have unhinged his mind. . . ." No longer did men and women have faith in reason; rarely did they invoke its name in consoling the bereaved, for the mind had become a frail organ, subject to the senses. Most Virginians, then, would have echoed Wilson Cary's simple statement that "grief . . . weakens the mind. . . ."[44]

The common belief that grief weakened the mind explained and thus perhaps encouraged the melancholy of the bereaved. Typically, Eliza Parke Custis grieved for her mother. "The loss of my last, so much loved Parent . . . has pray'd upon my mind, and injured me, a few more years will pass . . . & her often wretched child will leave this world, & fly to her bosom for refuge & Peace." Similarly, although her adored father was resigned to his death, although she was convinced he was "going to a nearer, happier home," Betsy Ambler never recovered from the loss. Five years later she would write, "The truth is, from the moment I was deprived of my dearest Father, everything in nature, wore a saddened aspect. –"[45] Attached to her father throughout his life, shattered by his death, she continued to be severely depressed for the remainder of her life. Again, we see the grief at separation from a loved one; both women used that loss to "explain" and thus, in a sense, to legitimate their continuing melancholy.

Mourners found solace in self-pity. Truly, the bereaved were to be pitied, and perhaps because that was the only emotional indulgence fully permitted by the sentimental culture, men and women swam in it almost to its farthest shores. Consider Ebenezer Pettigrew, a North Carolina planter, the son of a Virginian. His father was an Episcopal minister, a man of reason, wit, and equanimity, but the son was always of a more sober and emotional bent. His darkest fears were realized with the premature death of his wife, Nancy. In a letter to his sister-in-law are compressed most of the elements of nineteenth-century grief: "I grieve for the suffering of one of the best of women. O my Nancy, my dearest wife! I grieve that she was taken in the prime of life from her dear family. I grieve because I was blessed and knew it not. I grieve for myself because I have lost that which the whole world could not replace. I grieve that I did not know the author of my blessing. I grieve that my dear Nancy did not live to see that change in my heart towards the great author of all good. I grieve because I required such a heart rending affliction to bring me to a knowledge of my own weakness & my dependence on him. I hope & pray God that this curse of sorrow, which is now overflowing may be lessened." It is his great loss that convinces Pettigrew of his own insufficiency and brings him closer to God. He slides easily from grief for his wife to mourning for himself. Half a year later, the forty-seven-year-old widower still wept for himself (as he would the rest of his life); one night, on a piece of writing paper, he wrote his own prayer: " . . . it is hard to live, and a dreadful creation for mortal existence. Poor Dear Nancy! Poor Dear Nancy! Poor Dear Nancy! and Poor disconsolate Old man! Poor forelorn old man! Amen, amen." Pettigrew worshiped, finally, his own loss and grief; he clung to his isolation and self-pity, finding in them his creed: "To court nobody and expect no court from any, is a happy condition, a golden age, and the most natural state of man."[46]

Death ruptured the ties between the living and the dead, and surviving Virginians found in that sense of separation and loss the kernel of their religion. Yet it was a curiously unspiritual age. Rare was the genteel Virginian who could envision God more clearly than his own self-pity. Their peculiar mixture of sentiment and creed confirmed men and women in a despair from which they drew no more heavenly reward than a family reunion in the world to come.

4
"Little ambitions"

SUCCESS

"HABITS OF INDOLENCE"

BY 1824 Peachy Gilmer reckoned himself a failure. This scion of a prominent Virginia family confessed to an old friend, "The little ambition I once had is extinguished: a farm, a snug cottage after the English manner, food & raiment, & education for my children, with patience to buffet the rippling waves of life until they cast me upon the shore of Eternity." Gilmer's goal was modest, as he himself acknowledged, yet it proved elusive, for he found that the profession he had chosen – the honorable and respectable practice of law – could not bring him peace. He complained, "I am weary (not of life) but of both John Doe, and Richard Roe, and still more weary of those who appeal to them." His clients and his fellow Virginians "derange and subvert: that tranquility & domestic repose; so becoming and so desirable to advancing years; Really I am apprehensive there can be but little consolation, in retrospect upon the life of an old lawyer. . . . I would fly, as from the plague, from the profession, if fortune had not clipt my wings: . . . when we are ascending the hill of life, all buoyed it is a fairy land filled with joyful expectation, but when we reach the top, and look upon the regions, that lie, between us and the grave. It is in truth, little better than a wilderness, abounding more in thorns, and in bitter fruits than in flowers. . . . blessed are they, who look still farther, to that peace which passeth understanding." There is much in Gilmer's lament that by now should be familiar: Gilmer has sought a life of "tranquility & domestic repose," only to find his world a "wilderness"; true peace will be found only on the other side of the grave. If Gilmer's dream – "after the English manner" – was shaped by convention, so also was his complaint, for he spoke a language common to Virginians of that time. What is puzzling is why a son of Virginia's planter elite would have set for himself so modest and conventional, so carefully studied a goal, only to find his fairyland turn into a vision of hell. His wings were clipped, but Gilmer had been no Icarus, defying the gods. He was merely a country lawyer who loathed "compulsitory intercourse with . . . [his] fellow creatures."[1]

No more than William Byrd or any other eighteenth-century gentleman could Gilmer brook being subject to what one planter had scorned as the "humors and vices of others."[2] But those planters, in the years before the Revolution, had boasted not only of their "independence" but also of their wealth and power. Gilmer seemingly has struck a bargain: He asks for neither fortune nor fame; these he will forgo if only he may retain independence, tranquillity, repose. Gilmer would sacrifice the wealth of his fathers in order to secure their independence, but why should a son of the elite think such a bargain was required?

Peachy Gilmer never addressed himself to our question, but he was not the only Virginian of his generation to strike an imaginary deal, to aspire to less than his father had, and to find even his modest hopes dashed. From the writings of other men and women we can reconstruct a picture of the glittering fairyland of the pre-Revolutionary gentry, a world that seemed to offer opportunity to the ambitious and satisfaction to the proud. And we can see how, in the decades after the Revolution, that world turned into a nightmare, frustrating the little ambitions of honorable men. It should be made clear that the story to be told here is not about the changes in Virginia's economy – although that is an important part of the tale, but rather of the notions that men and women held of proper economic activities, of the nature of work and reward, of the relationship between character and success; that is, we will concern ourselves with the values, attitudes, and perceptions that men and women brought to their work, that they used to understand their work and that of others.

It will be remembered that Virginians had long cherished independence, and this would remain the ideal into the nineteenth century. Independence, freedom from entangling relationships with others and especially from debt, was considered the precondition for a life of comfort and ease, a life free from trouble. So widely shared was the ideal that it required no explanation. J. H. Coles spoke for many men when he proclaimed, "My crede [*sic*] of Happiness is a Virtuous, improve[d] mind, a happy female Companion, and independent situation." Again and again, independence was equated with happiness, as when one young man predicted to a friend, "If I was independent – I should be happy." Independence was not merely a prerequisite for happiness: It was joy itself. More than love or salvation, fortune or fame, young men aspired to independence, so much so that it could seem like a state of spiritual grace. Consider, for example, the words Bathurst Jones used to inform a kinsman that he had recently purchased a plantation: ". . . if I have not (bought a good bargain) comfort at least I *have*. for with truth may I say since I have got fixed on my farm, in the Language of the Scripture; that I experience a peace and comfort which passeth understanding."[3] In the nineteenth century, as in the eighteenth, Virginians worshipped independence; it was their faith and their creed.

Independence, then, was divine, a veritable heaven on earth, assumed to be within the grasp of the gentry (or even the majority of respectable white farmers). Consequently, dependence and its forerunner, debt, were despised. When Virginians spoke about dependence, they wrote in the same shorthand they used for discussing independence; no elaboration was required when assumptions were so widely shared. Thus, a woman could inform her daughter that "Dependence, surely, is one of the capital evils, inflicted on the human species." Dependence was cause for shame, apology, and anxiety. Richard Meade, falling into debt, confessed his fears to his brother. "I have a wife & two children, whom I am happy enough to fancy equal to any – . . . & well is this for me, or I should have but little comfort, for my pecuniary affairs disturb me greatly," he wrote. "Your abhorrence of debt cannot exceed mine – I am in debt, which sours almost every scene of my life – tis a state of dependence which a man of honor & feeling can by no means reconcile or sleep soundly in; I am naturally disposed to be content with this world. I study to be more so – & ask for no more than I have just title to. . . . These are the circumstances that disturb my peace."[4] Again, the language and the feelings are familiar: The goal is peace, and peace lies in freedom from debt and compromising dependence upon others.

At one level, gentry thinking was simple: Avoid debt, be self-sufficient. By the time of the Revolution, such a creed had become part of the prevailing republican ideology, for the virtuous, independent farmer was seen as the ideal citizen of a republican society and – because he was subject to no one else's will – the surest guarantor of liberty. So also did the abhorrence of debt reflect an abiding distrust of commerce and all those complex financial interactions that were so necessary in a mercantile economy but that could – in a popular simile of the age – burst like a bubble, splattering a man with droplets of his hope.[5] Independence, then, was woven into the fabric of the political, social, and economic ideology of the age of the Revolution. It became part of the garment in which relationships, economic and social as well as political, were clothed.

Yet if the ideal was simple in one regard, it was more puzzling in two others. First, even if Virginians abhorred debt, they did not and could not avoid it. Even ignoring the mounting spiral of planter indebtedness in the years before the Revolution, a certain amount of debt was unavoidable in an undeveloped economy that relied upon a seasonal cash crop. Planters needed credit from merchants until their crops were in, and in the absence of a plentiful, sound circulating medium, the local economy consisted of a complex net of I-owe-yous, payable in hogsheads of tobacco. Add to this the fact that the planters were dependent upon their slaves and that, in the colonial period, everyone depended upon the whim of the British crown, and it becomes obvious that the sort of independence that was worshipped could be achieved not by a planter who depended upon the marketing of his tobacco but only by a farmer who was by himself capable of satisfying all his family's needs.[6] Independence, as it was rhapsodized, was not a plausible goal, yet the gentry invoked it as if it were.

Instead, its origins were partly literary – "after the English manner," as Peachy Gilmer had put it – and it is puzzling, too, that the aggressive, grasping pre-Revolutionary gentry should have bequeathed to their sons a notion of economic and social life that partook more of fiction than of sociology. Here we resume the story begun in our first chapter. Remember Richard Ambler, who had sent his sons to London in the mid-eighteenth century for a gentleman's education, proud that his offspring would not be "condemn'd to the necessity of Labouring hard" for a living. Pre-Revolutionary planters such as Ambler had amassed fortunes not "after the English manner," that is, not by the desultory farming or professional dabbling that nineteenth-century Virginians assumed was the practice of the English gentry. Instead, the great southern fortunes were built not by tobacco planting alone, but by commerce, land speculation, and money lending as well.[7] The most successful planters in the eighteenth century were entrepreneurs and merchants in addition. The accumulation of wealth and power required energy, skill, and aggression. William Fitzhugh, an emigrant from England, declined to visit his brother in the homeland, "For in my Opinion none under the degree of a settled annual income which can be advantageously managed in their absence, can give Regency & power to fancy & delight, as to neglect Interest or their particular concerns. . . ." For such men, business came first, and "settled incomes" would not be derived solely from tobacco. In 1751 John Smith hoped his son would develop a fondness for "some business. . . . for planting alone is poor doings. but with other business it will answer very well." On the one hand, such men engaged in a variety of economic endeavors, many of which Revolutionary ideologues would tar with the brush of "commerce," as if to reject not only the centralizing and modernizing tendencies of contemporary economic and political life[8] but also the source of their own fathers' rise to fortune and prestige.

It was partly the fathers' own doing, for if they struggled in a colonial wilderness it was only to – again Richard Ambler's words – set themselves "above the lower class and thereby [enable] them to . . . [preserve] their children in the same class & Rank among mankind."[9] Here is the dynamic: Parents *rise* in the world, only to *preserve* their children at the same level, as if the parents were self-made aristocrats, creating also the rank to bequeath to their offspring. Clearly, parents intended to give each of their children an "independence," an estate upon which each child could subsist in comfort. Such was the goal in the eighteenth century and so it was in the nineteenth. As John Taylor told a friend, ". . . I have six sons, plantations only for two, money to buy them for two more, and the remaining two I propose to provide for by dying in time to divide between them that whereon I live." Again, we are in a realm of widely shared assumptions in which parents discuss how best to fulfill their obligations to their children. Thus, Peter Carr could congratulate his sister on a wise investment her husband had made: "I suppose that the property . . . is now very valuable, and that its value will be much enhanced by the time your children stand in need of it, as a fund, which will make them independent, and you happy; – for your happiness will certainly be increased by the reflection that they are independent."[10] The parent who could give each of his children – daughters included, for they were usually given movable property or cash as a dowry to be combined with the groom's land – independence might rest satisfied.

If the fathers – and this term will be used to include all those members of the planter elite who turned Virginia into a tobacco colony in the century before the Revolution – were self-made men, their sons were not. The fathers, to the best of their ability, gave their offspring both landed estates and a set of notions about how to conduct themselves in the world. We know that many, if not most, in the Western world at that time had ambivalent attitudes about commerce, the marketplace, and the increasing modernization and interdependence of economic life; recent historians have skillfully shown how such misgivings could fuel a variety of social and political movements and ideologies throughout the nineteenth century.[11] In the South and in Virginia, the dilemma was particularly complex. First, the attempt of the fathers to create a New World landed gentry flew in the face of countertrends toward both democracy and an increasingly commercial economy. Second, in grounding their ideal of independence in plantation slavery, southerners wedded their vision to both the land and a form of labor that the modern world was finding increasingly repugnant. By the mid-nineteenth century, southerners would be twisting and turning on their own rack, fighting rhetorically, at least, against commerce and justifying slavery, all the time proclaiming themselves true democrats. But in the heady years before the Revolution, no one more than the Virginians had tied together the loose ends of a logic that legitimated quasi-aristocrats as independent citizen–farmers, all the more admirable as Americans because their aspirations were modest, "after the English manner."

Rejecting commerce and mercantile pursuits more categorically than their Northern counterparts,[12] much of the Virginia gentry by the early years of the nineteenth century clung both to planting and the professions of law and medicine and to the notions that extolled those occupations as the most virtuous. Here we find Virginians living by their own rhetoric, striking Peachy Gilmer's bargain. "When last you wrote me you seemed discouraged as to the farm," John Lewis responded to his son in 1806. "Do you think of any other business to engage in. the farming is an Independent business, one slow in making money. but if a man will be content with moderate living I believe it is the most happy. as well as the most desirable."[13] Lewis thought that happiness derived from independence rather than wealth; his son should be content with"moderate living."

The presumption was that a young man could not enjoy wealth and happiness both. So Virginians explicitly warned one another; such was the advice young Dabney Smith Carr received from relations when he set out to choose a profession. James Carr, a planter whose own farm was failing, warned his cousin against continuing as a merchant: ". . . abandon a pursuit which at best, affords only temporary wealth: a man may amass great wealth by mercantile pursuits; yet in ninety-nine cases out of a hundred, either the Parents or children are sufferers in consequence of that very wealth; it creates habits of luxury, and extravagance which disqualifies one entirely for supporting the loss which is almost sure to be sustained." James Carr recommended either law or farming. An uncle who was an attorney also warned young Dabney Carr against the perils of a "mercantile business." "It presents," the older man intoned, "a much more alluring prospect [than the law] – in it, we see men accumulating in a few years, princely fortunes; but a fatality seems to attend them – they know not where to stop – the thirst for wealth increases with its possession – success makes them bold – they adventure more & more, & at length by some unlucky step, or some unforseen misfortune, the labour of years is wrecked in an hour. . . . [It is] a game of hazard. the law, is very different – it presents no splendid prospects . . . but to every man who will make himself reputable in the profession, & pursue it with diligence, it assures an independence at least, if not affluence."[14] The older man's fears of commerce are reflected even in the style of his writing: Short, breathless clauses bespeak a deep-seated panic, anxiety about a nameless "they." The cadence becomes less restless only when the attorney writes of the law and the security it offers the (note the change from plural to singular) individual. Mercantile professions, Virginia gentlemen believed, promised inevitable ruin, whereas farming, law, and medicine offered modest success and independence, if not great fortune. Further, both the acquisitiveness and the aggression required to reap enormous profits and the effects of that wealth itself were dreaded; the character necessary to procure wealth and the effect of wealth on character were scorned. Here we see the traditional critique of commerce – that it was chancy, that it led inevitably to luxury (which, in turn, would sap the character so necessary for the success of a republican government) – combined with an injunction to settle for a modest living.

Rather than hazarding fortune, Virginians were told to seek only moderate wealth and, in fact, moderation "in every pursuit, action, or undertaking. . . . a little is enough for all the necessities. . . ." A clear conscience and a tranquil mind were more important than worldly success. John Jacquelin Ambler's father encouraged him to preserve not the family's great estate but its good name. "As to worldly affairs, remember, you have left a *respectable* & *worthy family,* who have preserved their reputation, for three or four *generations blot it not* my *son,* for recollect it would take the same time to *regain it,* if ever."[15] Significantly, young Ambler was not told how that great estate had been acquired. The young were told to settle, and fearing that the pursuit of wealth and true happiness were mutually exclusive, they fastened their hopes upon a vague notion of "happy independence." Yet it is too simple to say that Virginians after the Revolution so internalized contemporary rhetoric that they rejected out-of-hand all commercial enterprises, for in so doing they were making not merely political statements but personal ones as well, saying that they neither could nor would be like their own fathers.

It is not uncommon in history to observe that the children of the nouveau riche scorn their parents' brashness and vulgarity and even that the parents wish their children to be more polished than they. Surely we have seen this in Virginia, with Richard Ambler's desire to educate his sons in London, for example. If the parents and children both wanted for the younger generation the refinement that had eluded the founders of the colony, and if refinement came to be defined as independence and a modest living, we must remember Peachy Gilmer's lament: Even so modest a goal would, for the sons, prove unreachable. The sons struck a bargain, sacrificing the founders' grandeur, perhaps in unconscious recognition of the fact that an aristocracy had no legitimate place in a democratic nation, or perhaps in expiation for their parents' supposed sins in acquiring such great fortunes, and perhaps reinforced in their choice by the evangelical religion that held the rewards of this world illusory and vain. Whatever their conscious and unconscious motives (and here their private writings give no more direct evidence than what has already been here revealed), to strike such a bargain – in this case, for the children of the gentry to so reject the wealth and power of their parents – is a sign of defeat and a signal of submission to some outside force that required such tradeoffs to be made.

If the sons, those who came to maturity after the Revolution, were defeated, that had not been their parents' intent. Those who had given their children independence in the form of an estate hoped to give their children not only the material means for success but the psychological ones as well. In 1749 Richard Ambler, whom we have already met, warned his teen-aged sons, who were studying in London, "Don't trust yourselves in the hands of your own Counsel. . . . a few years more will shew the . . . folly of leaning on the understanding of yr selves." Forty years later, in reprimanding his adolescent stepson for misbehavior, St. George Tucker lamented "that I can not be ever present with you to warn you of the dangers which at your time of life are either overlooked or disregarded." Although independence was valued highly, self-reliance was considered dangerous. A woman reported that a young kinsman had established a business or law office, but had "thought best to dispose of it & return home – & I hope it will prove to his advantage – for he is too young to embark on the boisterous sea of life alone – oh! . . . did youth but know the value of a Parental Pilot in this stormy voyage they would not be so solicitous to escape from their guidance – or so desirous to direct their own course as they generally are."[16] Young people were counseled to rely upon their elders rather than themselves.

Children were dissuaded from seeking independence, for that was something their parents would give them. Ideally, a parent would provide each child with the means to support himself; such an estate did not have to be earned, and thus the only skills a youth would need, in theory, were those necessary to maintain or augment, rather than to acquire, a living. Such an ideal was static, for the children aspired to the standard of living that their parents had enjoyed and, in fact, hoped to give them. Children wanted to equal their parents, not to surpass them; for those already living in comfort, upward mobility held no attraction. Instead, the ideal of bequeathing independence would encourage passivity, as the offspring enjoyed their comfort and maintained their ease, or defensiveness, as they repulsed threats to their peace. Inheriting independence thus would not necessarily ensure a personality that was "independent," that is, aggressive, active, or creative; rather, it might foster the opposite.

How such a dynamic would operate can be seen in the relationship of the lawyer Joseph Prentis to his son, Joseph, Jr. The twenty-two-year-old man, also a lawyer, moved from the family home in Williamsburg to Suffolk, for the home town could not support them both. The young man still sought his father's advice, which the older man gladly gave. Prentis, Sr., regretted that his sons would have to live away from him. "However, it was to be expected and right that they would be prompted to seek out Establishments that might promise support, and place them in situations that might at least present the hope of Happiness." The absent son should nonetheless rely upon the father's counsel: "With the benefit of Experience on my part, I am the better able to judge of that conduct, by which [Happiness] is most likely to be attained. . . . A Young Man just entering into life, and whose character may be truly said to be unfixed ought to pay the greatest attention to the first steps. . . . [Youth] pursue with unabated Zeal the plans formed by themselves with the ardour of youth, and confiding in their own knowledge, become indifferent to the opinions of others. . . ."

The father consistently admonished the young attorney that integrity and peace were more important than worldly success. "Surrender your business, your most flattering prospects, nay my dear Boy even your Life itself; sooner than your charcter to be lost. . . . earthly honours . . . or the pleasures which wealth may present you in its train are mere trifling things compared to a tranquil Heart." Several months later, Prentis, Sr., warned his son, "Your own Happiness is of more importance than wealth, and reject every means to get forward in Life, that may be at variance with the strictest Rules of Honesty, Morality & Virtue –"[17] The older man believed both that his own son was in need of parental guidance and that the conflict between wealth, on the one hand, and integrity and happiness, on the other, was real. The young attorney was warned not to sacrifice character and tranquillity to worldly gain; adopting the rhetoric of the time and place, the father implied that wealth could come only at great personal cost.

Although success as a lawyer came extremely slowly, the younger Prentis remained optimistic. He lamented not his lack of fortune but his great distance from his father. Joseph Prentis, Jr., although separated from his father by perhaps only forty miles, felt himself "thrown upon the grand stage of action without the aid of a father's counsel to direct and govern all his actions: whose reputation and standing in society, is to be established by his own conduct, and action –"[18] Young men such as Prentis, Jr., were advised that happiness would come by practicing moderation, choosing an honest and independent profession, and following parental advice. Self-reliance and wealth could only shatter peace and tranquillity.

Told that they would be given an independence, admonished not to trust their own judgment, and warned that obtaining wealth while maintaining happiness was almost impossible, genteel youth after the Revolution were characterized by idleness and instability. So frequently was such language used that we know we are dealing not with aberration but with what Virginians believed was a serious social problem. A few examples, typical comments from typical letters, should suffice. An "unhappy Kinsman . . . is weak & thoughtless. . . ." A grandson is "not industrious." A son at school "added impudence to idleness . . . easily [led] astray."

A young woman regretted that her cousin was being sent to the University of Virginia: "I think he is quite too young to be trusted." The fears were well founded; a year later, the young man was reported to be leading a life of idleness and dissipation.[19]

Although some young men might outgrow such youthful folly, others would not. Larkin Smith complained of two candidates for senator. Dr. Jones, one of the aspirants, was "an indolent, and almost useless member of any deliberative political body; if he can engross the attention of a private circle, or a dinner party, he appears to be fully gratified. he is certainly a man of brilliant acquirements but his talents are lost to the public from a total want of energy. [Peter] Carr is a man of more energy but the same objections apply to him with considerable force."[20]

We have already suggested that such habits of indolence, so often described, may well have been encouraged by patterns of childrearing. We may return to the Prentis family for further confirmation. Joseph Prentis, Jr., despite an overweening attachment to his father, would eventually establish himself as a lawyer. He and his sister Eliza worried greatly, however, about their brother John and sister Mary Ann. Before his death, Prentis, Sr., too, had worried about John: "I fear that [he] has not that steadiness of mind, and evenness of manners which will promise himself Happiness in Life –." Two years later, Eliza was "pleased . . . to hear that my dear Brother has determined on going to work. It is really what I never expected to hear, as he has so often declared that he never would follow that business." Her anxiety now was focused upon her sister: ". . . could she but conquer her aversion to study, what pleasure it would give us. . . . If she could only prevail on herself to persevere in her studies, she would soon become habituated to them, and find she had only to exert herself –." Although Mary Ann's progress in her studies is unknown, John apparently never developed "steadiness." More than twenty years later, his sister Eliza prayed, "I wish to God, he was established in business somewhere."[21] Habits of idleness, acquired early, often could not be overcome.

Again and again, Virginians faulted themselves and each other for their idleness, unsteadiness, and lack of discipline. It is interesting to note that those contemporary thinkers who favored commerce did so on the grounds that it encouraged industry and vanquished indolence.[22] If Virginians, in eschewing business and gain, sought to avoid the Scylla of luxury, the product of too much wealth in which to indulge, they foundered upon the Charybdis of indolence, thought inevitable without productive activity to keep body and soul engaged.

Nonetheless, although Virginians lamented the laziness they saw, their attitude toward it was frequently ambivalent, for indolent people were often quite likeable. James Greenhow spoke of a friend as a "damn Lazy inat[t]entive fellow th[ough] a very good hearted of one; he has passed a deal of his time in idleness & now cannot Break himself of that habit." Another man described one of his own sons as "the most listless of mortals – who never did any good in his life – . . . he has been a very disrespectful Son – but has a heart I am happy in believing more disposed to virtue than vice." Time or attention, it was hoped, would provide the steadiness that early training had failed to instill. Thus, Neil Jamison was "a pretty sensible young man, he seems at present a little wild but a few years will probably tame him. . . . he seems of a friendly affectionate disposition. . . ." And a mother believed her son "as good as the generality of Boys at his Age. . . . he has a very irr[i]table temper but it is very soon checked. he has capacity to learn, but he wants Industry and Energy. he has a mind which requires to be expanded and cultivated, and if properly directed I think he may make a fine man, but the vine requires pruning. . . ."[23] See how the woman wavers! Again and again, young Virginians, like the woman's son, were seen as idle and wild but fundamentally good-hearted.

Although Virginians so often described young, and sometimes older, persons as indolent but affectionate and seemed to accept these traits uncritically, occasionally a perceptive man or woman would seek their source. Twenty-year-old Ellen Randolph described for her mother a Mr. Barksdale: "Nature appears to have endowed him with talents[.] his education is very good, his temper mild, & he seems free from vice of any description; his greatest fault is a want of stability, he has no firmness of character & of course has been often misled & . . . engaged in some acts of folly & dissipation of which I suspect Mr. Barksdale has been since ashamed. his large fortune has been upon the whole a disadvantage to him, for as every wish is gratified as soon as it arises, he can never be stimulated either by hope or by fear; he has been from the age of eighteen completely his own master & has contracted habits of indolence which make him the victim of languor & ennui; he has nothing to do, nothing to think of, and yet if anything in the world offends him it is to hint at these little defects."[24] Barksdale, as the young woman realized, had been disabled by receiving a fortune without the judgment to manage either it or himself.

Even the prospect, preceding the realization, of inheriting an independence might encourage idleness. Billie Aitchison, for example, had "unfortunately been brought up with the Idea of possessing a fortune when he becomes of age and he gives himself little trouble to acquire kno[w]ledge of any business, so as to add to what little fortune he may have –." Six years later, Aitchison's widowed mother was uncertain about how best to help her son. Although Rebecca Aitchison's brother-in-law advised investing her money and living off its interest, the son wanted "the whole of it . . . to engage in Trade but I am afraid he has not stability & industry sufficient for such an undertaking. . . . but it hurts my feelings very much to refuse a beloved son anything that might contribute to his future advancement in life."[25] Indulgence, it seemed, bred indolence, but indulgence was difficult to avoid.

Virginians often recognized their own unsteadiness but seemed powerless to overcome it. Peter Minor wrote a kinsman, "You ask if I intend to prosecute the study of Medicine? The Volatility of my conduct, first applying to it with ardour, & then abandoning it for months, might well justify such an inquiry." Another young man had a similar confession: "I do not apply very close to business, but still resolve at the end of one week to do better the next & when in a fair way sometimes to put my resolution in practice I find myself under a necessity to apply or rather to attend to something else." Idleness, of course, was not without its charms. Ellen Randolph, so critical of Mr. Barksdale, found herself succumbing to the allures of Richmond: ". . . here there are so many comforts of life, so much *warmth* and ease, so few duties to perform, so many hours of indolence and luxury. . . ."[26] Men and women who prized comfort and ease often had little incentive for choosing industry over indolence.

Habits of indolence acquired early might prove impossible to break. Young Wilson Miles Cary spent brief periods at William and Mary College, Hampden-Sydney College, and the University of Virginia. After dueling with one of his instructors, he was expelled from the last institution. A kinswoman hoped the nineteen-year-old's widowed mother would "place him in the *country* to read Law. This may change the comple[x]ion of his future character which is certainly not a very favorable one at present. good tempered, plausible (they say *clever*) vain, self-conceited, with ungovernable appetites." Although a year working in a rural county clerk's office was reported to have effected "the most surprising conquest over [young Cary's] pride and love for dissipation," by the young man's own admission, the improvement in his character was not complete. In 1828 he told his mother, "Though I am conscious of a great change in my character and that my propensities for wildness and irregularity are considerably shaken yet I feel every day a want of industry and perseverance . . . and the difficulty of acquiring them stares me frightfully in the face[.] nevertheless I *shall Try* and I think I *must succeed.*"[27] Everyone knew what the problem was, including the young man who struggled in vain for self-mastery.

Two years later, by now twenty-four years old, Wilson Cary planned to marry a cousin, Jane-Margaret Carr, but her relatives were not enthusiastic about the match. When one woman proposed a "scheme" for the young couple to prosper, another feared it "might be feesable for a very industrious, energetick man, but for a man of [Wilson's] Indolent temper it would be madness. Under such a pressure of debt, he would be the most miserable man living. let them keep out of debt, and they may avoid complete wretchedness." His father's failure had left Wilson with very little fortune, and Jane-Margaret could expect only a small dowry. Perhaps the couple should postpone marriage until their prospects were "more flattering." "Jane M . . . could accom[m]odate herself to any situation . . . but Wilson . . . becomes gloomy under difficulties. And to encounter abject poverty, and a gloomy tempered husband would be too much for Mortal Woman. . . ." The pessimistic kinswoman concluded, as might many Virginians: ". . . I who have seen so much trouble by beginning the World in debt, have an invisible horror of any scheme that includes debt."[28] Acknowledging that the young man's flawed character made his success improbable, his relations could do no more than counsel that he avoid debt and further responsibility, thereby compounding the cultural problem of which Wilson Cary was so stunning an example.

College, as young Cary's attendance at three illustrates, was not the place for a young man to "get the right end in front." Many of the teenagers attending Virginia's colleges seemed only to spend their parents' money on fancy clothing, gambling, and drink, and in fact, southern colleges were well known for the unruliness of their students.[29] Wilson Cary, writing from college, asked his mother if she could "spare any more money." William Cocke, at the same school, told his father, "I am in great want . . . of money.

About a hundred and ten dollars will be sufficient." Parents honoring such requests urged their sons to be more frugal. Peter Minor sent $100 and the suggestion that "Oeconomy would very well suit our circumstances." But circumstances at college were otherwise; appropriate clothing was a necessity. When his older brother was at college, Robert Hubard was a "little surprised . . . to find that you are in want of money. . . ." Three years later, the younger man better understood how such situations could arise. "I find," he wrote his brother, "that unless I dress decently while here, I shall not be thought much of – or rather *anything*."[30] Philip St. George Cocke told his father that his debt of $130 "may seem to you at first view extravagant, but I am sure it will not when I tell you that I shall not have one single article of dress fit to wear off. . . ." Although parents often indulged their sons at college, such extravagance might produce a rebuke. Young Cocke explained that a debt had been contracted "for the purpose of furnishing myself with some articles of clothes almost indispens[a]ble. . . . I am mortified to find that you consider the fact of my *'owing a debt* of any amount to *any body'* . . . should evince any disregard to your 'earnest and affectionate admonitions.'" The young man conceded that "Debt . . . is an evil . . . above all others . . . since its consequences are often degrading to personal independence as well as ruinous of prosperity."[31] The young man mouthed the conventional wisdom about debt but seemed powerless to follow it.

The protestations of young men at college, their attempts to justify their extravagance and dissipation: These matters would be more amusing were they not indicative of problems within genteel culture, problems of which Virginians were acutely aware. One of the problems was that belief and temperament combined to create patterns of childrearing and education that, in turn, frustrated the original goals. Virginians extolled independence and manly virtue; they got indolence and dissipation instead. The correspondence of the Blow family offers us a rare insight into both the thinking and the practice of one family as they confronted this troubling issue. Our story begins in 1804, when George Blow was a student at William and Mary. His father asked him to explain his "misconduct" there. The young scholar was shocked. "I draw the natural conclusion," he protested, "that some vile, malicious, slanderous calumniator has been casting aspersions on my conduct; of which I am not only innocent, but entirely ignorant. I confess to you that the young men have been dissapated this course, and I have sometimes joined them; but Sir, I must also inform you I have always avoided inebriation." Young Blow acknowledged that some gambled; he did not, nor had he been the second in a duel. He hoped his father would realize that he had not "expended more money than was necessary" for him to maintain his respectability. "You would not have penuriousness imputed to me. . . ."[32] All that distinguished young George Blow from other college students is the vehemence with which he protested his innocence.

As a grown man, Blow regretted his youthful folly and hoped his own sons would behave better. Believing that "at School Boys are too apt to acquire bad Habits which it is difficult even after to shake off," Blow resolved that until college his sons "would always be with me, I should be their constant companion – . . . no bad habit could be acquired, because no bad example would be before them. –" A number of years later, in deciding to send one of his sons to Presbyterian Hampden-Sydney College instead of the University of Virginia, Blow offered a justification based upon his own experience at college and the widespread belief that young people should not rely upon themselves: "Boys at the University are given up to their own controul. . . . & are masters of their own actions and conduct. if idly disposed – they are at liberty to run wild in the mad career of vice and folly intoxication Blasphemy Gaming Lewdness & what not."[33] Typically, Blow recognized the problem but resolved it in favor of parental control, which was to prevent his sons from engaging in the wild behavior expected of young men who were "masters of their own actions."

Despite his determination, George Blow's sons followed in their father's path. Blow's resolve to monitor his sons' behavior proved difficult for a busy planter. "Robert [aged eleven], Richard [nine] and the other children are as playful, as Idle, and as Happy as possible," the planter reported. "My business prevents my attending to all their instruction at this time. But a little relaxation of the Bow will increase its elasticity. and I wish them to run wild with delight. . . ." Again, we see the characteristic preference for pleasure, the shying away from discipline, with the result that two years later, Blow was somewhat alarmed. "The Boys are so Idle that I can do nothing with them. Robert's perversity is unmanageable. Richard I can controul." The young men continued in indolence at college. The eldest son, Robert, often found himself short of money. The next son, Richard, followed his brother's example. Their grandfather lamented, "Rich'd is like Robert, both too full of their pleasures and amusements." The seventeen-year-old

Richard proved unable to account for all the money he had spent at college one year. The next year, he assured his father that he had "not laid out a Dollar for Liquor" and that after he had paid for "books cloth[e]s a straw hat . . . horse hire[,] segars . . . I shall be clear and shall never . . . go in debt for a cents worth of anything so long as I live." The third son, George, resembled his brothers. At the age of fourteen, he was "becoming accustomed to being called a lazy fellow." Two years later, at college, he was "entirely out of money. . . . pennyless on account of the bad state of my wardrobe."[34] Like father, like sons.

Recognizing that discipline was necessary to check indolence, fathers such as George Blow determined to govern their children, only to abandon such plans. Fathers who intended to give their children an independence were not by temperament strict taskmasters. Indulgent and affectionate, they reared children who were, in turn, indulged, volatile, and good-humored. When such youngsters in their early to middle teens went to college, they promptly fell into debt and dissipation, and their parents wondered why.

Young men who insisted that fine clothes, straw hats, and cigars were the necessities of college life (it was these items and never books that sent them into debt) exposed yet another contradiction in Virginians' thoughts about success: Although they had fears about the effect on character of great wealth and the means necessary to obtain it, very few Virginians were prepared to live without money. Thus, one woman asked a friend, ". . . have you succeed'd in business. I hope you are making money – don't omit any opportunity to do so, for without a moderate portion of that vile dross which corrupts too many – there is no chance of living comfortably any where." Almost like adolescents beginning to indulge in hitherto forbidden pleasures, men and women both could become almost giggly when talking about "that great article money" or "that very essential article commonly called *money.*" Intoxicated, George Stevenson confessed to his stepbrother, "As you know my aim is money and money alone –." No less dizzy was Martha Terrell, an orphan who was delighted to find employment: "(Heaven pardon me for the groveling sensation!) I really do feel considerable regard for money and the conveniences which it procures." Although they deplored the "groveling sensation" – and here is the rub – Virginians loved money. Heaven might forgive them in the next world, but, as Sarah Clopton had told her sons, ". . . money is all in all in this world."[35]

People had a considerable regard for money because they needed a considerable amount of it to support a desirable standard of living. Despite the talk about cottages "after the English manner," an independence was not a yeoman farmer's self-subsistence but rather a planter's comfortable life. James Hubard, while studying medicine, shared with a friend his reflections about wealth: "What are the riches of this world but mere delusive Phantoms, they in fact embitter our minds upon reflection, and will make a discerning person readily sense the futility of what are called earthly joys." Dr. Hubard perhaps scorned "delusive Phantoms," but he had no contempt for what those phantoms could buy. Ten years later, he gloated to his wife, "I rec'd our Chariot yesterday – Every person here thinks it by much the most elegant carriage in Virginia. . . ." A year later, he purchased a house for $5,900, and a year after that, Hubard was embroiled in a bitter contest with his mother-in-law over his wife's dowry. "At the time that I married," Hubard explained to the older woman, "I certainly had a right to expect pecuniary or money assistance. Susan was wealthy and her funds quite sufficient. But what assistance have they afforded me. – None. I felt it my duty to entertain her as genteely as possible and to effect this I have been obliged to sacrifice almost everything I possessed. You are fully apprized of the fact that since our marriage Susan's Estate has not bro't to my hands more than one hundred dollars." The doctor subsequently sank into debt.[36] James Hubard and other Virginians felt compelled to live genteely, but genteel living required a great deal of money although genteel values deplored the "groveling" necessary to obtain it.

The predicament was real; men and women wanted wealth but scorned struggling for it. John Cocke suggested that his orphaned nephew might become a deputy to a rural county clerk. The young man was reluctant to accept the office, for he would have to be "during the whole of the winter and nearly all the spring and fall employed all day writing in the office, and at night till nine o'clock engaged in examining." In addition, he would have to sweep his own room, bring water, cut wood, bring it up from the woods two or three yards up a steep hill. "Now if you would wish me to accept such a place as that," the young man told his uncle, "I would think you had no regard for me." Such hard work was not thought necessary for success. One lawyer recommended the profession to a younger kinsman. "Look around you," John Davies instructed. "Behold the great men who now figure in Congress Hall – remember that the place now occupied by the proudest of them all, a few years of ordinary application in that profession which is in this country the road to riches and to honor, will enable you also surely to attain – Great application is not necessary."[37]

Virginians looked for money in areas where great application was not required. Bernard Carter continued to deplete his soil by planting tobacco. He told a more careful and progressive planter, "I too ought to be a farmer – but am devoured by the demon avarice at such a rate as to have already degenerated into a Tobacco worm. . . . But I must make tobacco – it brings so much money –." If Virginia's soils were depleted, a man could move elsewhere. Thus, one young man determined to "go where I find I can make the most money with the greatest ease." Another believed that in Tennessee people "could spend their days in comfort & live in plenty with a tenth of the labor requisite [in Virginia]. . . . and as we are all children of the world," he reasoned, "we have a right to look for those parts where we can live easiest & happiest." There might even be easier ways of making money. One man had been "buying lottery tickets for the last month, and he says he will not stop til he draws a large prize and then he intends moving to South Carolina – where he will end his days in peace and happiness he hopes."[38] As always, peace and ease were the goals.

Young men who were warned that the pursuit of wealth tarnished character hoped never to test that proposition. And when self-indulgence or bad luck, as they all too often did, ran them into debt, they chased legacies or lotteries or some other effortless and supposedly honorable way to recoup the position into which their parents had placed them. They asked for no higher station than their parents'; they would even settle for a bit less, as if the modesty of the aspiration could magically ensure its success, if only they might be spared the strenuous efforts required to accumulate such fortunes. Virginians in the early years of the nineteenth century craved a life of ease bought with easy money. Like Peachy Gilmer, they inhabited a fairyland. No wonder that so many seemed unstable. A young law student, John Lewis, spoke for them all. He reported to a friend that he was "sometimes reading constantly for a week[.] Then flying off at a tangent to some folly or other. then melancholy sei[z]es me. There is one piece of information which I wish to obtain as soon as possible. . . . I mean the way to get an independent living in the short time of one year with ease and honour. . . . In spite of all the philosophy which the old and new schools have kindly given to the world I still am fool enough to think [a] th[ous]and guineas would make me happier than I am now."[39] The tone was jocular; the question was serious. And if that was the question of youth, what would be the answer of age?

"THESE THE WORST OF TIMES"

Charming yet passive, expecting independence to be given instead of earned, the youth of Virginia were not prepared for the economic decline that would wither their region in the decades after the Revolution. Virginians themselves recognized the signs of impending troubles in the 1770s. They began to notice that they and their friends were encountering increased difficulty in making a living. They discovered that without "care and frugality . . . the best Estates in Virginia soon dwindle & come to little. . . ." One planter, although intending to sell a thousand acres and eight slaves, still feared ruin: ". . . when I consider a good Wife & seven fine children must be involved in that ruin nay perhaps may even want Bread the thought is too melancholy to dwell on –." The economy in Virginia was beginning to show strain. Robert Wormeley Carter, an inveterate gambler, chastised himself for a $500 loss: "Cursed folly to throw myself into such difficulties in these the worst of times."[40]

Times in Virginia would not get better. In the decades after the Revolution, the region entered a period of decline. Land values, exports, and slave prices all fell, forcing thousands of Virginians to leave their native state. The tobacco boom was a distant memory; merely producing an adequate return from that old mainstay became quite difficult. A century's planting had depleted Virginia's soils; as a result, the advantage with tobacco was on more fertile lands to the west. Consequently, well before the Revolution, many planters, small and large both, shifted to grain production, where an expanding market promised a good return. Yet growing cereals was not the stuff of grand fortunes; if anything, it was better suited to smaller farmers and certainly to those who were careful, steadfast, and energetic in their cultivation of the soil – not characteristics we have found in abundant supply among the sons of the gentry. Those young men who turned their backs upon their fathers' entrepreneurial past hoped to maintain their fortunes by planting alone. Yet planting was in a period of transition. Vast holdings in land and slaves were no advantage unless carefully managed, with a close eye to the market.[41] Those Virginians who were unable or unwilling to adapt to changing circumstances believed themselves to be living in the worst of times.

"We have nothing new here," a man wrote his nephew in 1824. "The old song Hard times &c." By the 1820s, "hard times" was indeed an old tune. For perhaps half a century, Virginians had been reporting economic distress and failure, much as they had always cataloged common events such as births, deaths, and marriages. Typically, Thomas Mann Randolph in 1785 advised his sons of the "low state of my Finances, I mean the bad crops of every kind together with the heavy Taxes, we yearly experience." Another man wrote more dramatically to implore his brother's aid, without which he would not have a "she[e]t If I Should Die to put in the Coffin with me." The examples could be multiplied, but one – from 1805 – is particularly interesting. Thomas Jones told a kinsman, "I have never experienced the want of that article [money] more than I do at this Time – There is a general complaint of the scarcity of it, and my almost constant employment for some months past – has been putting off Duns. and Lengthening out a poor feeble Existence –." A century earlier, William Fitzhugh had accepted the necessity of remaining on his plantation and making it profitable. Jones, however, lamented his being "confined to one spot," unable to visit his kin. "If I could avoid such a disagreeable situation [want of money] by participating in the common amusements of men: it might be an aleviation. . . . these are serious matters to the feeble and wearied Body whose only comfort is in retirement and ease of Mind."[42] Bad times were made worse by the necessity of attending to business.

The general economic decline was punctuated by even more frightening episodes, such as the Panic of 1819 and the subsequent depression. Edward Graham's experience will serve as our example. Graham described the situation to his son: "McCrory at the ironworks has failed. Daniel Hoffman unexpectedly to everyone has failed. some of the merchants here were his endorsers at the bank of Lynchbg. that creates pressure on them. They press on others and so on." A year later (1820), the pressure was on Graham himself. He had lent his son money from the county school fund, of which he was treasurer, intending to replace it with his expected dividend from the James River fund. There was, however, no dividend that year, and Graham told his son to "procure money in any way you can short of dishonesty." A planter, about to be sucked into the vortex of collapse, could see the product of forces he could not comprehend: "general consternation & alarm prevailing –. . . . How long will this state of things last?" Although the economic situation subsequently improved, the generally bad "state of things" persisted in Virginia throughout the 1820s, and letters were filled with complaints of lack of money and tales of economic distress. The "great want of money"[43] had become a common and sorrowful tune.

In such hard times, men and women were ill-served by their propensity toward indolence. Such was surely the case with Joseph Lewis. At the first sign of economic distress, when he was unable to rent his land, he welcomed the opportunity to farm it himself. "I cannot help hoping," he wrote, "It will ultimately prove to my interest in a pecuniary point of view, as well as make me more settled, give me an object to aim at, and eradicate habits of indolence [that phrase again!] I have acquired, before they become too deeply rooted." Lewis's hopes would never be realized. A year and a half later, disappointed in love and farming, he was considering moving to Kentucky but feared he would "never have energy enough to accomplish [the plan]. And perhaps to go so far from every friend, to set [?] down in a wilderness, and have nothing to commune with but a dead book, a stupid negroe or brutish whites would be but an exchange of evils." Lewis thus remained on his land, resolving to "try again. . . . because steady endeavors, must finally succeed." His resolve was inadequate, for he continued borrowing from his more prosperous brother and never became a successful planter himself.

In writing to his brother, Lewis often reflected upon his abilities as a farmer. "When I remember how sincerely I hate the wind & cold & heat, how many small matters I neglect, how often I act by proxy, how a book or newspaper can absorb me, how I hate to dirty my hands – I am almost induced to retract what I said of my being a tollerable farmer. But still," he insisted, "I am a very good cultivator . . . whose pleasures are chiefly of a sedentary cast, & who feels no very strong stimulous to action – not a good economist – a most indifferent maker of money – & upon the whole a tollerable farmer." Being "tollerable" as a farmer was not sufficient to maintain a comfortable life. In a less complacent mood, Lewis would confess, "My emulation & ambition, if I ever had any, are now asleep, or dead – my hopes are so subdued, that I trust to the contemptible means I possess, to gratify them. Wife, family, I shall never have. . . . If I can get a new coat now & then, fiddle strings, tobacco, why need I trouble myself for more." Farming poor soil, lacking energy, preferring leisure to planting, and, indeed, deriving no pleasure from farming itself, men such as Joseph Lewis were doomed to failure.[44]

Lewis adjusted to his failure by radically limiting his expectations; he would forgo wife, family, and the material comforts that Virginians usually enjoyed. Others would find such sacrifices more difficult. When he married Louisiana Cocke, John Faulcon declined his father's offer of a house and plantation, and instead accepted a plantation in Amelia County from his father-in-law, John Cocke. Typically, Faulcon reported that he would not risk depending upon the "precarious profits" of his profession as a physician; instead, he would support himself and his wife by planting. Faulcon borrowed heavily from his father-in-law, giving the older man detailed explanations of his financial status in return. Although he demurred, "No one can possibly have a greater horror at the thought of debt than I have," he borrowed about $4,000 to build a house, furnish it, and equip the plantation. He calculated upon an annual income of $2,500, which would enable him to discharge the debt in three years. A poor cotton crop, however, forced the young husband to ask his father-in-law for money to meet his obligations for 1828, now insisting that "It is with the horror of Death that I think of increasing a debt already too great for my comfort."[45]

Alarmed at his son-in-law's increasing indebtedness, John Cocke pressed him instead to decrease his obligations and, of course, extravagances, such as his horse. "While I admire a fine horse," Faulcon admitted, "I trust I have more regard for my interest than to indulge my propensity to keep one, at the expense of my purse." Faulcon sold the horse, one of the distinguishing marks of the gentry,[46] but he balked at disposing of another necessity for elite status, an old and trusted family slave. "Had he been a common cornfield hand, a brute of a man, without any feeling than his sensual appetites," Faulcon protested, "I might not . . . have hesitated to hoist him on an auction block & have sold him to the highest bidder – but I could not forget that he had been raised in my father's family [the father Faulcon was forsaking to live near his wife's family, incidentally], & amid scenes calculated to awaken his sensibilities that he had often exhibited evidences of feeling and that he had I have reason to believe some attachment towards myself – as I doubted therefore the moral rectitude of dissevering in one capable of estimating them the ties of nature & association, & of thus disregarding feelings which the coldest Humanity is prone to respect – it appeared to me worthy of consideration whether the evil of an additional debt of $350 was not to be preferred great as it was to the evil of turning adrift upon the world an old & not invaluable servant with all the consequences of doing so." We need not question the sincerity of Faulcon's regard for his slave or himself as a feeling man, and thus when he sold the old man for $400,[47] he put a price also upon his self-esteem.

Yet even that was not enough, and several months later Faulcon concluded that "it is injudicious . . . to calculate upon making money by cultivating an exhausted soil. . . . The farmer with the best land in the long run does little more than make a decent support for his family." Someone deeply in debt, such as himself, was without hope. He therefore determined to sell out, pay his debts, and commence "de novo in some favorable position . . . with a stock of dear bot. experience I think I could not but thrive better than I have heretofore done." Unprepared to live without a wife, a comfortable home, and a good horse, Faulcon hoped for better land and a new beginning.[48]

Joseph Lewis and John Faulcon are particularly interesting because the pressures of their circumstances forced them to expose their values and to sacrifice their pretensions. Other Virginians, suffering from bad times, would make similar adjustments at apparently less psychic cost. The matter of slavery merits close attention because although plantation life obviously depended upon slavery, slaveowners in their private correspondence almost never discussed slavery as an institution and rarely mentioned their own slaves.[49] Historians have shown us that southerners would accommodate to an institution increasingly repugnant to the modern world by styling themselves as Christian masters and men of feeling. They would even distinguish between those slaves who were "common cornfield hands" and those with "sensibilities."[50] Thus, when Faulcon parted with his oldest and most trusted servant, he struck at that man's feelings, his very moral base, as well as his own. Feeling seemed a luxury the prudent planter could ill afford. In yet another way, Virginians such as John Faulcon chafed at the economic imperatives of their time. Still, at some level, most planters accepted the fact that slavery was part of their money-making venture. Why else did so many of them choose selling a slave as the quickest way to raise cash?

John Faulcon was exceptional only in his qualms about parting with a treasured servant. Wison Cary, for example, was almost giddy when he reported to his wife the prices their former slaves had fetched: "Martha and her 3 children are sold to Mr. Hopkins of Goochland . . . for eight hundred dollars – which is considered a very good sale, as Negroes have certainly fallen since they were valued. . . . Polly is also sold with her 2 children to a Mr. Farrar who lives in Fluvanna. . . . We were obliged to abate 50 dollars in her price – so that she sold for 550 dollars – we think we shall be able to make up this difference in the sale of the others." Cary had been offered $1,200, which he acknowledged was "an enormous price," for his family's cook, Billy. "I merely mention this . . . in the way of conversation, and not with any serious idea of depriving you of your cook who is so valuable and trusty." Whether to sell Billy would be, then, his wife's decision, and Wilson Cary continued to consult with his wife about which of their slaves they could most easily do without. Cary's primary (and only) concern was his family's comfort: "All I would have desired to keep for you and my children but that cannot be. I am determined you shall not in the future, feel the evils of Poverty whilst I have properties." With a depleted soil but a prolific labor force, Virginians often discovered that their most valuable commodities were human. Thus, Richard Blow found that he could sell ten young slaves for $5,000, thereby reducing his bank debt to $4,500. He reckoned that the sale of ten females might nearly erase the obligation. As he explained to his son, "I think it useless to raise up families of them for any other purpose but to sell –"[51]

Virginians in the early decades of the nineteenth century spoke so freely with each other about selling "excess" slaves that it is clear that they did not consider the slave trade a form of business, that enemy to character they so deplored. Instead, slavery had developed as a sine qua non of their plantation way of life, that which distinguished them from a more commercial North. As we have already seen, Virginians refused to consider their very commercial agriculture as commerce, and so they were disinclined to view their own slaves as a form of merchandise, even when they treated them as such.

Virginians held high their ideal of the planter's life, and so, those who could not extricate themselves from debt looked to more fertile lands for a new beginning. Men and women believed that money could be made with great ease farther to the west or south; one Virginian had estimated that comfort in Tennessee required only one-tenth of the work necessary in Virginia. Another described that same state as "the land that Moses viewed at a distance abounding with milch and honey." The same sort of hyperbole would be extended to the Ohio River Valley, to Kentucky, to Missouri, and to Louisiana, which a Virginian who had moved there described as "the land of promise." His assertion that his crops that year alone would bring $20,000 was reported "to have dazzled the eyes of our gentlemen here not a little."[52] Descriptions of richer lands hinted at salvation of more than the family fortune.

Such descriptions were bound to dazzle, and thus families were enthusiastic when one of their members headed out. Agnes Cabell was pleased to see her brother depart for Tallahassee "in fine health and in good spirits, full of hope and disposed to use every exertion to retrieve his lost fortune." Perhaps Florida would also offer the Cabells opportunity. "In [Virginia] I see but little chance for my *poor* sons

– and they will have to seek their fortunes somewhere." The next year, Abram Cabell followed his uncle, and the young man's parents believed he had "the means of making a fortune." Young Cabell, however, had already displayed the unsteadiness so characteristic of much of Virginia's youth. Several years earlier, he had abandoned his study of medicine against his parents' advice and set off for Kentucky. Now they hoped he would have the "energy and perseverance necessary in his new situation." When young Cabell sent back glittering reports from Florida, his father urged his other children also to depart their home state. In a new land, they would be able to purchase estates, independences to bequeath their children, whereas in Virginia, "All that you can expect is to bring them up in good habits, with good principles, & give them an education, if they will take it and then turn them loose to shift for themselves."[53] To the extent that they identified their problem as poor soil, Virginians looked to the richer lands of the Deep South and West. Better to give one's children an independence in Florida than to ask them to "shift for themselves" in the Old Dominion.

Agnes Cabell was unusual in her willingness to see her children move away, for men were more often eager to leave Virginia than were women. One recent historian of the westward movement has observed that migration was frequently a man's idea that was reluctantly accepted by a wife, who valued her home and family more than her husband's notion of success.[54] The personal writings of Virginians reveal that, indeed, men were more inclined to pull up stakes than were women, but women reconciled themselves to what they believed was necessity. That was the situation in the Trist family. According to Nicholas Trist, he had no real future in Virginia, despite his wife's enchanted childhood as one of Thomas Jefferson's grandchildren. Instead, he could practice law in Washington, D.C., or he could join his parents in Louisiana. Although she had heard the same glittering reports of Louisiana as everyone else, Virginia wavered. Her brother Thomas Jefferson Randolph, the grandson and namesake of the author of *Notes on Virginia*, was "full of the idea of our going there *in a body*. . . . he is completely disgusted with this state which he calls the 'last of nature's works.'" Still, Virginia was reluctant to move until a year later, when, with her husband about to go into debt, she realized that "he must make money." She had heard good reports of Florida, but although she believed that it was in her husband's and child's best interest to move to a more promising land, Virginia Trist feared she might never see her mother and sisters again. Like many women, she determined to sacrifice her own feelings to the needs of her husband and child; she would resign herself to the inevitable. "What *can* be done?" she asked. "When we have become reconciled to our state of exile," Virginia Trist hoped, "we should have more tranquillity than we have known of late years."[55]

Whether to move West, then, was a family decision as well as an economic one, and any migration became a family drama as much as an economic endeavor. If some families would move in nuclear groups and some en masse, in others only the young men would depart, hoping to succeed and provide for the rest of the family at home. About to be crushed by the debts that would shorten his life and leave her a struggling widow, Wilson and Peggy Nicholas (and their children) were already proposing to quit Virginia for a

Plate 14. Nicholas P. Trist. Trist, here as a young Byron, later would persuade his wife that he had no future in the Virginia of her family and ancestors. "He must make money," she realized. "What *can* be done?" (From the collection of Mrs. Charles B. Eddy, Jr.)

more prosperous area. In 1819 their son Robert left the family "as undecided as ever what he shall do," and their other son, Wilson, was talking of going to New Orleans. "These are dismal times for all young men, but particularly my sons," Peggy Nicholas concluded. Several months later, the parents themselves were considering moving to Kentucky. Their married daughter was reluctant to be separated from them, but realized that "to be independent is so essential to everyone's happiness. . . . You would in Kentucky have a provision for the girls." After the death of her husband, Peggy Nicholas relied upon her sons to recoup the family's fortune (and expected them to make their own provision). With her small inheritance, they invested in and settled on a Louisiana sugar plantation. On periodic visits to Virginia, they awed friends and relations with their boasted prosperity. The Nicholas brothers, however, had not been as successful as they claimed, and in 1829 Peggy Nicholas discovered that although the plantation had every year realized great profits, they had been used to discharge equally large debts. Then, with the failure of the current year's crop, that year's obligations could not be met, and the plantation was plunged deeply into debt. It became clear that fortunes could be lost in the West as well as in Virginia. Peggy Nicholas was "completely horror stricken . . . at this sad disclosure." The widow could now "only look forward to being a burden to my children as long as I live."[56]

True, the West offered richer soil than weary Virginia, but it did not always prove to be the fairyland that distressed Virginians longed for. They sought a land of milk and honey; such extravagant hopes were not to be realized in this world.

Men, nonetheless, continued to dream, whereas women, because of the conventions of the age, had to rely upon husbands and sons or – if they were even less fortunate – upon themselves. Widows and orphans had few choices. They might sell their slaves or their estates. They could sell

Plate 15. View of the west front of Monticello and garden. "My sisters wish to *work* for their own support, but [they are] the granddaughters of Thomas Jefferson," Ellen Coolidge ruefully observed the same year that she commissioned this watercolor. The young women in empire gowns are her sisters, Mary and Cornelia; the boy is her brother, George. (Jane Bradick [Petticoles], c. 1825. Collection of Thomas Jefferson Coolidge, Jr.)

patchwork quilts or sew shirts "for filthy lucre's sake." Widows, "delicate women, left in dependent circumstances," sometimes took in boarders. Women met some success as teachers,[57] and this was the possibility entertained by Thomas Jefferson's granddaughters, but they feared that their social position precluded such work. "I wish I could do something to support myself instead of this unprofitable drudgery of keeping house here," Cornelia Randolph complained to her sister Ellen. "But I suppose not until we sink entirely will it do for the granddaughters of

Thomas Jefferson to take in work or keep a school." At the bottom of her sister's letter, Ellen Coolidge added her own verdict: "My sisters are losing heart (. . . poverty was approaching with withering strides. the first great evil is sin, the second disease, the third pecuniary difficulty). . . . My sisters wish to *work* for their own support, but [they are] the granddaughters of Thomas Jefferson."[58]

Despite the great difference in the roles prescribed for men and women, in Virginia both sexes confronted the same problem: They were limited by their notions of gentility. For women as well as men, it was unseemly to work for "filthy lucre's sake." As it became increasingly difficult to maintain a comfortable life without a great deal of industry, however, such negative attitudes about work were challenged. Women, like men, began to find that their upbringing had poorly equipped them for the roles they were intended to play. Throughout the eighteenth century, well-to-do Virginians had trained their daughters to serve as decorations for society. Mothers were, by their example, to "inculcate [in their daughters] those feminine virtues which are the highest ornaments of the female character; and wch wou'd not only be a source of placid content & happiness to themselves, but the sure means of conjugal felicity." Such a sentiment, deriving from notions of British gentility, would create a suitable female partner for the lord of the plantation manor. Just as young men were advised of the virtues of planting, so young women were told of the rewards of an accomplished gentility. Richard Terrell, for example, instructed his nieces, "This is the time . . . to accomplish yourselves." They were to acquire habits that were "natural, easy, & graceful," to be attentive to their dress, and to be educated in musical instruments, voice, and dancing. Mouthing the assumption of the day that rigorous academic training was inappropriate for women, Thomas Mann Randolph believed that "The *elegant* and agreeable occupation of *Poetry* and the fine arts, surely become the delicate sex more, than tedious & abstruse equiries into the causes of phenomena."[59] Significantly, both sexes were to receive genteel educations. Women were to decorate their homes; like men, they were trained to enjoy leisure.

In the decades after the Revolution, such training would prove inadequate for Virginia's women, even those from the most prosperous segments of society. Nancy Cocke, on her deathbed, requested that her daughters not be given a town education such as she had received; it would be inappropriate for a woman "destined to spend her days in rural retirement." In less elegant prose, John Lewis conveyed the same message; he warned his son not to marry "one of you[r] high dames of quallity." His son should select a woman "who will not think it degrading to attend attentively to domestic affairs and be content with such living as you can conveniently afford." As for his own daughter, Lewis wished her to be "brough[t] up to know how to spin knit or make butter, rather than suppose herself a fine Lady and be reared a worthless being which I think is the case with nearly all those girls who are brought up in idleness."[60] A man in straitened circumstances might wish for a genuine helpmeet more than a "high dame of quallity," an adornment he could no longer afford.

Such adjustments were not always easily made, and just

as John Faulcon had balked at parting with his horse and servant, badges of his gentry status, so too would women be reluctant to dispense with the perquisites of a privileged life. Peggy Nicholas, for one, regretted that her daughter's husband had purchased a new plantation. She asked another daughter, "Are you not sorry for your poor sister, to be obliged to enter once more on the drudgery and dreariness of a farm, a life she abhors so much and again to have a house to build, a house to furnish, and servants to qualify is certainly too provoking." Hard times did not allow leisure, however; instead, they confined women to what Cornelia Randolph had termed the "unprofitable drudgery of keeping house." Another woman voiced the same complaint: "The fact is that fortunes are too moderate in this country to allow a mistress of a family time for any occupation but attending to domestic economy."[61] Hard times doomed Virginians, men and women alike, to that which they dreaded: a life of dull work and limited pleasure. A life of independence, comfort, and ease presupposed leisure, yet the kind of independent life nineteenth-century Virginians desired precluded the hard work, the grubbing thought necessary to procure that rest. Virginians' attitudes, ironically, condemned them to a life not of comfort and ease but to its opposite: drudgery. Men and women were trapped by views they had not fashioned themselves. Rather, they had inherited their values from their ancestors as a legacy that went along with the horses, the slaves, and the estate. But the beliefs proved easier to maintain than the fortune, and in fact, the beliefs militated against the aggressiveness and acquisitiveness necessary to preserve or secure an independence. For reasons they did not understand, such a legacy proved to the Virginians a rather mean bequest.

"HABITS OF INDUSTRY"

Eighteenth-century parents had tried to give their children independence, somehow believing that this state was more a social position than a personal quality, that it had more to do with one's relations with others than with the individual psyche. Thus, they gave their children settlements instead of character. Those Virginians who were to escape from the ironic legacy of their ancestors would have to alter their psychological predispositions in order to shed their habit of indolence.

Ellen Coolidge, whose father, Thomas Mann Randolph, had advocated the study of poetry and fine arts for women, found herself poorly prepared for her responsibilities as a wife and mother. She did not realize "how deficient I was in useful qualities until called on for the exercise of them; . . . I am constantly trying by the sacrifice of my brilliant qualities to acquire those of ordinary usefulness." She attributed her "present uneasiness" to her "unfortunate education": "I was brought up far too tenderly, rendered unfit for an ordinary destiny – . . . Nature gave me a timid and affectionate temper, great flexibility and docility, quick feelings, & a lively imagination." She thus shared the more charming qualities of many of Virginia's other youth. "As severity was evidently unnecessary in the education of one so ready to yield & to obey," Ellen Coolidge continued, her friends and relatives "neglected to enforce even the wholesome discipline which was wanting to give strength to my character. . . . The voice of affectionate commendation was sounding always in my ears – I was constantly hearing my own good qualities." As a youngster, she was "a darling with all"; as an adult, by her own account, she was "a sluggard, fond of ease, averse to any employment which does not happen to fall in with the humor of the moment."[62] Ellen Coolidge defined her problem as one of character and discovered its roots in an overly indulged childhood.

The solution she found in a children's book published in Boston. There she read that "energy" was "the power of doing whatever we do at all, with the same spirit and promptness which we exercise in doing what is agreeable to us." It was energy that she lacked, but she could make up for her deficiency by giving it to her children: "I will try to give my children the *habit* of energy, for it should be a habit, not an occasional impulse – so should be all our virtues. So is all Virtue, for nothing deserves the name which is not steady in its course."[63] In choosing to give her children the habit of energy, Ellen Coolidge made a break from her past, her family, her upbringing.

More perceptive and also more cosmopolitan than most Virginians, Ellen Coolidge was able to analyze herself and her situation with eloquence and insight. Less gifted men and women arrived, however, at the same conclusion as they discovered that failure to give their children the habit of energy might doom them to financial failure. As Virginia's economy faltered, its children began to realize that they would have to find their own independences; their parents could no longer provide them. In his monumental study of *Democracy in America,* the French sociologist

Alexis de Tocqueville coined the term *individualism* to describe Americans, a people who were "apt to imagine that their whole destiny is in their own hands."[64] If elsewhere Americans embraced individualism, Virginians of the gentry class awakened to it reluctantly. Again and again, parents wrote of thwarted plans and dashed expectations that would make it necessary for their children to establish themselves. St. George Tucker's blunt declaration to his stepsons will serve as a counterpoint to Tocqueville: Their patrimony had been consumed by debt. The unfortunate "consequence, my dear boys, must be obvious to you – your sole dependence must be on your own personal abilities & Exertions."[65] His children and so many others would now have to provide their own independence.

Parents who found themselves unable to settle their children hoped instead to provide them with the proper training to support themselves. Martha Randolph wanted her sons "to have professions that will enable them to make their own way in the world." In fact, some Virginians began to believe that education and character were better for a child than a bequest. One planter was "thoroughly impressed with the belief that it is better to give a boy a good education and bring him up correctly, morally, & with good habits, than to give him a large Fortune."[66] Another man similarly intended to educate his children "so as to provide for themselves. far better I think than finding them a house and a fortune to spend in Idleness." The way in which each man phrased his choice shows that giving a fortune instead of the proper habits was considered not only an alternative but a preferable one. Fathers who would not or could not give a fortune were forced to rationalize their behavior, and such justifications were often combined with the persistent complaint about the indolence of youth in forming new patterns of thought. Thus, Edward Graham explained his failure to settle his son: ". . . the young man who sets out with competent qualifications & circumstances moderately favourable, to make an independence for himself, is more likely to pass through the world comfortable than he who sets out with an independence ready made for him," Graham suggested hopefully to his son. "The one has an object constantly before him to engage his attention & animate his exertions, & on virtuous & successful exertion the happiness of life chiefly depends; – the other being without any suitable stimulus to excite his exertions is likely to fall into a state of lassitude & torpor & to be consumed with ennui. Perhaps to relieve himself from the gloomy blank of existence to which he finds himself sinking, he has recourse to riotous excesses which are a worse evil than the one he wishes to avoid."[67] Perhaps the necessity of providing for themselves would rescue young gentlemen from deficiencies of character.

Virginians thus began to recognize the necessity of industry. They recommend it to others, particularly sons without inheritances, but they also accepted it for themselves. Hard work once had been scorned; now many noticed its value. "Grow up with habits of industry and order," a young woman advised her younger sister. "No one . . . can be so happy as a person who is always employed." A new language of individualism and self-reliance now crept more frequently into Virginians' correspondence: industry, order, perseverance, and enterprise. As one advised, simply and emphatically, *"Rely upon your talents &*

exertions & you will do well." When his cousin complained that he had nothing to anticipate but "hard work, industry and perseverance," James Carr assured the young man that "nothing more is necessary. With your talents, enterprise and perseverance with prudence to balance them must in a few years ensure a fortune." Most young Virginians resigned themselves to their new responsibilities. Thus, Thomas Jefferson Randolph explained to his father-in-law, "My prospects from my father I consider blank. from my grandfather not very cheering. . . . [but] with the motives which I shall have for exertion I hope for much from industry and perseverance."[68] Personal qualities would have to take the place of an inheritance.

Young Virginians came to the realization that their destinies were in their own hands regretfully. A young man in 1828 observed that at college "there is no great deal of pleasure in studying anything." He knew, nonetheless, that "upon my conduct here, depends my character and standing hereafter." Note the tone. Young people spoke as if in disbelief. Self-reliance was neither a mandate nor a challenge, but an unhappy fact of life, and in their correspondence, Virginians traded back and forth this unfortunate truth. Thus, John Peachy, a young law student, observed, "My happiness depends on my own exertions," and a mother was relieved to find that her son was giving "uncommon assiduity to the acquirement of his Profession. . . . it is the only shield he has, against the wants and vicissitudes of this changeable world."[69] In a changing world, children would have to rely upon themselves, not their elders. Inner resources would be more important than advice or bequests.

In early-nineteenth-century Virginia, perseverance and industry were necessary for success. Poor land haphazardly or halfheartedly farmed would produce a poor yield. A planter might profit, but only with a great deal more effort and steadiness than those Virginians who prized ease were inclined to supply. George Blow was one who discovered in mid-career what success as a planter demanded. As a youth at William and Mary, young Blow had been typically wild and improvident. From college in 1805 he had explained to his father that "a young man must of necessity be extravagant if he wishes to associate with the best company." Several years later, Blow was meeting with little success as a Southside planter. Unable to pass the bar by himself, he hoped to persuade a judge and family friend to get him a license "without my being examined at all." As might have been predicted, he fell into debt and observed "my time as well as my prospects is so gloomy as almost to discourage exertion." The young planter became increasingly pessimistic about his future and thought of moving, but his father reminded him that any move would require capital. Blow remained on his plantation, where he suffered from the poor economy in 1819, bad weather, sick slaves, and a failed crop. "The times continue to grow worse with me," he complained. "It seems as if Providence intended to crush me this year."[70]

George Blow was not crushed; instead, he experienced a change of attitude. He abandoned the plans he had had for a political career and determined to "have nothing on earth to do or think about, but my own *private* Business. a man who has much public business must of necessity neglect his private affairs. . . . now as I have a plenty of Business to engross my time . . . [the] best way is to give up public offices – and have no body's business to attend to but my own."[71] It would not be for almost two decades more that Tocqueville would identify this impulse to withdraw from public life as central to individualism: "Individualism is a mature and calm feeling, which disposes each member of the community to sever himself from the mass of his fellows and to draw apart with his family and friends, so that after he has thus formed a little circle of his own, he willingly leaves society at large to itself." The sociologist could have been describing George Blow. The Virginian was a convert to individualism, and he confessed to his father, "I have received a new impulse, a strange & strong hankering after making money lately – and I begin to think I shall get in the way soon."[72]

Blow's prediction was accurate, and with his newfound energy, his plantation began slowly to prosper. In 1828, at the age of forty-one, Blow found himself a successful, if not affluent, planter. He boasted that "all my plans & purchases have so far answered a good purpose, and turned out well." With the "economy – industry & management practiced on this worn out plantation," he had been able to add to his "exhausted lands" "a very valuable Mill, and about 300 acres of the best land I own. besides doubling the Value of the Estate by very expensive Improvements. besides doing this, I have made out to live comfortably; to send my sons to college; and to keep out of Debt." Achieving such success had required Blow to content himself at home. Far removed from his days at college, he was no longer extravagant, nor did he "associate with the best company." Rather, he wore clothes in which a "city Negroe would not be seen in the streets." "I have even incurred, and borne with secret satisfaction," the planter noted, "the nickname of 'the Stingy George Blow.'"[73] For his success, this son of Virginia's gentry paid no small price.

The most successful Virginians were generally those who, like George Blow, devoted themselves to their work, sacrificing thereby their pretensions to ease. The case of John Cocke, who became one of Virginia's most successful planters, is instructive. He had early acquired habits of industry, which he maintained as a young planter. He explained to his mother-in-law that he would be unable to visit because of "the multiplicity of my projects. . . . I think the secret of human Happiness is to be completely, rationally & vertuously employ'd." Cocke's attitudes served him well even in adversity. Although many Virginians became depressed by reverses, Cocke, his father-in-law observed, was "the happiest man, who has lost the most of his Crop; that you can imagine." He merely continued "planning & improving. . . . Happy man, who can thus control & limit the objects of his happiness within the sphere of his command!" Even his kin considered Cocke's perseverance remarkable. His industry paid off, and he proved wealthy enough to settle his sons. Nonetheless, he wanted them to be educated in a profession "which will fill up the period until [they] take possession of their property. . . . And will guard against the most dangerous enemy to young Virginians – Idleness."[74] John Cocke had discovered and wanted his sons also to know that continual employment – in other words, hard work – was the secret to success and happiness.

John Cocke's belief that idleness in Virginia was a cultural problem opened the way for broader criticisms of the

South. Cocke's own son, John, Jr., who inherited his father's passion for work and order, was delighted by his visit to Frederick, Maryland. "The Sperit of Yankey-dom is coming south," he proclaimed. "Much is to be seen on the northern borders of the ancient dominion – God speed it to the Southernmost parts –" Those who considered indolence and unsteadiness enemies often thought such qualities peculiarly southern. When her sister feared that because of her deficiencies as a homemaker she would not be able to make her husband's income cover their household expenses, Ellen Coolidge confessed, "I have the same fears and the same doubts. . . . you know not how difficult it is to make the exact calculations & exercise the rigid self-denial strict economy requires. . . . economy is an art not to be acquired without great study & pains, and," she concluded, "we southerners know little enough about it." Virginians lived "in a sort of rude plenty which gives us habits of waste and disorder."[75]

Ellen Coolidge would later attribute both her and her region's peculiar habits to that region's peculiar institution. Northern girls, she observed, always picked up after themselves, whereas southerners might relax indefinitely, knowing a slave would put away what her mistress had left out. The young woman's mother also found much to criticize in Virginia. She admonished her son, "Your success in life will depend as much upon the habits formed in youth as in your natural talents and disposition. how many men of fine and excellent dispositions are lost for want of the early habits of self command and industry." Such good habits, Martha Randolph reflected, "are more rarely to be met with to the south than they ought to be. the number of slaves, make people indolent and idle, and consequently encourage a habit of self indulgence as ruinous to the moral character as to one's fortune."[76] Critical and reflective Virginians blamed slavery for their region's ills.

Few Virginians, however, were disposed to that sort of cultural criticism and, in any event, there were rather clear limits to such analysis. To the extent that southerners saw slavery at the root of their region's ills, they virtually foreclosed hope of change, for they were unprepared to live without their slaves.[77] For the vast majority of southerners, even self-critical ones, such a cure was worse than the disease. It was not only that by 1820 their society was too tenaciously wedded to racial slavery seriously to consider altering that social, political, economic, and racial relationship; it was – even more simply – that they did not want to. If by 1820 or 1830 indolence could be seen as particularly southern, then industry was considered a "Yankey" attribute. Thus, as Virginians began to analyze their dilemma, they could conceptualize it only in an either/or, Cavalier/Yankee way. The tendency to think of economic life in either/or terms had been present since at least the eighteenth century, when thinkers had assumed that their society might choose either the path of agriculture or that of commerce, independence or vice. To a certain extent, many historians believe, such a dilemma seemed to confront the entire North Atlantic community as its economy became increasingly modern, its economic and political relationships ever more complex.[78] As we have seen, Virginians rhetorically favored agriculture and an ideal of independence at the time of the Revolution; such a stance legitimated the colonists and denigrated the commercial empire from which they were rebelling. The rhetoric of independence, then, served a useful political function at the time of the Revolution. After the Revolution, however, many Virginians clung to that rhetoric and accepted it as a cultural ideal.

Seemingly, by the third decade of the nineteenth century, many Virginians were questioning the usefulness of notions that crippled their youth with habits of indolence and intense longings for patrimonial milk and honey. Yet by that time, the Virginians were confronting a problem more serious than habits of indolence; bad habits, after all, can be broken. More important, industry and all it entailed was now seen as the province not of London but of Philadelphia, Boston, and New York. To acquire habits of industry would necessitate, men and women believed, abandoning their beloved homeland for the despised North, either/or.[79] In other words, the difficult problem of how to adapt to a changing economy and a changing world was complicated for Virginians by their conviction that adjustment required adopting not only habits of industry but also a whole host of loathsome Yankee characteristics. A cultural problem was cast in sectional political and moral terms.

As a result, Virginia gentlemen faced their dilemma with ambivalence and dread. Beverley Kennon, typically, feared that his nephews were becoming indolent; yet he feared even more sending them to school in the North: "Do you not think it would be hazardous to let a boy grow up among the Yankeys? . . . I admire their industry – temperence – economy – enterprise &c but in other respects I detest the New-England character in which I have generally found . . . a great deal of duplicity – low cunning – roguery – and meanness. – I prefer, with all its faults, the character of the Cavalier to that of the Puritans."[80] Many Virginians, by the 1820s, felt some uneasiness about their culture, about the indolence and unsteadiness it encouraged. But "with all its faults," they still preferred it to what they believed was the only alternative: one that seemed to breed duplicity, cunning, roguery, and meanness.

Like many Americans of the time, Virginians drew simple moral equations. Industry and cunning, enterprise and theft, as if perseverance and hard work necessarily entailed deceit, as if indolence, conversely, were a badge of honor. The legendary attributes of the southern gentleman – hospitality, graciousness, and chivalry – are no more accurate as description than deceit and cunning are for the northerner. Rather, these are moral code words, used to suggest that southerners were unselfish, whereas northerners were not. As Americans in the early years of the republic sought to reconcile their economic endeavors with their spiritual longings, they often resorted to simple pieties and sectional stereotypes that might ease an economic transformation or a troubled conscience. Yet such notions in the long run offered but cold comfort to those Virginians who feared that the habits of industry necessary for worldly success would undermine southern virtue.

Genteel Virginians used a moral vocabulary to link character traits with economic activity. Thus, with time, many were willing to recognize, but despise and brand as "Yankee," certain characteristics among themselves. Although George Blow had smiled at being called "stingy," the nickname was in truth an insult; and John Cocke had acquired a reputation as a stiff, hard-bargaining man.[81]

Peachy Gilmer in 1827 complained bitterly that "Virginians have become Yankeys as to all that is bad, retaining at the same time all the original stock of bad qualities incident to their peculiar situation. They have become coarse, rude, dishonest and in all things fraudulent –. . . . Delicacy is considered as a hindrance to enterprize and business; refinement hypocrasy; politeness affectation. . . ." Yankees were indeed "cautious, circumspect, prudent, provident of the future, systematick, persevering, [and] intelligent to all useful pursuits," but inescapably "coarse, and selfish . . . in which particulars we are rivalling, and will soon surpass them, abandoning . . . our . . . moral habits, chivalrous, hospitable, and manly & generous spirit."[82] Virginians believed that in order to acquire habits of industry and energy, they would have to forfeit all that they found most pleasant about their culture. Although many, if not most, Virginians, in theory at least, would have preferred to retain "with all its faults" the "character of the Cavalier," they no longer seemed to have that choice. Unwilling converts, they resigned themselves to an economic world they neither wanted nor liked.

Changes in Virginia's economy, as well as in religion and consolation, had thrown Virginians back upon themselves. By the third decade of the nineteenth century, Virginians knew that success would require hard work, industry, energy, and exertion. They realized that their destiny was theirs to create, that their happiness depended upon their own efforts; but they were not happy with their new responsibility. As an orphaned young man lamented, "It has been my misfortune to be thrown upon the world, *entirely dependent on my own* exertions."[83] Self-reliance was not a challenge; it was a calamity.

It is no wonder that those thrown upon the world in such a manner found it an inhospitable place. After his father's sudden death, John Caruthers told a cousin, "I had always hoped (and indeed thought of nothing else) that he would have lived to start us all in the world. . . . But a wise providence has ordered it otherwise. we are left to shift in this hazardous ocean of life without a pilot –." We have already seen that sentimental religion depicted the world as a wilderness; such a vision was reinforced by popular thought about the economic realm. Virginians felt themselves rudderless, adrift on uncharted seas.[84]

The injunction to be industrious ran counter to the culture's values and thus necessarily contributed to the perception of the world as barren. To succeed, it was believed, one had to sacrifice his soul. Many young men, facing these assumptions, became despondent. William A. Graham's sister urged him not to be "depressed"; she tried to cheer him with the observation that "your prospects are as good as any Young Man's I know who has to begin the World on nothing as most of them have to do." Perhaps Graham had learned his response to the necessity of self-reliance from a cousin who, dissatisfied with his prospects, found "melancholy sat heavy on my brow [because of] . . . my own uncertain & doubtful situation. . . . when looking forward into the wide world I could see no prospect to animate or allure me –." Or perhaps Graham was mimicking his own father, who wrote: "Although I always did & still do, hold in very low estimation, a griping, swap[p]ing avaricious disposition, yet . . . I have gone to the other extreme, and have not had that reasonable attention to my own interest which is necessary in such a world as this." As a consequence, the older man fell into debt, and "the subject press[es] on my mind . . . & produce[s] a considerable despondence & depression of spirits."[85] With such examples before him, is it any wonder that the young man was depressed?

Virginians' letters in the early nineteenth century tell many such stories of depressed young men, the victims, apparently, of the burden of self-reliance or, more precisely, the conviction that self-reliance was a grave misfortune. Seventeen years old and orphaned, Hardress Waller thought, "I must look out for myself." He never did. Instead, he drifted from one apprenticeship and clerkship to another until, two years later, he became too depressed to work at all. His relatives could discern "no Fever, or any complaint, except Melancholly. It is very difficult to get him to speak a word. He goes to bed early and dont get up in the morning till he is called. yet he says he dont sleep any." Clearly, the young man was suffering from the symptoms of depression and, although he recovered somewhat, he never found steady employment. He asked his brother-in-law, George Blow, for advice, which the more successful man gladly supplied. Predictably, Blow suggested "*Sobriety,* Steady undeviating perseverance, regular Habits, temperance and solidity of character – to ensure success." "Say, if you please," Blow continued, "that you are desolate, forsaken – self condemned – melancholy – miserable. – Say even, that your Life is a Hell to you, and all your moments torments. even then is there no talisman to dissipate these shades that encompass you. Yes! there is: and you possess it. You alone, are the Magician to chase away those foul Friends of a disordered Mind, . . . the Wand is in your hand and only requires that you should use it, to reverse the scene, and change all to joy and gladness."[86] Hardress Waller was told that he could command his own success and happiness. His brother-in-law told him to drink more deeply from the jug that had poisoned him in the first place. Waller died at the age of thirty, unable to profit from his kinsman's advice.

The pressures of self-reliance were so great that some who were actually prospering imagined they were not. John Camm "became serious and gloomy. . . . his friends are at a loss how to account for his situation, he began by saying he was overwhelmed in debt, but . . . his friends knew this to be only Imaginary. . . . I suppose [his] Estate worth Sixty thousand Dollars altho it never was profitable to him." Camm, his friend explained, was "a bad manager." Camm shortly thereafter succeeded in taking his own life. Men and women, confronting and adjusting to new economic imperatives, began to trade stories of failure and despair, associating psychic distress with the pressures of self-reliance even as they denied the source of the woe. Consider the words a young woman used to describe a kinsman's peculiar behavior. William Buchanan, she wrote, "has had one of his desponding fits upon him for the last three months." Although he appeared to be prospering, "notwithstanding this he has taken it into his head that everything has gone wrong, that his well has limestone in it. which is admitted on all hands to be the softest purest water in town and no limestone within miles of it. . . . and in short that all his plans have been the most foolish and impracticable that were ever laid. . . . it is in vain to try to convince him that he has no grounds for alarm." Buchanan's friends and relatives were unable to explain the young man's strange state of mind. After all, "every one that knows anything about the business says he has his fortune in his own hands."[87] Need we add more?

Letters and diaries do not provide adequate proof of the incidence of mental distress, nor are they a reliable indicator of the source of such ills. Instead, such sources are suggestive, and what they do show clearly is that in the early decades of the nineteenth century Virginians shared with each other tales of despair; such vignettes did not appear in the correspondence or diaries of the eighteenth century. At the very least, then, men and women talked about distress more, and that talk in itself created an atmosphere, a set of expectations and fears; even men who had no apparent cause for worry could become despondent. It was indeed a world of woe.

5
"Earthly connexions"

LOVE

DEATH, which had robbed the Terrell children of their parents, increased the love among the survivors. As Martha Terrell explained to her sister Virginia, "My sisters are both my parents and my children." Death threatened always, however, to cut the threads that were woven so tightly by the orphans in compensation. In 1814, Lucy Ann Terrell told her sister Virginia of "the delightful sermon which I heard yesterday. It was the funeral of a gentleman in the neighborhood and never was I so powerfully affected by a sermon. His three sisters were there apparently in deep distress and at the grave his brother sobbed like a baby. The circumstances and the discourse together reminded me so forcibly of sister Martha's ill health that she has scarcely been absent from my mind a moment since I heard it." Lucy Ann Terrell, reflecting upon death and love, observed, "I sometimes tremble to think how much my all of happiness depends on earthly connexions especially on my sisters."[1]

The scene and the way it is rendered are instructive. A bereaved family sob like infants, and a Virginia woman, moved by both their tears and a minister's words, is tied to them by bonds of sympathy; she shares in their grief and thinks of her own ill sister, the happiness that comes from love, and the precariousness of life. The minister's words and the family's grief stimulate in Lucy Ann Terrell sympathetic emotions; she enjoys the experience – the minister's sermon, after all, was "delightful." The thought that arises, however, is not narrowly religious. Lucy Ann Terrell thinks of her own happiness, which depends upon love.

As we have seen, sentimental religion enjoined against resting one's security upon the evanescent things of this world. Lucy Ann Terrell did not say so, but quite likely the minister voiced the same warning. Did Lucy Ann Terrell tremble because she, in resting her happiness on mortal beings knew she defied one of the tenets of her religion? To love, perhaps, was to sin.

To love, surely, was to court disaster. Landon Carter, pre-Revolutionary self-styled patriarch, feared divine retribution when he invited his disobedient daughter back to his home. "Thus my God have I suffered myself to destroy thy divine order in governing this world," Carter confessed. Aware that he had broken his God's laws, Carter hoped that the God of justice would also prove a being of love who would forgive him just as he himself had forgiven his daughter. He begged that his forgiveness "not be imputed to me as a crime."[2] Clearly and consciously – all the while that he anthropomorphised his God from his own example – Landon Carter feared punishment for the sin of affection, as if to love and forgive were to violate the natural order.

We have seen that Virginians could interpret the death of a loved one as chastisement for the sin of idolatry. Such a view was consistent with contemporary Protestantism and the contemporary wisdom of the eighteenth century, which called for moderation in all things. Yet by the early nineteenth century, at the same time that Virginians were warning themselves about the dangers of love, they were also – as if in the same breath – like Lucy Ann Terrell, linking their earthly happiness almost exclusively to earthly "connexions." Thus a woman, unavoidably separated from her husband, asked him to dampen his ardor: "Not withstanding I think and feel that loving and being beloved is the most exquisit[e] happiness of life, I wish our tender affections could lie in a state of insensibility. . . ."[3] Here is a double paradox. Why would Virginians so willingly follow a path whose destination they feared? And why would they seek happiness in an emotion?

Doubly Virginians broke with their ancestors, both in their surrender to emotion and in their belief that happiness could be found primarily in one realm of life. Doubly the bonds of moderation were snapped. Virginians in the years prior to the Revolution had given priority to neither family life – the home of affection – nor the emotions. Both were managed to serve a higher good, domestic tranquillity. The family was conceptualized as a counterpoint to a tumultuous world, and activity in that world was considered significant and exciting. Family life, in contrast was designated as pleasant, yet simple. Consider, for example, one young man's formula for "Happiness": "a Virtuous, improve[d] mind, a happy female Companion, and independent situation."[4] Cultivation, property, and an amiable yet anonymous mate were the elements of contentment. Significantly, no one aspect tipped the balance, and just as significantly, the image of the family was warm, simple, and vague.

Sociologist Richard Sennett has argued that in eighteenth-century cosmopolitan Europe, public life was more compelling, more vital to men than the private realm.

Who would want a private life that was dangerous or challenging when public life was all that and more? Instead, at home, a man could express a different side of himself: his natural sympathies, a set of benevolent, compassionate impulses supposedly common to all men. Thus, at home when one acted "naturally," one acted like all men, that is, without individuality. Home life was intended to be warm and affectionate, yet simple and restrained.[5] Neither the individual expression of emotion nor even happiness, as Lucy Ann Terrell used that term to designate a psychological state, was expected or desired. Happiness, instead, was a product of measurable, material relationships, of one's position and role more than one's personality.

Although Sennett's work is sociology more than history, the ideal of eighteenth-century family life that he depicts seems to fit nicely recent descriptions of the British upper-class family at that time.[6] Presumably, this ideal of family life "after the English manner" was imported into pre-Revolutionary Virginia along with issues of the *Spectator* and *Tattler* and copies of those novels that were so popular on both sides of the Atlantic. Indeed, a recent study of eighteenth-century Virginia family life shows it to resemble markedly its British counterpart; on both sides of the Atlantic among the well-to-do, the affectionate family was in vogue.[7] Yet the affectionate family was not an end in itself; an impressive study of William Byrd's world has shown him to be as fully devoted to his public life as any Parisian.[8] Virginians in the years before the Revolution intended family life to be pleasant, but not central. From it no Virginian would derive his all of happiness.

Instead, happiness or, more appropriately, satisfaction

would come from playing a variety of roles, of which family member was only one. And within the family, relationships would be managed and arranged so that obligations could be met easily and simply. Yet, as we have seen, there was a certain amount of artifice in this endeavor to keep family affairs pleasant and restrained. The domestic peace Virginians achieved was fragile and, as they were aware, could all too easily be rent asunder if emotions were not checked. That realization, combined with religion and the prevailing currents of thought, all acted to keep the potentially disruptive passions in rein.

But, as we have seen, sentimental religion unleashed emotion, and so it was with good reason that the gentry had feared the effects of religious revival. Indeed, the Baptist Awakening in Virginia had been designed partially to counter the mannered restraint of the gentry with a warm emotionalism, to oppose the exclusivity of reasoned manners with the democracy of feeling.[9] The rising tide was with democracy, and just as democratic political ideals would triumph in Virginia, so also would a more democratic, more emotional form of worship.[10] In the years after the Revolution, even the gentry came to accept certain elements of revivalistic religion: its emphasis on feeling and its negative valuation of the world, if not its more radical and communal impulses.

Yet the emotion unleashed by religion would not find its object in God. It is almost a given of certain trains of sociological thought that modern religion, in the increasingly secular nineteenth-century West, was hard pressed to satisfy mankind's deepest longings for spiritual fulfillment and compelling answers to the riddles of human existence.

Forced to compete with other modes of explanation, not only by the First Amendment but also by the changing patterns of thought and knowledge that made it necessary, diverse religions lost their majesty.[11]

Instead, people turned to one another for fulfillment in what Ernest Becker has identified as "the Romantic solution" to mankind's quest for meaning. Alexis de Tocqueville, of course, long ago recognized a similar impulse in individualism, "which disposes each member of the community to sever himself from the mass of his fellows and to draw apart with his family and his friends, so that after he has thus formed a little circle of his own, he willingly leaves society at large to itself." Here is the same nineteenth-century retreat from the public sphere that Richard Sennett so deplores, and here also is an explanation of why it occurred. Tocqueville traces the origin and growth of individualism to the breakdown of older, more stable hierarchical forms of relationship. "Men living in aristocratic ages are . . . almost always closely attached to something placed out of their own sphere, and they are often disposed to forget themselves. . . . Aristocracy had made a chain of all the members of the community, from the peasant to the king; democracy breaks that chain and severs every link of it."[12] In the disruption of older patterns of social order, individualism and the isolation of the family were born.

Virginia, of course, had never had an aristocracy, despite the earnest hopes and best efforts of some members of the gentry. Nonetheless, in the years before the Revolution, the gentry had dominated civic and cultural life and had established a corresponding family style: affectionate yet formal. Particularly between parent and child, love was demonstrated tangibly and materially, most often by the gift of property. We have seen in the foregoing chapter that, in the years after the Revolution, economic success and property became more problematic, and although it is tempting to link new forms of family relationship in Virginia to the poor state of that region's economy, it is more accurate to say that a troublesome economy made more palpable and pressing an alteration in family form that was considerably more widespread. Family life would become more intense, less restrained, in areas where the economy was less halting as well.[13] What was at issue in Virginia, as elsewhere, was the notion that property was central, that family life would or could be restricted and restrained.

In a series of remarkable letters from a young man to his father, we can see how two individuals confronted their changing world and tried to steer their way through the uncharted rocks and shoals of altering forms of material and emotional relationships. James Parker had been a Loyalist during the Revolution and ultimately chose to return to Britain. His son, however, decided to remain in the Norfolk that had always been his home. The two men tried to maintain their relationship by correspondence. In 1786 the younger Parker wrote his father of his plans to establish himself as a merchant; he "would not have taken this step but as you wrote me it was entirely out of your power to do anything for me I thought the sooner I could do anything for myself the better." Twenty-two-year-old Patrick Parker was optimistic: "It is well known that a man of industry may allways get a Living any where allmost –"[14] The younger man thus seemed to accept his new responsibility to earn his own fortune. Although James Parker was unable to provide his son with an independence, he would not relinquish his right to filial obedience; and even though Patrick Parker hoped by hard work to make his own way through the world, the young man craved his father's approval and could not help feeling that approval should be expressed with money. The patterns of the eighteenth century were becoming outmoded, yet parents and children still clung to them.

James Parker vigorously opposed his son's plan to work in Norfolk. He thought success would come more readily in the West Indies, South Carolina, or virtually anywhere but the Virginia that had treated him so cruelly. He persuaded his son to move to South Carolina, where the younger man remained only several months. Patrick Parker returned to Virginia to marry his cousin and to try to make his fortune. He hoped his actions would receive his father's blessing. The father, however, withheld it, objecting that the couple were "without a farthing between them." The son, finding it difficult to maintain "that respectfull and submissive manner I ought," argued that his "industry" would overcome his "poverty." He begged his father's sympathy and approval and acknowledged his own "imprudence." "God help me I am really to be pitied – My Duty to my Parent – my own personal Interest leading one way – and on the other an affection and esteem which I never shall be able to surmount."[15] The young man was torn between an older ideal of family relationships, duty (to his father) and a newer one, affection (for a fiancée). Much like Landon Carter, who had worried about welcoming home a disobedient daughter, Patrick Parker conceptualized unchecked love as profoundly disruptive. Following one's emotions was not in one's "personal interest."

The romantic young man married with neither fortune nor parental blessing and spent the rest of his life struggling to acquire both. Crippled by bad judgment and worse times, Patrick Parker went into debt. He both drew upon his father's credit and borrowed from him, further incurring the older man's scorn. The father relentlessly demanded repayment, which the young man was unable to remit. Whereas the father was convinced of his own righteousness, the son wavered, often in the same letter. In his father's letters he could "clearly see . . . that you are quite disgusted with me – every error of omission of mine is repeated and magnified to a crime – upon a Cool & sincere reflection however on past transactions, every man who has acted so dramatically opposite to the commands of a Father deserves it."[16] Young Parker alternated between two modes. First, he tried to read his father's heart, to seek the source of his own mistreatment; then he retreated to a conventional analysis: There is no more than meets the eye; disobedience merits punishment.

Patrick Parker, looking for a God of mercy, found one of wrath. When his two-day-old infant died, the young man conjectured to his father "this is the method heaven takes to punish me for disobedience in marrying contrary to your inclinations." Like God, like father, and Patrick begged his parent "for God Allmighty sake don't run me distracted with your cruell [censures] on my conduct. . . . my spirit cannot stand it nor do I deserve it – particularly from a Father – . . . if a son cannot make free with a Father I think it is hard indeed." Several years later, deeply in debt and rapidly succumbing to tuberculosis, Patrick Parker embarked for Britain to obtain his father's forgiveness before he died. "On my Languid sick Bed I have reflected what a just Prophet you have been respecting my settling in Virginia," the son confessed to his father. "To God I had gone home [Britain] when you asked me. . . . Adieu my Dear Father May the close of your days be much h[appier] than those of your affection[ate] Son's have. . . ."[17] Only a week out of port, the young man died aboard ship, alone.

James and Patrick Parker had been unable to fulfill eighteenth-century expectations of the proper behavior of fathers and sons. The father could not provide the settlement to which the younger man felt himself entitled, and the son could not yield the obedience that the older man demanded. Thus, neither man was able to give what tradition said he should, but neither man was willing to forgo what tradition said he should receive. Such a relationship proved "hard indeed" for both men, for in their failure to fulfill traditional responsibilities they were forced to surrender both traditional benefits and the peace of mind derived from knowing and filling their roles. Whereas the older man was rigid when faced with his new situation, the younger one was beginning to think and act in ways that were to become more common in the nineteenth century. He married before he was independent; he reasoned with his father, "How hard in your young days did you labour for a fortune and when acquired how suddenly was it snatched from you – this convinces you of the uncertainty of all human events – ought we not then endeavor to be happy and not let every little [trifle] prey upon our minds."[18] In a thought characteristic of the nineteenth century, Patrick Parker concluded that the uncertainties of life, not the least of which was property, mandated a search for individual happiness, yet he found his own impossible to secure without his father's approval.

As emotions would come to replace property as the fulcrum in the balance of love, that scale would be tipped toward the parents. Eighteenth-century children had known how to repay their parents for the financial investment they made in their offspring. Deference and obedience were required, both of which could generally be expressed by behavior, by deportment, rather than by psychological compliance with the parents' requests; parents expected and were satisfied by the expression, the show, more than the feeling of love. As parents' investment in their children became largely emotional, however, children found it difficult to reciprocate adequately that love. Once parents and children had exchanged different "currencies," ones specific to their roles; parents had given money, and children had reciprocated with duty. Later, parents and children dealt in the same currency, feelings of love.

Whereas once children had demanded the proper "testimonies of love,"[19] they began to feel grateful, even guilty, for whatever their parents might offer. The confidence of the pre-Revolutionary decades dissipated, and nineteenth-century children became obsequious, exposing feelings of profound inadequacy. Adolescent Thomas Bolling was typical. He told his father, "I [k]now very well that your situation of business is very important and it was never my wish you should do anything for me that would interfear with it." The young man was "conscious how much trouble and expense I have already been, and should be much better satisfied if I had the smallest expectation of compensating you. . . ." Since he was a poor student, he could not repay his parents by performing well on his examinations. ". . . should I be last among the number," young Bolling confessed, "I will feal ashamed to meet you: the best of Fathers; I regret that I had ever been born; being unfortunate in all my pursuits. . . . I smile to recollect the fealings which my Parents entertain of me, and frown at my undeservedness." Reciprocating his parents' care and affection was "an obligation which I can never expect to repay, and can only comfort myself by reflecting, that I am by Nature deprived of the means." As a married man, Thomas Bolling still felt himself unworthy of his parents' love. They had, he assured them, "made too many great and unreasonable sacrifices" for him, "but I would have done the same for you. . . . you must be contented and satisfied for my love and sincere attachment in return for your better evidences."[20] Nineteenth-century Virginians believed themselves incapable of repaying their parents' love. Because of the parents' many years of care and devotion, the children's love given in return was insufficient compensation.

Fearing their inadequacy, children opened their hearts to their parents, to show that the proper feeling was there, to demonstrate their thankfulness for the parental gift. Ellen Randolph told her mother that she had "no principle of either happiness or virtue which you have not given me, whilst my faults are all my own." "How much pleasure it gives me," the younger woman reflected to the older, "to recollect all the claims which you have to [your children's] devoted gratitude and affection & to feel that your cares are repaid, as far as our utmost tenderness *can* repay them." Ellen Randolph was consumed by her love of her mother. "How sincerely I love you," she wrote to her. "In fact how completely my affection for you is the passion of my life. . . . no human being ever loved a mother as much as I do you, but then no one ever had such a mother."[21] Nineteenth-century children often expressed an ardent love of their parents. Perhaps their emotions were no deeper than those of earlier men and women, but we have no evidence of such warmth of feeling in earlier periods. That absence, surely, is significant.

Earlier Virginians had checked their emotions; later ones felt a need to show them, particularly to their parents. George Thompson informed his father that "the fact is you have no idea how much I love you." No idea, that is, unless the son told him. So also Joseph Prentis revealed himself to his father, whose letter afforded the young man "uncommon gratification and a tear trickles down my cheek at the perusal. The joy, the insuperable bliss which I derive from your letters can be better felt than imagined." Such devoted children often considered themselves inferior to their parents. Young Prentis felt "more and more sensible of the obligations" that he owed his father. He hoped to prove a worthy son, although unlike his father he would "never occupy a conspicuous stand at the bar." Another loving son lamented his social maladroitness. "With my father's manners," he sighed, "I would stake the world on my success."[22]

It was often the most devoted children who believed themselves the most inadequate. John Cocke, Jr.'s, devotion to his father had not gone unnoticed. The young man's stepmother commented to his father, who had left the son temporarily in charge of the home plantation, "Poor John has been sadly out of spirits [as] usual since you left home: indeed you seem to be almost necessary to his existence." The young man realized that he suffered in his father's absence. Although himself an extremely competent planter, he promised his father to "do my best towards executing your various directions but alas! I have so bad a head for contrivance & particulars that your going from home is always a matter of regret lest you should find things in greater confusion on your return than when they were put under my charge." Although the older man may not have consciously encouraged his son's feeling of helplessness, he may have fostered the great devotion upon which the young man's conviction of inadequacy depended. After a visit to an aunt, the young man received her praises. He was a "dear boy" with "an excellent heart." The more she was "with him, the more I am convinced of his worth – his good conduct through life will I hope make his Father amends for all the anxiety he feels about him."[23] Children who believed that they had to make "amends" for the anxiety of their parents might well feel inadequate.

Some parents consciously fostered their children's feeling of undeservedness. St. George Tucker reminded his daughter, "Rightly have you said, my child, that you never can repay [your mother's] kindness in this world! I trust it will be held in remembrance by you to all Eternity, & that your love & gratitude to her will increase with time itself, till time itself shall be lost in Eternity."[24] So great was the daughter's debt, she and her father both believed, that it could not be repaid on this side of the grave. Note that the mere rhetorical acknowledgment of her inacapacity would not serve as a means to discharge the obligation; instead, the young woman's father demanded a feeling of eternal incompetence.

Parents sent signals that their children were certain to see. A young man at college could not help noting a comment in his mother's letter: ". . . it was this (speaking of the money [which you sent]) 'which I hope will give you pleasure and be off service to you, as you may be sure I do not forget you.' It seems to imply, Mama, that you thought sending me that money was requisite to make me remember you." The money came with strings attached, strings that joined the son's to the mother's heart. Eliza Blow concluded a long letter of advice to one of her sons with the reflection, "My dear Son this long letter is very tiresome to you, but it is for your own good, and knowledge." Perhaps to assure that her suggestions would be heard, the mother told her son that before long "the head and heart that dictates it may be in the cold grave, and for this reason I would have you have this letter which may animate your exertions and encourage you."[25] Eliza Blow was not ill when she wrote the letter; she merely alluded to her own death as a sure means to reach her son's heart.

Images of death and separation lace parents' letters to their offspring, as if to impress upon the children the gravity of their flaws. Thus, a widow lamented that her sons had moved so far away from her. She felt herself "bereav'd of my two elder sons," and she told one of them, "Could I have foreseen this I would now have [been] the wife of a worthy man – but I thought only of my children & promoting their fortune."[26] Parents manipulated their children's emotions by suggesting that they had put their offsprings' welfare ahead of their own, that they themselves were self-sacrificing, and that their children were either ungrateful or incapable of returning the same kind and amount of love. Confronted with such a charge, no wonder the adolescent Thomas Bolling had replied, "I regret that I had ever been born."

Why did nineteenth-century parents make such enormous demands upon their children's frail hearts? True, since at least the eighteenth century, parents had believed that their children should be comforts to them.[27] Virginians continued to believe that the blows of old age would be cushioned by their children. F. H. Allison, for example, thought that the birth of her friend's child would "compensate" the mother for "all your sufferings and bless you with an infant to amuse you while young and be your Future Comfort." One man was not "ashamed to acknowledge . . . that a very great portion of my happiness results from the hope that my declining years will be cheered by the virtues & talents of my children." Virginians invariably described babies as "little darling" and "pet" and could already see in such infants the promise of their parents' future happiness.[28] Such sentiments were common, even conventional, but it is perhaps significant that adults wrote much more frequently of the pleasure their children would bring them than of what they might do for those children. Men and women maintained great, if vague, expectations of the blessings their children would bestow.

Indeed, sentimental notions of childhood had been in vogue in the Western world since at least the early eighteenth century.[29] What distinguishes parents of the early nineteenth century is their insistence that their little darlings were their only comfort in life, their sole source of happiness, their only reason for being. As one father wrote of his children, "They are the ties which [now] bind me to the earth."[30] The same message was conveyed directly to the children when one widower wrote, "O my dear Sons! let me entreat you to make your conduct such that your poor father may have it in his power to say it is well that I have lived. But for you my dear children can I live, and let me not live in vain."[31] Parents' enormous emotional expectations of their children grew out of their own huge emotional needs. Children were asked to perform the impossible, the unreasonable. Consider the plight of a young man whose sister had just died, a victim of bilious fever. The mother asked that the sad news be broken to him in this way: "Hanging now on [her] only child as the last comfort in her maternal Struggles, she begs to admonish him not to neglect the opportunity now afforded him [at school] of acquiring learning; but to contribute to her comfort, and essentially to secure his own happiness."[32] The grief-stricken mother made no acknowledgment of her son's equally great loss, for she thought of him only as an instrument of her happiness. His emotions were appropriated; his happiness was not his own to secure.

Parents who felt that their happiness would come solely from their children could not resist playing upon what must be any child's greatest fears. Consider as an example the letters Hetty Carr, a widow, addressed to her son. The mother was "sure I love my children more than they do me. they are all anxious to leave me & I would never part with them if I could help it. . . . perhaps," she pointedly told her son, "we may all meet again tho we perhaps will never live together again." She was disconsolate when her children failed to write her, explaining, "I have my dear son but little to make me happy. but if my children neglect me. what have I then left, poverty I can skuffle with. but the loss of affection in my children for me would kill me[.] it is all I have to comfort me."[33] As if in search of a weak spot, the widow tried several popular themes: self-sacrificing mother, ungrateful child, separation and death, and – finally – her own gaping need, an emptiness that could be filled only by her child's affection. The mother concluded with a telling thought: A son who would not offer the love that she required was nothing less than a matricide; the lack of love could kill.

Hetty Carr's letters to her son are wild and charged in the way no pre-Revolutionary letters ever were, and her desperation seems in some ways disproportionate: What she asked of her son was only that he write. But no piece of paper could have filled her need; indeed, when her son wrote, she scrutinized his every letter for the appropriate words and thoughts, once complaining that she did not see her "affectionate son" in the letter, for he had neglected to use that customary closing.[34] The son was not allowed to discharge his filial obligations by formula, by voicing the right words, or by comporting himself in the appropriate way. Instead, the mother tried to look behind the words, behind the convention, into her son's heart, in order to draw from it the sustenance of life. Could any child have fulfilled such a demand?

Thus, in the breakdown of traditional modes of parent–child interaction, emotions were freed. Parents with great need and limited ability, conceptualizing the world as cold and barren, looked to their children for comfort and warmth. In the balanced world of pre-Revolutionary Virginia, comfort was thought to come from material independence; hence, that is what parents wanted to bequeath to their children. In the decades after the Revolution, however, "comfort" became increasingly a state of mind, the product of human relationships. Social critics such as Richard Sennett and Christopher Lasch have lamented such a turn of events, which they consider characteristic of the modern West. Each has suggested that modern families and private life have been asked to fulfill needs incapable of being met. Hetty Carr and her son would be a case in point. Although their analyses diverge, these critics suggest that the elevation of the private and the withering away of the public life – in effect, major changes in the social structure with attendant results for the culture of the past two centuries – are the culprit.[35]

It is tempting to agree, to see the glorification of feeling and the private life as a dependent variable, an unfortunate by-product of the disappearance of older, more stable forms of social relationship. It is tempting to echo Tocqueville and suggest that the demise of the aristocracy and – more relevant to Virginia – the advent of individualism awakened longings whose satisfaction was denied. Again, think only of Hetty Carr and her desperate need. But think also of Lucy Ann Terrell and her trembling affection for her sisters. Or of Landon Carter, forgiving his daughter despite his fears. Perhaps the affectionate yet restrained family of the pre-Revolutionary years embraced a contradiction. Perhaps love, once awakened, could not be indefinitely chained. Again and again, we have seen Virginians telling themselves that to limit love was to limit pain, yet they could not deny themselves their measure of joy, their "exquisit[e] happiness."

Affection had its own logic, and we have just seen that in

relationships between parent and child, that logic could be devastating. But we have examined only one facet of family relationships, that of parent and child. What of those of man and woman, husband and wife? The rich public life of pre-Revolutionary Virginia, with its horse races and courthouse activities, had been almost exclusively a male world. Surely the glorification of the private sphere must have had an important meaning for women. If happiness were to come solely from the family, where all of a woman's duties lay, then women would necessarily acquire a new and significant role. Perhaps it was one that they themselves advanced, for both the obvious reason that to do so was to increase their stature in their society[36] and also because in love they found something that they could offer and something to which they could lay claim.

Both men and women believed that marriage should be based upon affection. Most parents were thus reluctant to interfere in their children's choice of a mate; the couple alone knew their true feelings. John Cocke was typical; he had hoped that his eldest son might marry the daughter of his best friend, Randolph Harrison. Harrison and his wife would have been delighted with such a match; the choice, however, was Polly Harrison's to make, and her parents would not interfere. They were "both happily taught by experience that mutual & unbiased affection form the principal ingredient in matrimonial felicity, & therefore it is our custom to leave our children very much to the influence of that Holy passion, which . . . makes a heaven on earth, & without which the connubial bond is a chain of misery throughout its duration." Similarly, a pious woman prayed that her stepdaughter, in choosing a mate, "may be directed by the good spirit of God." Parents might influence their children's decisions by pointing out a potential mate's good or bad qualities, but they generally exerted no other pressure.[37]

When parents frowned upon a match, it was most often because the young man was not yet independent. Such an objection became more prevalent in the nineteenth century than it had been a century earlier, as young men had to establish themselves in the world. James Parker had been displeased with his son's poverty, not his choice of mate. Likewise, one woman was unhappy with her daughter's marriage to a young doctor who had "not . . . yet established himself in the business and therefore she thought it wrong for her daughter to marry him now particularly as she could not give her a fortune to enable them to set up Housekeeping." James Bowdoin told his father that he planned to marry a South Carolina woman who was "amiable & industerous & with her portion (which is not large) & his industry they can make a living." The father, however, was "distressed that James should marry so early before he had made a fortune & the more so as I fear he will take a permanent stand there [in South Carolina] where I cannot visit him & of course shall see him seldom if ever."[38] Since the fortune was the young man's to make, not the father's to give, the father had very little control over whom his son would marry or where he would choose to live. Parents might criticize their children's shortsightedness in marrying without a fortune, but unless they could convince their children that they were being foolhardy, the parents usually had no means of forestalling such marriages.

Although children were not unaware of the hazards of

marrying before they were independent, they often hoped, like James Bowdoin, that their "industry" would ensure them a living. John Coalter, for example, did not consider his poverty an insuperable barrier to his marrying Maria Rind. He wrote her instructively of a poor but happy couple. The man "by his industry means to make her happy." The woman had resolved not to let their poverty or the exertions necessary to overcome it "give her unnecessary trouble, because in the first place it could not help the matter, and in the second it might prevent her husband from pursuing with chearfulness and success those measure[s] absolutely necessary for both their Happiness." Although their lack of fortune was a hindrance to their marriage, Coalter believed that because the "whole happiness . . . of our whole lives" depended upon choosing the right mate, "we should let no considerations of wealth or poverty bias us in this determination."

Love, more than property, was to be considered in marrying, for poverty could be overcome; indeed, love would make it easier to do so. Married, Coalter would have "a tender Bosom into which I may pour forth my Cares – and I will have Maria to Love me! everything is contained in those two expressions!" Coalter told his fiancée, "You must not repine at my poverty – you must be chearful and happy – it is the only chance I have for ease – mine is interwoven with your happiness[.] I look to you for all the comfort that my present situation is capable of receiving."[39] Overcoming poverty, Coalter suggested, would be difficult, perhaps disheartening. For Coalter or any young man in similar circumstances to maintain his spirits, he would need his wife's encouragement. Coalter's happiness and success would depend upon his wife's "chearfulness," and her good spirits might, he implied, have to be generated and maintained consciously, as an act of will. Coalter's choice of language is instructive. He looked to his future wife for "comfort" and "ease." The pre-Revolutionary gentry had also used those words to describe the ideal life, but for them such a life would derive from their entire social, cultural, and economic situation. For later Virginians, such as Coalter, it would come almost entirely from love.

Virginia men who wanted their wives to bring them happiness selected their mates on that basis. Like John Coalter, they valued a woman for her "prudence, sweetness of disposition and sweetness of person." John Carr described a young woman as "all a man could wish. Clever, Affectionate, Good-natured, Kind Hearted." Joseph Lewis courted Adeline Ball, who was "mild and sweet as virtue and innocence can be[,] a cheerful and happy little creature." Such men were describing the nineteenth-century's ideal of womanhood, the national dream girl more than a peculiarly southern belle.[40] North and South, men wanted women who were sweet, innocent, and cheerful, or, in the words George Tennent used to describe his wife, "Sensible – good natured – beautiful and affectionate." Tennent called his bride his "dear Savior." Similarly, one man rhapsodized to his bride about "the happy reality of being all in all to such an heart as yours – . . . one so worthy of – *almost my devotions* – at least of my warmest and most constant Love."[41] A man who could find a truly amiable wife might almost worship her, for she represented the promise of earthly happiness.

An affectionate and cheerful wife ensured her husband's

happiness by encouraging his efforts, relieving his anxieties, and providing a haven from the tumultuous world. One young man married when he "found one on whom I can depend," and Thomas Gray's new bride was "the lovely, the beloved, and adored fair *one.*" She "gave me a *heart* which is destined to consummate my felicity; and support me through the numerous, perplexing, and painful difficulties of a professional life."[42] Such rapturous language was used not only in wooing and keeping charming ladies but also in writing to other men. Notions of ideal womanhood were widely shared.

One young man's letter to his fiancée expressed feelings about marriage shared by many Virginians of the time. Charles Nourse explained that the settlement he could expect from his parents, although small, would be "sufficient for comfort." Those parents, he was certain, would welcome her "as much from your own merit, as from my choice." Nourse himself had once sought his own fortune; at the age of twenty-one he had engaged in a merchant trade, but had failed. Then for two years he "did nothing," and next entered the army, from which he had just resigned. "I have been," he continued, "for some time sated with the bustle of life, and the only desire I can feel is for retirement, for domestic happiness . . . to you only I now look for the realization of those views." Nourse envisioned home not only as a retreat from "the bustle of life" but also as the source of his greatest happiness. Relying upon "the sweetness of [his fiancée's] disposition" and his own love and devotion, Nourse did not doubt "that we should be happy." He concluded his letter, "Suffer me to add to you as I do to my Mother, that I am ever truly and affectionately yours,

Charles J. Nourse."[43] The closing is revealing: Nourse seemed to hope that his fiancée could re-create for him the comforts of home and the kind of affection he had known as a child.

Many Virginia men found that their hopes and expectations of an affectionate, cheerful wife were realized, and that their mates created for them "domestic happiness." Sometimes, it is true, the letters addressed to wives partook so much of convention that it is not possible to ascertain the depth of their husbands' ardor. Wilson Cary, for example, voiced his dependence upon his family while he was in debt: "With a good and affectionate wife, who chearfully bears her lot, and with promising and dutiful children, such as mine, no reverse of fortune could happen to me, which I could not bear with fortitude." But there is no doubting the sincerity of Thomas Jefferson Randolph. Trying to arrange a lottery to save Monticello from his grandfather's creditors, he implored his wife, "For godsake keep up your spirits. . . . without you all events will be alike a blank to me. With you only I have known happiness. your arms have been the haven of all my passions, hopes, & fears." Another man, unavoidably separated from his wife, so loved her that his vision of heaven was eternal marriage to her. "We ought to try to be good, my dear," he wrote, "and pray to God that he would be pleased to grant us a long and a prosperous life, and that we may die in each others arms, and be conveyed away to those happy seats above where there will be no sorrow, no more pain, no more parting, there we shall dwell together in everlasting love."[44] For such men love was their protection from worldly reverses, their promise of spiritual bliss.

Plate 16. Virginia Randolph Cary. When in debt, her husband relied upon her for comfort: "With a good and affectionate wife, who chearfully bears her lot . . . no reverse of fortune could happen to me, which I could not bear with fortitude." After his death, she supported her children by writing books extolling woman's traditional role, what she once had been rather than what, of necessity, she had become. (Charles Cromwell Ingham. Virginia Historical Society.)

Love had become for many a new religion. So it was with Edmund Randolph. It was only after her death that Randolph fully appreciated "My dear angel Betsy." He had originally been attracted by her "cheerfulness and good sense, and benevolence. . . . qualities which I later found to be constituents of nuptial happiness." His wife had "explored and studied my temper, and anticipated the means of gratifying even my caprices. Innumerable were the instances, in which I have returned home dissatisfied with some of the scenes of the day abroad, and found an asylum in her readiness to partake of my difficulties and make them her own, or to divert them by despising them. On those occasions her features . . . assumed a species of glory, which angels always possess." After her death, Randolph found his "present situation is so greatly contrasted by its vacancy; regrets and anguish, with the purest and unchequered bliss, so far as it depended upon her for many years of varying fortune," that he daily visited her grave to maintain "a mental intercourse" with her; he prayed God "to keep me steadfast in my duty to her memory and that treasure of human happiness the holy gospel."[45] Edmund Randolph had adored his wife during her life and worshipped her after her death.

No argument is made here that all Virginia gentlemen were so happily married, or that notions of marital happiness were not shaped by convention. At the very least, however, men felt compelled to defer to popular notions of the family's importance and the wife's worth. Such had not been the case a century earlier, when William Byrd II joked about his wife's pregnancy and impending confinement: "I fancy if there were any such thing as seeing into Female hearts we should find, this is the reason the whole Sex wants to be marryed, that by being with Child they may have a chance to dye Martyrs [having become pregnant in obedience to the First Commandment]."[46] Such flippancy about the very real dangers of childbirth would have been considered downright irreverent in a later age; indeed, such a jest would not have been made, particularly in a letter to a woman. The nineteenth century in Virginia, as in the rest of America, would come to revere womanhood, to hold up an ideal of feminine merit to which men made willing bows. For many men, including those such as Edmund Randolph, who seemed literally to worship their wives, that adoration was considerably more than sham; it was love.

What of the women? They, too, married primarily for love, and their expectations of marriage were in many ways similar to those of men. Although she had suffered through one unhappy union, Eliza Custis planned to remarry. "I stand alone in the world," she explained to a friend, "& let no one blame me if I venture once more upon that state where my peace was wrecked before. . . . my heart wants some kind bosom to repose my cares in – a protector's arms to guard me from trouble – a man of talents & of noble qualities, who will deserve my esteem, & possess my affection." She had found the right man. "Next to God I revere him, & can make him the master of my destiny without one fear for my future happiness. . . . my *affection for him is as fixed as the Decrees* of fate, & no cause but death shall take me *from him*."[47] Whereas men saw women as providing an asylum from the world, women hoped men would protect them from the same world; although the roles were different, both agreed that in a hostile world there is no happiness in solitude.

Plate 17. Eliza Parke Custis. Perhaps it was her failed marriage that taught her what she wanted in a happy one: "Some kind bosom to repose my cares in – a protector's arms to guard me from trouble – a man of talents & of noble qualities, who will deserve my esteem, & possess my affection." (Virginia Historical Society.)

In marriage, women required love. A young bride made explicit her expectations of her husband: "Let me ever have the sweet consciousness of knowing myself the best beloved of your heart." Another young woman voiced the same hope in her diary. Several days before her wedding, Sarah Anderson wondered: "Will Dr. B. be all that I want in a Husband? In short will he love me as I desire to be loved? I dont look for perfect bliss, but the whole soul of my Husband devoted to love me. . . . I would be foolish to expect perfect happiness, but my heart will demand *perfect Love* Love tender ardent and constant." On her wedding day, the young woman was curiously resigned and detached. "Soon I shall be Sarah Bowen – soon I shall leave my home," she began the final entry in her diary. "Soon I shall get through all the troubles and joys of lifes eventful Drama – soon I shall meet my Maker, a disembodied Spirit, to know my eternal Destiny, and then what will it avail me who I married, or what my honours or enjoyment in this world."[48] If she were disappointed in this world, she might hope for greater happiness in the next. Other women had similarly high hopes and guarded expectations about the possibilities for "perfect bliss" in marriage. When a friend planned to marry a man for whom she had no great love, Elizabeth Williamson counseled her, "Although I by no means think that violent love is necesary in the marriage state, still I think there ought to be a sufficient quantity, when a person considers they are to spend thiere life together." Elizabeth Williamson, perhaps reflecting upon her own marriage, continued, "Though many cares attend a married life still it is the happiest."[49]

If women sometimes tempered their expectations of

blissful marriage, perhaps it was because they saw so many bad husbands. Whereas men often described ideal wives as cheerful and affectionate, women more often characterized good husbands as those free from a host of flaws. In explaining to her husband how she wished him to behave, Margaret Coalter asked him not to "brood," not to "praise too much in another woman any quality that you know I am particularly deficient in," not to "be too fond of company at home or abroad," and "never [to] speak harshly . . . to the Wife of your bosom."[50] The young woman provided a virtual catalog of the behavior women dreaded in a husband. She presented herself as an emotionally fragile creature; her happiness depended upon the care her husband would take not of her person but of her feelings.

Nineteenth-century notions held that women were naturally emotional and men just as naturally rational; in marriage, the woman was heart, the man head. Consequently, women were expected to minister to the emotional needs of the family, whereas men were to see to its material wants.[51] Virginia men who hoped for women to "support" them through "the difficulties of a professional life" thus had conventional expectations of marriage. Women, however, when discussing ideal mates, did not generally ask for men who were strong, decisive, or good providers; more often, they wanted husbands who were kind. They asked for an emotional quality in their mates, and perhaps because they were in this small way defying convention, they were sometimes disappointed.

That disappointment was voiced, and Virginians described husbands who were insufficiently kind. After visiting a cousin who had recently married, Sarah Nicholas had "given up the idea of our sweet Nell having a greater share of happiness than falls to the common lot of humanity." In her cousin's spouse she had observed "specimens . . . of a temper . . . the . . . most to be deplored in a husband" and a "morbid sensibility." The husband's temperament was the cause of his wife's unhappiness. David Meade expressed a similar thought when he wrote that he knew "no Wife [who enjoyed] . . . less felicity in the Hymenial connexion" than his own daughter. She "wants the solace of a well tempered – tender and indulgent husband."[52] If men required affection in marriage, so also did women, but unlike men, women did not necessarily expect to find it.

Jane Bernard certainly did not, and because her husband was insufficiently tender, she suffered grievously. In her diary Mrs. Bernard chronicled her unhappiness; indeed, when she wrote nothing for two weeks, she believed "the reason is that the time has passed tranquilly." During the summer of 1825, her "uneasiness" was caused both by her children's illness and by her husband's card playing. When he spent two nights out, she wished that she could act "on . . . such occasions as he wishes with indifference – but ere I can I must cease to love or *honour* him." Jane Bernard especially resented such absences; on one occasion when her husband seemed to be away from home longer than was necessary, she felt "mortified that he should be willing to stay away when he could get home." While brooding about that absence, Mrs. Bernard visited a young couple and reflected, "How delusive their dreams of happiness are." A woman's happiness depended upon the attentiveness of her spouse, and experience had taught Mrs. Bernard not to count upon a man's attentions. As a result, she was most often depressed and anxious, wishing for what she could not have. In fact, she could describe herself as "calm and happy" only when her husband had "been kinder than usual[.] when he is affec[tionate] I mind nothing. . . . no one knows the heart of woman[.] love governs all her feelings and when they are unamiable it is from some disappointment or fancied neglect perhaps [from him]. . . . a wife is vain of nothing but the love of her husband."[53] Women who defined happiness as an emotional state made themselves dependent upon the humors of others.

A woman's mood depended upon her husband's temperament. The home was an emotional orchestra where feeling cued feeling until the whole house reverberated, sometimes with clashing sounds. One woman was "distressed to hear [from her husband] many bitter & cutting things which caused torrents of tears to flow from my eyes." Her husband's reproach could make her miserable; so also could his mood. Her husband "seemed gloomy & displeased, & never did I feel so entire a willingness to give up this world & all it contained, if [I] might be permitted to enter into that rest which remains for the people of God." The unhappy wife found relief through prayer: ". . . my heart seemed suddenly to melt within [?] & I was enabled both to feel & to confess & bewail my faults – . . . I felt myself more united to my dear husband than ever."[54] Why would a woman with a difficult husband accuse herself? Perhaps because she did not fundamentally believe that a husband's affection was her natural right.

Modern analysts, looking back upon the pervasive unhappiness of many nineteenth-century women, have suggested that women's malaise may have been a product of their exclusion from power, their galling inability to control their own or anyone else's destiny.[55] Yet, the dynamic may have been considerably more complex. To be sure, as Revolutionary republicanism was transformed into American democracy and individualism, virtue was maintained with the insistence that all women were, by nature, self-sacrificing. Men might make their peace with self-seeking individualism if the home remained a repository of virtue.[56] Yet, as we have seen, in Virginia at least, men and women were ambivalent about the imperatives of individualism. Thus, whereas women may have been frustrated by their lack of power, that was not their articulated complaint. They did not, as a rule, demand to have the perquisites of men. Instead, when they complained, it was more often that their husbands were temperamental, thoughtless, and unkind – in short, that they lacked the admirable characteristics of women. It was in this hope, that their husbands might be more virtuous, that women defied convention. That small rebellion, wishing for good husbands, and the accommodation, blaming themselves for an inability to resign themselves to those who were bad, may explain both women's unhappiness and their tendency to voice loudly the claims of the home.[57] And men who in the early years of the American republic may have harbored doubts about the character required for worldly pursuits, likewise accorded increased importance to the home, even if they were less certain than their wives about what role they should play in it.

Still, despite the considerable requirements of a wife and the uncertain ones of a husband, some women found in marriage the love that they required. Nancy Cocke will speak for all the women who loved their husbands greatly and found in marriage what we cannot doubt was deep happiness. She was particularly moved by a letter from her husband: "I thought you had found every avenue to my heart, but these expressions, this whole letter, my husband, has entered one which has created as much emotion as any other your heart has dictated." Husband and wife spoke in the language of love; they knew the words to reach each other's heart. Thus, while her husband served as a general during the War of 1812, Nancy Cocke suggested that they make their separation "the seed time of a fruitful harvest – Let us ask ourselves what one of us would be in this world without the other, and how little happiness beyond our love, is to be enjoyed here."[58] Again the common theme: Happiness comes from love. For some women it was a hope, for others a proven conviction.

Both men and women hoped for domestic happiness, feelings of pleasure, enjoyed at home, created by one's family. Yet for men and women, such happiness had a somewhat different meaning. Since women were believed to be more emotional and giving, they were supposed better able to minister to others' needs. They were also, incidentally, more susceptible to others' moods and more often than men depicted themselves as dependent upon the tenderness of a spouse. Further, since the home was a woman's place, the burden of everyone's happiness, including her own, fell to a woman. Women were aware of this responsibility. Mothers, in fact, taught their daughters that their happiness depended upon themselves. Thus, Maria Armistead advised her married daughter rather bluntly: "Let it . . . my dear Girl be your resolution to be happy – we cannot enjoy our every wish – it is not fit we should. . . . Don't infer from what I have written, that I suppose *you* are not happy. . . . let it not be your fault, if you are not so." Happiness, presumably, was within a woman's reach. Moods could be overcome by an act of will. Agnes Cabell urged her recently married daughter to take "pains . . . to restore to yourself your wonted spirits and health. This, no Physician can do for you, it must be the consequence of your own exertions, the exercise of *your good sense, your correct principles, and naturally affectionate disposition.*"[59]

Tocqueville wrote of Americans that "they are apt to imagine that their whole destiny is in their own hands."[60] So it was with Virginians in the early nineteenth century. Men were advised that their fortunes were theirs to make. In fact, it was partially the anxieties attending such an endeavor that led them to seek solace and renewal within the family fold. So also were women urged to secure their own happiness: "Let it be your resolution to be happy." Whether seeking salvation, success, or domestic pleasure, men and women were told that the object was within their grasp. Surely so great a responsibility must have created a great deal of anxiety; to it must be attributed some measure of the early nineteenth century's pervasive gloom. Nonetheless, more unambiguously than with either religion or work, men and particularly women shouldered the burden of family happiness. It was within the family circle that men and women told each other to look for happiness, and there, if anywhere, that they found it.

Virginians romanticized family life. Typically a man away from home pined, "O! How I long to make one in the circle." Another man told a kinsman that he longed to be "in the bosom of your family [to] partake somewhat of their quietness & peaceful content." "How often when travelling in dark nights & bad roads did I reflect on the peaceful happy circle I had left behind! . . . how did I regret the loss of those joys I have left behind!" an attorney wrote his wife. Similar words came from a young man at college, addressed to his ailing father: "Without thee and the rest of our beloved family & a few friends this world would cease to have a charm for me. To these do I look for the little happiness which may be destined for me in this life." All of these declarations are conventional. One young girl at boarding school expressed the popular thought more simply. Although her school was "the most beautiful place you ever saw," she concluded that "after all there is no place like home."[61]

Virginians who rhapsodized about the family were creating and reinforcing an article of faith for their society, a belief perhaps more central to their lives than any other. Surely, their idea of family partook of myth, as their often pompous language suggests, and it would be impossible for any institution to fulfill such exalted expectations. Nonetheless, Virginians often found that their ideal of the perfect family was in fact the image of their own family. One woman, far from her family, begged her relatives to visit her. "It is true," she wrote, "I have good friends here but none of them are like relations." Another woman, also distant from her kin, reflected, ". . . when I think how completely severed from my home, my family, and my friends [I am], I have a sickness of heart as painful as it is indescribable." Men also knew the value of family. "When relations whom we love visit us," a man explained to his brother-in-

Plate 18. The Washington family. It would not do for the father of his country to be represented as childless, so Martha's grandchildren were drawn into the intimate family circle. Note, on the far right, the figure of a black servant, both literally and figuratively obscured. (Edward Savage, 1796. Andrew W. Mellon Collection, National Gallery of Art, Washington, D.C.)

law, "we have no reserves, ceremony is discarded, & what is all important, they visit us in times of Trouble and Sickness, when common acquaintances are apt to neglect us."[62] Love was a refuge from formality and reserve, and it was only love that could relieve suffering and pain. Unchecked emotion could heal.

Love was seen as compensation. For a decade, Jane Randolph's family had known little but death and failure. She did not think she could withstand any more, and she told her sister that she would insist upon her husband's selling their plantation so that they could move "near you all, for I love you too dearly to be so far from you; & we are so unfortunate; have so many bereavements to bear; that we ought all to be near each other; as being together is the only alleviation for such sorrows as we have felt."[63] For the sorrows of failure and death, love, it seemed, was the only comfort, the only consolation.

Love need not have been life's only comfort in early nineteenth-century Virginia. Religion and success might also have consoled. Religion at the time suggested that life was so bleak that consolation was needed, yet it withheld comfort. It tended to isolate people from one another and to suggest that isolation could prevent pain. Such a consolation was ultimately ineffectual, for most men and women needed love too desperately to relinquish it willingly. Neither did success console, both because material reward seemed difficult to attain and because Virginians' beliefs about success offered no relief; the thought that their destinies were in their own hands was not consoling. Instead, men and women thought of love as consolation. It proceeded from sympathy, a profound awareness of one another's need for comfort in the face of failure and loss. Hence, the more dismal the world seemed, the more necessary was love. Affection drew itself from the world and set itself up in opposition to it. Thus, love necessarily exacerbated the tendencies it attempted to counteract. Love denied the world its power to hurt by insisting that it alone had redemptive value.

It was in love, for better, for worse, that Virginians found their all in all. John Clopton had always lamented that his career as a congressman separated him from his family for so great a part of each year. Old, alone, and dying in Washington, he regretted the choice he had made. In his last letter he told his son, "Much distress of both body and mind do I suffer. To leave all the comforts of home to be here in my situation O what a fool I have been."[64] Worldly success and fame had not been worth the sacrifice of personal happiness. Ultimately love was more valuable to men and women than success, and it was more important than religion, too. Finally, it was love alone that could transcend the barrier of death and love alone that gave meaning to life. Ellen Coolidge reflected upon her long and not always happy life: "When I dream it is mostly of long past times. Night after night I have been surrounded by the friends of childhood and early youth – my grandfather, mother, brothers, sisters, those whom I dearly loved and who dearly loved me, and whom I hope in God's own time to rejoin. I think if anything survives the tomb it must be love."[65] Well might Virginians have trembled to find that all of their happiness depended upon earthly connections.

6

"The best feelings of our nature"

CONCLUSION

LIKE HIS father and his grandfather before him, Thomas Jefferson Randolph aspired to a career in public service, but the women in his family greeted the prospect with dread. "I [am] *in despair.* it's a paltry business," lamented his mother, the woman who had served as Thomas Jefferson's hostess during his presidency. Randolph's mother-in-law, widow of a man who had served Virginia as senator, representative, and governor, was even more agitated. "I have not a doubt but the happiest station (and nine times in ten, the most honorable too) is in private live," she wrote her daughter, who likewise believed that happiness began and ended at home. Her husband's career in public service began and ended with a brief sojourn in his state's house of delegates.[1]

To a certain extent, the circumstances of the Randolph clan were exceptional. The deaths of his father and grandfather, the burden of their debts, and the responsibilities of providing for both his younger siblings and his own children combined to make public service appear a luxury, a self-indulgence that Thomas Jefferson Randolph could ill afford. Yet when those sons of the gentry for whom civic affairs had been a way of life withdrew from politics to serve their families first and only, a tradition was broken, a way of life itself profoundly changed.

That change is most curious when it is remembered that the call to civic virtue, disinterested devotion to the public good, was the battle cry of the Virginia gentry in the American Revolution. The leading families of that colony had a long tradition of public service, which they idealized and sought to maintain in Revolutionary thought and deed. Thus, when Thomas Jefferson Randolph and others like him willingly left society at large to itself (to paraphrase Tocqueville), they in effect revised the republican notion that virtue itself lay in devotion to the common weal.[2] Fifty years after the Revolution, good women sniffed that politics was a "paltry business" and believed that true happiness lay at home. We see here not merely women voicing their claims, but also a recasting of political and domestic terms. Civic life is not self-sacrifice but indulgence, the abandonment of true responsibility. Such a notion makes sense only when the public arena is considered amoral or vicious and domestic life virtuous and pure.[3]

The strands of evangelical religion, republican belief, and domestic thought combine; in the era after the American Revolution, the pursuit of happiness took men and women home. It could be said that when the gentry closed themselves off from the outer world, they merely shifted the balance from the public to the private sphere of life. Such a reorientation is sociological in that it alters the function of the institution of the family. The modern family, as recent analysts have noted,[4] is not so much the society in microcosm as a haven from that increasingly complex and threatening world. Virginians who sought a retreat from a "howling wilderness of woe" joined with other inhabitants of the North Atlantic community in refashioning the family for the modern age.

Such a refashioning was also political, not only in that it retained for men the privilege and responsibility of action in the public sphere. What we conventionally call power was clearly the province of men, yet the new and separate importance accorded the domestic sphere necessarily enhanced the position of women. In increasing the status of women, Virginia once again took part in a historical transformation that reached not only the shores of the James and Potomac rivers but also those of the greater North Atlantic.[5]

In the preceding chapters, we have seen how these changes affected the men and women of the Virginia gentry, and presently we shall attempt to analyze those changes more clearly. Now, however, we should note that such transformations were not only sociological and political but psychological as well. Men and women recognized and hungered after the inner life. In fact – and this represents another change – literate men and women would begin to use the literary form of the diary expressly to explore that newfound wonder, the inner life.

A new psychology literally dictated a new form of expression. Consider the diary of a middle-aged woman. One evening in 1825, Jane Bernard sat down to write in her diary. "My *Journal* has slumber'd a long time," she noted, and "the reason of that is I believe owing to the times passing away so tranquilly nothing has occur'd to interrupt our harmony[.] my personal situation is at present critical and extremely uncomfortable but when there is peace *within* I without vanity can say that I bear *bodily* pain with some patience and fortitude but of mental pain I acknowledge myself an errant coward."[6] Mrs. Bernard distinguished between an internal world and an outer one; with peace within, the physical world could do her no harm. The inner life –

that miasma of passions, humors, and vices so threatening to her pre-Revolutionary ancestors – took precedence; inner resources were more vital than the traditional supports of property, status, and an active religion. Yet the inner life was not bedrock; it was mercury, driven up and down by the humors and vices of others. Nothing disturbed Jane Bernard's calm so much as a slight from her husband. So, when the woman checked her mood, she was registering the effect upon it of other moods as well. In order to understand and control herself, she had to learn a new language, the language of feeling and mood. In the years before the Revolution, Virginians had urged thought to control emotion, fearing the disruptive effects of unbridled feeling; as a consequence, they expressed themselves formally, using the form to shape and check the feeling. Several decades later, Virginians such as Jane Bernard would crave emotion, finding in it the proof of their existence. Like explorers of the unknown, they would pass the boundaries of form and restraint to chart the recesses of the human heart.

When depressed or anxious, Jane Bernard would turn to her diary to quell the tremblings of her active heart. In so doing, she put the diary to a use not conceived by her ancestors. Changing forms of personal expression illustrate new modes of feeling as well.

All extant Virginia diaries from the pre-Revolutionary period were, as might be expected, catalogs of events and transactions. Although contemporary New Englanders and dissenting Britons, prompted by their religion, used their diaries to examine their souls,[7] the activist Anglican religion of the Virginia gentry had no such requirements of its followers. Consequently, Virginia diaries were neither religious nor introspective. Even Robert Rose, a minister, conceived his diary primarily as an account of his external life: "Having frequently found the inconvenience of not keeping an account of the most precious [gift], Almighty God has intrusted with Man, Time, and having been often accused of advising what I never said or thought, particularly by Mr. Morthland, very lately I resolve from this day during my life to keep a Diary."[8] The diary was intended as a reminder of social or economic transactions; it was, in most cases an expanded account book or farm record book in which a planter recorded the events of his life with as much detachment as he noted the changing of the seasons. Even Landon Carter's diary, the most introspective of all pre-Revolutionary Virginia diaries, expresses a preference for reason over passion and a reluctance to dwell upon feeling.[9] The gentry, beneficiaries of leisure and education both, also used diaries to display their wit and learning – intellectual account books, as it were.

Eighteenth-century diaries recorded external events. Men and women wrote about the crops, the weather, their horses, their slaves; who was born, who died, who was sick, who was well; what they read, and what they did. Diarists could be quite candid. In a journal written in code, William Byrd II recorded his sexual activities. Sarah Nourse charted her menstrual periods.[10] Such diaries provide a wealth of information about gentry life in eighteenth-century Virginia. They do not tell us, however, what the people felt. They reveal little about motivation. Even so frank and intelligent a diarist as William Byrd seemed driven by a crude behavioralism. "The Captain's bitch killed a lamb yesterday," Byrd wrote, "for which we put her into a house with a ram that beat her violently to break her of that habit." Byrd also attempted to break slaves of bad habits: "Eugene pissed abed again for which I made him drink a pint of piss."[11] Pre-Revolutionary Virginians did not live in a psychological realm. They did not examine motivation, nor did they muse about the complexities of human behavior. They had neither the taste nor the skill for self-examination. They did not probe the depths of the human heart.

Nineteenth-century Virginians continued to write diaries to keep their various accounts. They also began gradually to write diaries to explore and to soothe their feelings. Sentimental religion, by holding that purity of heart was more important than correctness of action, encouraged Virginians to record and examine the motions of their hearts. Louisiana Hubard called her journal "A Diary of my religious exercises and feelings." An exceptionally devout woman also used her diary for regular self-scrutiny. "I have been looking a little into myself, & am filled with despondency at the view" was a typical entry.[12]

Although religion encouraged self-examination, not all introspective diaries were religious. Sarah Andrews, a young school teacher, wrote a diary so devoted to her internal life that names, places, events – the usual stuff of earlier diaries – were almost never mentioned. Instead, she analyzed her feelings and moods. She kept a journal "to have something to refer to in future days to tell me how I felt, and how my time passed at certain periods, and lastly and principally, to become the anatomist of my heart and conduct." Although fascinated by her moods, Sarah Andrews found her life uneventful. "Really laughed heartily tonight, when one of my Scholars seeing me take out my diary, said 'she should be delighted to read *my life'!!!* Suppose by this, the poor little rogues think I am writing 'my life'!! Ha, ha, ha. . . . My life has been so eventful, so useful, so interesting! Oh. Jehu! Write my life!! Preposterous." Journal writing was a private ritual, an escape from a tedious life. "Well my Diary, I can say what I please in your ear and you never disclose my secrets. 'Tis a great relief to tell one's feelings and notions, though to an inanimate object." Sarah Andrews recommended this release to others: "I think all the victims of ennui, had best *make a Diary* and just say what *they* please. Let every freak and whim of their disordered minds be fully disclosed."[13]

Diary writing was nothing less than therapy, a balm to the suffering psyche. As Sarah Andrews turned from the outer world to the inner reaches of her mind, she came to fear that it was disordered. Her life was uneventful; she was exceptional only in her moods, but those feelings were so extraordinary that she could confess them only to the silence of a sheet of paper. As she turned from the outer world to her own feelings, she also turned from communion with others to an intense isolation. She found comfort only in elaborating her distinctiveness, insisting that what made her different and real was hidden from the world's view. The true self was hidden and could not safely be revealed.

Sarah Andrews displayed what some sociologists have described as a "modern" personality, in which "the individual's experience of himself becomes more real to him than his experience of the objective social world. . . . the individual's subjective reality . . . becomes increasingly differentiated, complex – and 'interesting' to himself. Subjectivity acquires previously unconceived 'depths.' . . . the self becomes an object of deliberate attention and sometimes anguished scrutiny." Such sociologists, following the lead of Max Weber, believe that the fragmentation of an increasingly urban, bureaucratic, and technological world drives the individual to seek certainty in himself more than in the no longer unified outer world.[14] Such an analysis, however, must prove inadequate for Virginia, which by 1830 had not experienced the major social, political, and economic transformations upon which such sociological theories are based. Nineteenth-century Virginians such as Sarah Andrews exhibited characteristics of a "modern" personality, yet their world was not – as the term is usually understood, modern. We must look for other causes for the historical transformation that would encourage a young woman to become the anatomist of her own heart and mind. In so doing, we may come better to understand not only the changes that swept Virginia but also those that transformed the wider Western world that has attracted the sociologists' interest.

Although sociologists and social historians have often linked the modernization of family and personality to the structural transformations associated with the industrial revolution, such an analysis cannot directly explain changes that occurred in the late eighteenth-century slaveholding, agricultural society that was Virginia. We will have to seek our understanding elsewhere than in the factories and cities of the modern age. We might more profitably fix our gaze upon eighteenth-century Europe, particularly England. As we have already seen, the same currents that bathed Virginia washed the shores of other North

Atlantic communities. By the eighteenth century, a cult of sensibility was in vogue on both sides of the Atlantic. Feeling, if not passion, was admired, and family life was intended to be affectionate and to provide a realm where a person might display his sympathy. Such widespread phenomena had their roots in Britain, at least, in the weakening power of kinship groups, in the increasing prominence of the landed gentry and an affluent bourgeoisie, in a standard of living and a frame of mind that could create literally and figuratively a domestic space, and in the growth of both literacy and works addressed to the "man of sentiment."[15]

Indeed, some of these trends would only be amplified in the New World and in Virginia. Older forms of authority would there be further undermined, culminating in the first of the democratic revolutions and in the institution of a democratic ideology and the concomitant idealization of the middle – or, as it was put at the time, "middling" – class. As the standard of living rose, families could afford the luxury of separate bedrooms, sets of tableware, carpets, curtains, and other marks of middle-class privacy and gentility. Such concepts of domestic life were refined by the magazines and books that men and women – an increasing proportion of whom were literate – read. And the importance of literacy itself cannot be overemphasized, for as one historian has recently observed, "when private readers withdrew into a secluded realm where discourse reached them in solitude, modes of silent thought developed – thus was engendered 'individualism.'"[16]

It is the development of individualism that we are tracing, but it would be both premature and inaccurate to locate it in the eighteenth century's cult of sensibility. Vir-

Plate 19. Woman reading in garden. Reading tames nature in this Virginia folk art painting. The growth in literacy and the spread of sentimental literature allowed men, and especially women, to retreat from the wild and boisterous world into the romantic privacy of the printed word. Here, Eve has returned to the garden with a book. (Caleb Davis, watchmaker, c. 1830. Abby Aldrich Rockefeller Folk Art Center, Williamsburg, Va.)

ginians imported their notions of gentility and tried to fashion for themselves a New World gentry class. Yet this sentimental mode adopted by Virginians should not be misunderstood as an embracing of individuality and passion. To the contrary, the formality required in the expression of feeling acted as a check upon the individual expression of emotion. The very newness of the Virginia society and the precariousness of its self-made elite, in fact, would serve to retard more than to encourage emotional display. Peace and passion seemed incompatible.

Sentiment, in some sense, then, was an import from the upper reaches of British society. Yet the general trend would be realized in the province in a particular way. In Virginia, the mannered display of feeling – the conventional display of the sympathetic heart – would be rejected by the lower classes in favor of a more deeply felt, individually expressed emotion. Waves of religious revival swept Virginia in the second half of the eighteenth century, enshrining feeling, more than position, behavior, or manners, as the surest test of individual merit. Revivalists sought release from the difficulties of rural life as well as from the emotionally barren Anglicanism of their gentry betters. They found communion in the sharing of feeling with life's fellow sufferers.[17] Evangelical religion released the individual's emotions, and although it bound him in fellowship with like-hearted others, it consequently must be seen as the source of both the valuing of profound feeling and the impulse to examine the heart.

Evangelical religion was not, however, the source of the sentimental family, particularly if by that we mean the adoration of children, the lavishing of sentiment, and the indulgence of joy. If anything, as one recent study has shown, evangelical families could be austere and forbidding – making a release in communion all the more devoutly desirable.[18] By the time of the American Revolution, then, the Virginia gentry hoped for a family life that was warm but restrained. Emotional heat was the province of lower-order evangelicals.

If there were social tides sweeping Virginia, so also were there political ones, and for a number of reasons well documented by historians, members of the gentry and the lower orders both would join in that Revolution, not always from the same motivation or always with the same goals.[19] Thomas Jefferson, member of the gentry, could gloss over differences of aspiration with the lovely phrase "pursuit of happiness." The success of the Revolution would unsettle the gentry, for it would render illegitimate their pretensions to social sway. More than their Church was disestablished as the lower orders came to assert their just claims. No argument is made that the gentry surrendered their power, but they certainly lost their self-confidence.[20] In a democratic society, aristocrats were acceptable only if doomed, a nostalgic reminder of a now-vanished way of life in which planter–entrepreneurs were supposedly Cavalier–emigres. By internalizing the Revolutionary rejection of commerce, Virginians could adopt a patriotic stance and endow their political struggle with an even broader meaning. But by adopting such an ideology, they forced themselves either to reject commerce in deed as well as word, and thus deny themselves the sine qua non for a gentleman's life, or to condemn themselves to unredeeming work.

With no solace coming from work, it is little wonder that the post-Revolutionary gentry turned to religion and to love. Evangelical religion – the faith of the lower orders – of course, argued that the business of this world was without sacred meaning, that it all too often turned a man's heart from the worship of his God. Such a creed seemed increasingly plausible to the gentry, but if they absorbed that part of evangelical religion, they would not adopt its more radical and communitarian aspects. Indeed, by the early decades of the nineteenth century, evangelicals were less inclined to challenge the standing order; they came to accept, for example, both slavery and the individualistic assumptions of Virginian culture.[21] The gentry would absorb the sentimental impulses of evangelical religion, and even a tinge of its asceticism, as private self-indulgence fell under a cloud (although it is true that the negative example of the British, as much as the preachings of the evangelicals, cast the display of luxury into disrepute). In sum, gentry and evangelical values would meld, creating for Virginians what we recognize as nineteenth-century middle-class culture.

Separate streams would merge into a main current of thought and feeling. This confluence is nicely illustrated by Virginians' accommodation to what was increasingly regarded as a peculiar institution, slavery. Revolutionary talk about self-evident truths, along with evangelical convictions about equality before God, made repugnant what had once been an accepted part of the social hierarchy; slavery became intellectually and morally outdated long before it had lost its economic usefulness. But that usefulness would not be denied, and so prospering Virginians reconciled themselves to the servitude they enforced by forging for themselves the new roles of Christian massa and missus. Evangelicals redefined themselves as Christian slaveholders, bringing the gospel to needy Africans. Simultaneously, the spread of sentiment among the gentry encouraged the man of feeling to sympathize with his slaves. The streams merged into what one historian has aptly termed "the domestication of domestic slavery."[22] It is telling that southerners in search of justification would call slavery not business but a family affair, themselves not taskmasters but people who cared. It is telling, too, that the sanctification for slavery would be sought not so much in religion and its creed as in the metaphor of the plantation family, with masters as parents and slaves as their kin. Slavery might be moral if planters loved their slaves.

Redemption, like happiness, was to be found at home. As we have observed, historians have noted the increasing importance of the domestic sphere in the early nineteenth century, and they have concluded that as the early stages of industrialization took work out of the home into the amoral world – always the antithesis of heaven – the family was styled as a haven and endowed with consolatory and redemptive value.[23] Yet Virginia was far from industrialized; planters still labored at home, all the while proclaiming it a haven as loudly as any northerner. The idealization of the family extended further than the reach of the factory's smoke. It perhaps can better be understood as a response to the ambivalences created by the growth and spread not so much of industry as of commerce and the complexities of interdependent economies, forces that had been transforming the Atlantic communities for well over a century. As the world became larger and more problematic, the home profited from the comparison.

The feelings awakened by religion wended their way home. As the pre-Revolutionary gentry had seemed to grasp, to embrace emotion was to court disaster. Individualistic feeling, intense and uncontrollable, might disrupt not only the sweet peace of domestic tranquillity but also a person's innermost calm. Evangelical religion indeed had sought such a revolution, shattering a person's precarious defenses in order to prove his ultimate dependence upon God. Yet religion was unable to reshape or harness the feelings it exposed. It could only suggest, particularly in consoling the bereaved, that trembling men and women deaden their senses to the hurts of the world and put to sleep what religion had just aroused – and was continuing to arouse with the insistence that feeling was crucial to faith. Religion thus denied full rein to the emotions. The home, however, would allow what elsewhere had been forbidden.

Virginians came to prize emotion. It would transform their family lives and their very sense of being. We have already seen how religion and its form, the introspective diary, imposed isolation. It cut men and women off from the wide and exciting world of their ancestors. In letters, the form of affectionate social relations, men and women recreated their world, making it not the vast tableau of the pre-Revolutionary years but a more intimate and richly detailed canvas, a work of shadow as much as light.

Pre-Revolutionary letters allowed men and women to trade information, gentlemen and ladies to display their learning and wit. Maria Carter, for example, sought to amuse a correspondent with a "merry & comical Letter" about a typical day in her life.[24] Others exchanged tidbits of information or bits of poetry, original or copied. All displayed the buoyancy characteristic of the gentry in that time and place. That rosy self-confidence evaporated after the Revolution, and people began to write apologetically.

A young woman excused herself for not writing her aunt: "I am always backward in beginning a correspondence, because I know I can write nothing to interest or give pleasure to others." Quite similarly, a young wife forgave her friend for not writing. "I know full well by experience that the duties & occupations of a married life precludes the possibility of devoting much time to the pen," Maria Randolph sympathized. "Indeed, so uniform are the days of a matron, that she rarely can find subjects sufficiently interesting to commit to paper – Thus it is with me, I know When I have spoken of my health & wishes to see you, all is said that is of any value."[25] Like Sarah Andrews, such Virginians did not find their own lives of any interest; they consequently suffered from a very precarious sense of self.

If the diary, however, could turn a sufferer only further inward, away from a life that no longer had charm, the letter allowed people to share feelings of isolation; it created a community of common feeling. It made people feel somewhat less alone. Thus, an elderly widower could remark that letters were "one of the few comforts now left" him. Letters operated upon the feelings; words affected mood in the therapy of choice for unhappy Virginians. As Ellen Randolph explained to her mother, "Your letters produce a beneficial effect upon my mind. they strengthen and confirm my good resolutions, they comfort me for every trifling mortification & remove every uneasy feeling."[26] Men and women of the early nineteenth century offered both the diagnosis and the cure. A woman wrote her friend because "I wish'd to soothe a little my depress'd spirits." She was willing to reveal her unhappiness in order to alleviate it. So personal a strategy became a creed when another woman observed, "How delightful to pour forth the effusions of the heart into the bosom of affection; it is indeed the only real relief the agonized soul can experience."[27]

When a woman could confess her "depress'd spirits" and another would stylize and generalize that sort of individual malaise into the "agonized soul," the buoyancy of the pre-Revolutionary years was gone. With it went that era's restraint. Men and women knew what they were doing as they tore down the walls of moderation, the complacent fronts they had once presented to one another. The impersonality of cold form was roundly rejected; instead, Virginians demanded communication that was direct, personal, and warm. The keen awareness of the disjunction between world and home was mirrored in a growing preference for the language not of the head but of the heart. To restrain oneself, to express oneself correctly and conventionally, was to show oneself defective in qualities of the heart.

Men and women rejected the conventions of restraint and the formal letters they had dictated. As one young woman put it, "I had rather have one letter *warm* from the heart than all the cold studied ones from the *head* you could send me." As if in response, another woman dispensed with the conventional closing and signed herself "Harriet Anderson, genuine; warm from the heart and to the heart addressed." No ordinary closing would do, for the young woman was determined to assert her individuality, her sincerity, and her warmth. In fact, all were variations on the same theme: to express, to feel, to be. Another woman, perplexed by the coldness of her aunt's letters, noted, "When I receive letters from my friends and relations – I expect they are to be affectionate and friendly. . . . [Aunt

Elmsly's] are so frigid – she dont write as if she felt."[28] The cold aunt seemed remote, unnatural, unreal.

The language of the heart was informal and expressive, in the words of one man, "as if you were conversing with me." It was supposed to be, in the words of another, "free and undisguised," as if cold form necessarily masked genuine emotion. The new assumptions became conventional wisdom when a man opined, "*Friendly* letters (such as only communicates the soul) require no studied phraseology of diction, but such as the heart will dictate." This philosophy was in fact a directive as to how letters ought to be written. Thus, a doting mother chided her son for a letter that was well written and "correctly spelt, but . . . I never wish you my dear son to write me a letter in any language that is studied or dressd, & never to copy one – the thought from your heart send me."[29] Literate Virginians demanded not those sentiments held in common – the "sympathies" of the eighteenth century – but those that were individual, "free and undisguised," as if any conventional sentiment could not be fully genuine, as if common feeling were suspect.

Family and friends were a haven from the cold formality of the world, its style and pretense. Yet here, letter writers created for themselves a new dilemma. Consider one woman's confession to her sister: "I am not ashamed to write carelessly, weakly, foolishly to you whom I do not wish to think better of me than I deserve."[30] With family one could be oneself – a weaker, more feeling person than the mask presented to the world. There is the suggestion that to be informal, to reveal one's feelings, to be one's true self was cause for shame. Why else the hesitancy about revealing one's heart to the wider world? Free and undisguised, one was foolish, weak, depressed. In encouraging feeling yet hiding it from the world, the nineteenth century once again gave with one hand what it took with the other. The language of the heart was the language of the soul, and the heart asked for absolution. It could expose itself only to another affectionate heart, the nineteenth century's equivalent of an all-forgiving God. Again, redemption was sought in earthly love.

Virginians believed they were rejecting convention in their demand for words that were "genuine, warm from the heart," and indeed, they did reject the particular assumptions of the pre-Revolutionary years, which had forbidden a too explicit reference to either individual emotions or topics that might be distressing. But at the same time, nineteenth-century Virginians were in fact creating for themselves new conventions, ones of warmth, individuality, and, to a certain extent, malaise, as talk of "the agonized soul" would suggest. How this process took place is well illustrated by the letters exchanged by Joseph Nourse and his fiancée Maria Bull. In 1784, Nourse received a letter from his fiancée with "heart felt joy." The letter afforded him "a secret pleasure, from the purity and elegance of the style. . . . how widely different were my sensations, from that of a person receiving a Letter from his Love, illspelt, badly written, & devoid of sentiment." Maria Bull had proven her affection by expressing her sentiments in a careful and correct way. Twelve years later, Joseph Nourse wanted something different from his wife, and he implored her, "Don't fail to write me – not along but a very *kind* Letter; tell me I do nothing wrong, that I am the dearest – you could know, but enough." Now he needed a more direct expression of his wife's love, but in making that demand he literally put the words into her mouth. Thus, Maria Bull Nourse dutifully replied, "To shew my obedience I echo back 'you are the dearest - you can do nothing wrong.'"[31] Love voiced new expectations, new words, and - finally - new conventions.

The nineteenth century awakened feeling and gave it form. Emotion could often be devastating, and we have examined the enormous grief of the bereaved, for example. Perhaps the very popular sentimental literature of the day may be understood as a socially acceptable and psychologically safe way to stimulate and shape feeling in one stroke. To show feeling was to prove oneself fully alive; as one man had told another, "I like you better for the grief that you feel."[32] Yet unbounded grief could incapacitate, as could unanswerable demands for proof of love. Thus, Maria Nourse had answered her husband with the words he wanted. The nineteenth century, to a certain extent, merely provided a new script for personal relations, one filled with words of love and feeling, grief and despair. If Virginians were no longer willing to check emotion, they would have to find ways of curbing its disruptive effects. Sentimental modes of expression may have filled that need, either by allowing men and women to portray themselves as more deeply and widely feeling than they may in fact have been or by providing new channels, in affectionate relationships, for the new feelings.

Men and women struggled with their culture's new dilemma: Feeling was prized, yet many feelings could hurt. Other societies might try to blot out the unhappy feelings and encourage only the most joyous.[33] Such was not the route taken by Virginians; if anything, they tended to prize feelings of melancholy and to mistrust those that were more cheering. Sometimes a perceptive man or woman might even see through to the heart of the dilemma. As her family was about to depart Monticello for the last time, Ellen Coolidge told her sister Virginia to reject self-pity: "The most disinterested and self-sacrificing people are sometimes the least able to deny themselves the dangerous gratification of musing & melancholy recollection. they have relinquished so much, they think, done so much, and suffered so much, that it is hard they should be refused the luxury of regret. but the cup which they cannot dash from their lips is drugged; although the best feelings of our nature, our best affections are mingled in the draught, it is only the more alluring, for being so compounded. drink deeply and often if you would become useless, enervated, repining, unfit for the situation in which you are placed & incapable of its duties."[34] Ellen Coolidge realized that her culture's balm was also its poison, that feeling itself could maim.

Yet in urging her sister to resist the seduction of feeling, Thomas Jefferson's granddaughter would surrender to the embrace of the era's other great deceiver, the notion of the all-powerful, ever-responsible individual, master of his or her fate. But neither individualism nor unbounded feeling could provide the happiness that men and women so greatly craved. Thus, Ellen Coolidge sometimes "felt like a weary thing to live on with so many cares and so few enjoyments, but I presume this is the history of more lives than mine. . . . It is," she concluded, "a poor consolation to be compelled to acknowledge that we are ourselves far more to blame than our destinies."[35] There is more than a little irony in the fact that the first generation of Americans to commit themselves to the pursuit of happiness would find so much sadness instead.

Abbreviations used in notes

Archives

DLC	Library of Congress
MiU-C	William L. Clements Library, The University of Michigan
NCD	Perkins Library, Duke University
SHC-NCU	Southern Historical Collection, University of North Carolina Library, Chapel Hill
ViU	Alderman Library, University of Virginia
ViW	Earl Gregg Swem Library, College of William and Mary
ViWC	The Colonial Williamsburg Foundation, Research Archives

Journals

AQ	*American Quarterly*
JAH	*Journal of American History*
JEH	*Journal of Economic History*
JSH	*Journal of Southern History*
JSocH	*Journal of Social History*
VMHB	*Virginia Magazine of History and Biography*
WMQ	*William and Mary Quarterly*

Notes

PREFACE

1 Garry Wills, *Inventing America: Jefferson's Declaration of Independence* (New York: Doubleday, 1978), 164; see also 149–64, 240–55. For other interpretations of what Jefferson and his contemporaries understood by the phrase, see Carl Becker, *The Declaration of Independence: A Study in the History of Political Ideas* (New York: Knopf, 1942; repr. 1965), chaps. 2 and 3; Cecilia M. Kenyon, "Republicanism and Radicalism in the American Revolution: An Old-Fashioned Interpretation," *WMQ*, 3rd ser., XIX (1962), 143–82; Dumas Malone, *Jefferson and His Time*, vol. 1, *Jefferson the Virginian* (Boston: Little, Brown, 1948), 227–8.

2 Thomas Jefferson Randolph to Jane Randolph, January 30, 1826, Edgehill-Randolph Papers, Vi.U.

3 Kenneth A. Lockridge (in *Literacy in Colonial New England: An Enquiry into the Social Context of Literacy in the Early Modern West* ([New York: Norton, 1974], chap. 2) has estimated that female literacy in the West, including Virginia, gradually climbed from 20 percent in the early seventeenth century to 50 percent in the mid-nineteenth. Male literacy rose at the same rate, approaching 75 percent in the mid-nineteenth century. Such statistics, as Lockridge explains, are difficult to estimate and complicated to use. Surely, only a small proportion of Virginia's population would have been well enough educated to write with facility (or, for that matter, to read with ease).

4 T. H. Breen, "Horses and Gentlemen: The Cultural Significance of Gambling among the Gentry of Virginia," *WMQ*, 3rd ser., XXXIV (1977), 240 n.

5 Peter L. Berger, *The Sacred Canopy: Elements of a Sociological Theory of Religion* (New York: Doubleday, 1967), 22; Peter L. Berger and Thomas Luckmann, *The Social Construction of Reality: A*

Treatise in the Sociology of Knowledge (New York: Doubleday, 1966).

6 From "Men Made out of Words," in Holly Stevens, ed., *The Palm at the End of the Mind: Selected Poems and a Play* (New York: Knopf, 1971), 282.

1. THE WORLD OF THE PRE-REVOLUTIONARY GENTRY

1 Dumas Malone, *Jefferson and His Time*, vol. 1, *Jefferson the Virginian* (Boston: Little, Brown, 1948), 10, 4, 31–2.

2 For Thomas Mann Randolph, see William H. Gaines, Jr., *Thomas Mann Randolph, Jefferson's Son-in-Law* (Baton Rouge: Louisiana State University Press, 1966).

3 Mary Randolph to Ellen W. Coolidge, November 26, 1826, Ellen Wayles Coolidge Correspondence, ViU.

4 Virginia Trist to Ellen W. Coolidge, March 23, 1827, ibid.

5 Henry James, *Hawthorne* (New York, Harper & Row, 1879), 42–43.

6 Allan Kulikoff, "The Colonial Chesapeake: Seedbed of Antebellum Southern Culture?" *JSH*, XLV (1979), 532–3; Russell R. Menard, "Economy, Population, and Society in the Chesapeake Colonies, 1607–1730" (unpublished paper), esp. 18–19. My understanding of colonial Virginia has been shaped by Bernard Bailyn, "Politics and Social Structure in Virginia," in James Morton Smith, ed., *Seventeenth-Century America* (Chapel Hill: University of North Carolina Press for the Institute of Early American History and Culture, 1959), 90–115; Edmund S. Morgan, *American Slavery, American Freedom: The Ordeal of Colonial Virginia* (New York: Norton, 1975); and Rhys Isaac, *The Transformation of Virginia, 1740–1790* (Chapel Hill: University of North Carolina Press for the Institute of Early American History and Culture, 1982).

7 Richard and Elizabeth Ambler to Neddy and Johnny, August 1, 1748; Richard Ambler to Neddy and Johnny, May 20, 1749; see also Richard Ambler to Neddy, February 28, 1752, Elizabeth Barbour Ambler Papers, microfilm from ViU at ViWC.

8 Catesby Cocke to Sr., March 11, 1752; C[atesby] C[ocke] to [William Cocke], November, 1752; C[atesby] C[ocke] to [William Cocke], December 3, 1752, Papers of the Jones Family, DLC.

9 I am indebted to Professor Rhys Isaac for the suggestion that William

and Catesby Cocke represented two different modes of gentry life.

10 For an interesting discussion of the ideals of the gentry, see Robert Dawidoff, *The Education of John Randolph* (New York: Norton, 1979), esp. 73–8. Dawidoff draws from Jack P. Greene's excellent *Landon Carter: An Inquiry into the Personal Values and Social Imperatives of the Eighteenth-Century Virginia Gentry* (Charlottesville: University Press of Virginia, 1967); esp. 13–27.

11 See especially Gordon S. Wood, *The Creation of the American Republic* (Chapel Hill, N.C.: University of North Carolina Press for the Institute of Early American History and Culture, 1969), 65–107.

12 For a discussion of the emotional self-restraint of the eighteenth century, see Richard Sennett's provocative *The Fall of Public Man* (New York: Knopf, 1977).

13 Quoted in Michael Mullin, ed., *American Negro Slavery: A Documentary History* (New York: Harper Torchbooks, 1976), 56–7.

14 For illuminating discussions of Byrd, see Mullin, *Documentary History*, 98–9, and Mullin's earlier *Flight and Rebellion: Slave Resistance in Eighteenth-Century Virginia* (New York: Oxford University Press, 1972), chap. 1, esp. 64–7; David Bertelson, *The Lazy South* (New York: Oxford University Press, 1967), chap. 4 –6; and especially Michael Zuckerman, "William Byrd's Family," *Perspectives in American History*, XXI (1979), 255–311.

15 Peter Fontaine to Brothers John and Moses, April 15, 1754, in Ann Maury, *Memoirs of a Huguenot Family* (New York: Putnam, 1853), 340–2.

16 Mullin, *Documentary History*, 58. The reference was Micah 4:4.

17 Philip Fithian, February 6, 1774; September 3, 1774, in Hunter Dickinson Farish, ed., *Journal and Letters of Philip Vickers Fithian, 1773–1774: A Plantation Tutor of the Old Dominion* (Williamsburg, Va.: Colonial Williamsburg, 1943), 84, 240–1.

18 *Orange County Order Book*, vol. 1, November 23, 1738, microfilm from Virginia State Library; W. W. Scott, *A History* (Richmond, Va.: Everett Waddey Co., 1907), 136.

19 For county formation, see Albert O. Porter, *County Government in Virginia: A Legislative History, 1607–1904* (New York: Columbia University Press, 1947), 47. See also the petition of the inhabitants of Frederick County to Governor Gooch, asking that the organization of their county be expedited. In *Calendar of Virginia State Papers (Richmond, Va., 1875–93)*, vol. 1, 223.

20 *Orange County Order Book*, vol. 1, March 16, 1735; July 27, 1738; Scott, *A History*, 136.

21 *Orange County Order Book*, vol., 1, June 27, 1737; Scott, *A History*, 135.

22 Much of this argument about the nature and purpose of local justice proceeds from an analysis of the Orange County Court records between 1734 and 1741. For a fuller, albeit somewhat different, discussion of the nature of county justice, see A. G. Roeber, *Faithful Magistrates and Republican Lawyers: Creators of Virginia Legal Culture, 1680–1810* (Chapel Hill: University of North Carolina Press, 1981).

23 *Orange County Order Book*, vol. 2, October 25, 1739; November 23, 1739; February 1739 (old style).

24 See, for example, Wiliam E. Nelson, *The Americanization of the Common Law: The Impact of Legal Change on Massachusetts Society, 1760–1830* (Cambridge, Mass.: Harvard University Press, 1975); Michael Zuckerman, *Peaceable Kingdoms: New England Towns in the Eighteenth Century* (New York: Knopf, 1970).

25 For the period 1763–88, Jackson Turner Main has established that 30 percent of white Virginians were landless dependents (see his *The Social Structure of Revolutionary America* [Princeton, N.J.: Princeton University Press, 1965], chap. 2), but a significant number of this group would have been sons of planters and farmers who would expect some day to own land. Access to justice in Virginia was thus tied very closely to property ownership or the ability to command patronage from a property owner; politics, in the widest sense of that term, were shaped by the owning of property.

26 Mullin, *Flight and Rebellion*, 16. In 1763, according to Mullin, Virginia's population was about 340,000, divided equally between blacks and whites. In 1790, 442,117 of Virginia's population of 747,610 were white. Charles S. Sydnor, *American Revolutionaries in the Making: Political Practices in Washington's Virginia* (1952; repr., 1965, New York: The Free Press), 37.

27 Zuckerman, *Peaceable Kingdoms*, esp. chaps. 2 and 3; Nelson, *Common Law*, 36–40. For the psychological source of New Englanders' anxiety about aggression, see John Demos, *A Little Commonwealth: Family Life in Plymouth Colony* (New York: Oxford University Press, 1970), 48–51, 134–9. Philip Greven suggests that members of the southern gentry were considerably more comfortable with anger

and self-assertion. *The Protestant Temperament: Patterns of Child-Rearing, Religious Experience, and the Self in Early America* (New York: Knopf, 1977), part four, esp. 318–20.

28 For the parallel origins of slavery and freedom, see Morgan, *American Slavery.*

29 For an examination of the philosophical implications of Virginians' concept of independence, see Daniel J. Boorstin, *The Lost World of Thomas Jefferson* (Boston: Beacon Press, 1948), esp. 194–204.

30 Thomas Jones to Elizabeth Jones, October 27, 1736, Papers of the Jones Family: "Journal of Col. James Gordon of Lancaster County, Va.," *WMQ*, XI, (1903), 219.

31 For discussion and examples of visiting, see Philip Fithian to John Peck, August 12, 1774, in Farish, ed., *Journal of Fithian*, 217–21; "Journal of Gordon," *WMQ*, XI (1902–3), 98–112, 195–205, 217–36; XII (1903), 1–12. See also Zuckerman, "Byrd's Family," esp. 299–311.

32 Dr. T[heodorick] Bland to John Randolph, [c. 1770], Bryan Family Papers, microfilm from ViU at ViWC.

33 Robert Wormeley Carter Diary, May 25, 1769, typescript, ViWC.

34 Landon Carter, September 5, 1772 (Saturday), in Jack P. Greene, ed., *The Diary of Colonel Landon Carter of Sabine Hall, 1752–1778*, 2 vols. (Charlottesville: University Press of Virginia, 1965), vol. 2, 772.

35 Francis Taylor Diary, July 5, 1799, typescript, SHC-NCU.

36 Frederick Jones to Thomas Jones, February 10, 1765, Papers of the Jones Family.

37 See Edmund S. Morgan, *Virginians at Home: Family Life in the Eighteenth Century* (Williamsburg, Va.: Colonial Williamsburg, 1952), 30–4.

38 Jane Swann to Elizabeth Jones, September 7, 1757, and Samuel Swann to Thomas Jones, September 8, 1757, Papers of the Jones Family.

39 William Fitzhugh to Oliver Luke, August 15, 1690, in Richard Beale Davis, ed., *William Fitzhugh and his Chesapeake World 1676–1701* (Chapel Hill: University of North Carolina Press, 1963), 279. See also Catesby Cocke to Sister [Elizabeth] Jones, speaking of "those desirable purposes of making a decent provision for my children, & of finishing my days with as much peace as this world can afford" (September 1753, Papers of the Jones Family). Henry Fitzhugh to John Bland, 1764, Henry Fitzhugh Papers, NCD.

40 Henry Fitzhugh to Capt. Francis Thornton, April 1757, Henry Fitz-

hugh Papers. See also Richard Corbin to Messrs. Hanbury, June 18, 1760, Richard Corbin Letterbook, Richard Corbin Papers, ViWC.

41 Frederick Jones to Thomas Jones, June 5, July 7, 1758, Papers of the Jones Family. For a genealogy of the Jones Family, see *VMHB*, V (1897), 192–4.

42 Samuel Swann to Thomas Jones, July 7, 1758, and Frederick Jones to Thomas Jones, June 8, 1762. See also Frederick Jones to Thomas Jones, May 22, 1763, and January 10, 1765, Papers of the Jones Family.

43 Frederick Jones to Thomas Jones, January 23, 1770, ibid.

44 Walter Jones to Thomas Jones, April 4, 1767, ibid.

45 Thomas Jones to Walter Jones [c. 1760], and Thomas Jones to Walter Jones, March 10, 1770, ibid.

46 Thomas Jones to Elizabeth Jones, September 12, 1736, ibid.

47 The phrase is Edward Shorter's from *The Making of the Modern Family* (New York: Basic Books, 1975), 6. Shorter believes that the presence of "romantic love" in eighteenth-century New England and Virginia distinguished New World families from their more "traditional" European counterparts (65). Both Daniel Blake Smith, in *Inside the Great House: Planter Family Life in Eighteenth-Century Chesapeake Society* (Ithaca, N.Y.: Cornell University Press, 1980), and Philip Greven, in *The Protestant Temperament* (part four), describe an affectionate, intimate Chesapeake gentry family. It should be noted that Greven little concerns himself with change and eschews "modernization theory," whereas Smith embraces it and concludes that after 1750 "planter family life changed significantly" (21). Because his evidence is drawn, however, indiscriminately from both halves of the eighteenth century, Smith's contention that family life after mid-century became noticeably more affectionate is unpersuasive.

48 For the South, see Russell Lindley Blake, "Ties of Intimacy: Social Values and Personal Relationships of Antebellum Slaveholders" (Ph.D. diss., University of Michigan, 1978).

49 Elizabeth Ronald to Madam, May 21, 1775, Parker Family Papers, microfilm from Liverpool Record Office, ViWC.

50 William Fitzhugh to Henry Fitzhugh, April 22, 1686; William Fitzhugh to William Fitzhugh, January 30, 1686/7, in Davis, ed., *William Fitzhugh.*

51 John Clopton to William Clopton, September 31 [*sic*], John Clopton

Papers, NCD. See also Theo[doric]k Bland to Frances Randolph, September 26, 1777, Tucker-Coleman Papers, ViW.

52 For the implications of such a conceptualization of the ideal family life, see Sennett, *Public Man*, 89–107.

53 Landon Carter, July 25, September 3, 1774, in Greene, ed., *Diary of Carter*, vol. 2, 835–6, 856. For Carter's father, Robert "King" Carter, see Louis Morton, *Robert Carter of Nomini Hall: A Virginia Tobacco Planter of the Eighteenth Century* (Williamsburg, Va.: Colonial Williamsburg, 1941), chap. 1.

54 Landon Carter, July 6, 1766, in Greene, ed., *Diary of Carter*, vol. 1, 314–15. By Carter's own reckoning four years later, he was in debt "but a very trifle"; thus, he was teasing his son more than a little (July 19, 1770; ibid., 447).

55 July 19, 1770, and August 12, 1774; vol. 1, 447, and vol. 2, 848–9, ibid.

56 March 15, 1776, ibid., vol. 2, 1002; Robert Wormeley Carter Diary, August 25, 1766.

57 A succinct statement of the case for the traditionalism (and hence the social importance or "familialism") of the supposedly patriarchal southern family can be found in Bertram Wyatt-Brown, "The Ideal Typology and Ante-Bellum Southern History: A Testing of a New Approach," *Societas*, V (1975), 1–29. See also, typically, Eugene D. Genovese, *The Political Economy of Slavery: Studies in the Economy and Society of the Slave South* (1965; repr. New York: Random House [Vintage Books], 1967), 28: "The planters . . . set the tone of social life. Theirs was an aristocratic, antibourgeois spirit with values and mores emphasizing family and status, a strong code of honor, and aspirations to luxury, ease and accomplishment. In the planters' community, paternalism provided the standard of human relationships." See, similarly, Anne Firor Scott, *The Southern Lady: From Pedestal to Politics, 1830–1930* (Chicago: University of Chicago Press, 1970), 14–21.

58 William Ronald to James Parker, October 14, 1769, Parker Family Papers.

59 Edmund Randolph, "Mrs. Edmund Randolph," March 25, 1810, Edgehill-Randolph Papers, ViU. Randolph was aware that times and conventions had changed, that marriage had become – in the ideal, at least – more romantic.

60 Landon Carter, July 27, 1774, in Greene, ed., *Diary of Carter*, vol. 2, 837, 814–15.

61 Margaret Parker to James Parker, April 31, [*sic*], 1765, Parker Family Papers.
62 "C. Cibber, Jr." [after the British poet] to Benjamin Waller, July 2, 1746, Waller Collection, ViWC.
63 For example, William Byrd II, October 31, 1710, in Louis B. Wright and Marion Tinling, eds., *The Secret Diary of William Byrd of Westover, 1709–1712* (Richmond, Va.: The Dietz Press, 1941), 250–1.
64 See ibid., esp. 125–33. See also Zuckerman, "Byrd's Family," and Bertelson, *Lazy South*, chaps. 4–6.

2. RELIGION

1 Ellen W. Coolidge to Virginia Trist, June 24, 1828; Mary Jefferson Randolph to Ellen W. Coolidge, October 20, 1825; Cornelia Randolph to Ellen W. Coolidge, October 31, 1825, Ellen Wayles Coolidge Correspondence, ViU.
2 For this point, see Nancy F. Cott, *The Bonds of Womanhood: "Woman's Sphere" in New England, 1780–1835* (New Haven, Conn.: Yale University Press, 1977), esp. 98–100.
3 Wesley M. Gewehr, *The Great Awakening in Virginia* (Durham, N.C.: Duke University Press, 1930), 212–13; see also 203–12.
4 Ibid., 49. The statute was not, as a rule, strictly enforced.
5 See Lester J. Cappon, ed., *The Atlas of Early American History: The Revolutionary Era, 1760–1790* (Princeton, N.J.: Princeton University Press, 1976), 39, 118.
6 See Mary Beth Norton, *Liberty's Daughters: The Revolutionary Experience of American Women, 1750–1800* (Boston: Little, Brown, 1980), 184.
7 Philip Fithian, April 3, 1774, in Hunter Dickinson Farish, ed., *Journal and Letters of Philip Vickers Fithian, 1773–1774: A Plantation Tutor of the Old Dominion* (Williamsburg, Va.: Colonial Williamsburg, 1943), 119.
8 Philip Fithian to John Peck, August 12, 1774, ibid., 220.
9 Peter L. Berger, *The Sacred Canopy: Elements of a Sociological Theory of Religion* (New York: Doubleday, 1967), 32. For the relationship of religion to society, see also Peter Berger, Brigitte Berger, and Hansfried Kellner, *The Homeless Mind* (New York: Random House [Vintage Books], 1973).
10 Henry F. May, *The Enlightenment in America* (New York: Oxford

University Press, 1976), 67. For other recent revisions of the prevailing historical assumption that eighteenth-century Virginians were unchurched and indifferent to matters of religion, see Rhys Isaac, *The Transformation of Virginia, 1740–1790* (Chapel Hill: University of North Carolina Press for the Institute of Early American History and Culture, 1982), 58–68; Patricia U. Bonomi and Peter R. Eisenstadt, "Church Adherence in the Eighteenth-Century British American Colonies," *WMQ*, 3rd Ser., XXXIX (1982), 245–86.

11 Landon Carter, February 28, 1771, in Jack P. Greene, ed., *The Diary of Colonel Landon Carter of Sabine Hall, 1752–1778*, 2 vols. (Charlottesville: University Press of Virginia, 1965), vol. 1, 544; Greene, *Landon Carter: An Inquiry into the Personal Values and Social Imperatives of the Eighteenth-Century Virginia Gentry* (Charlottesville: University Press of Virginia, 1965), 35–36.

12 James Gordon, July 27, 1759, in "Journal of Col. James Gordon, of Lancaster County, Va.," *WMQ* XI (1902), 107; E. Ambler to [William Dabney], July 14, 1767, Charles William Dabney Papers, SHC-NCU; Frederick Jones to Thomas Jones, February 10, 1765, Papers of the Jones Family, DLC.

13 See Sydney E. Ahlstrom, *A Religious History of the American People* (New Haven, Conn.: Yale University Press, 1972), 366–8; May, *Enlightenment*, 136–43.

14 Norton, *Liberty's Daughters, 126–7.*

15 "Mrs. Edmund Randolph," by Edmund Randolph, March 23, 1810, Edgehill-Randolph Papers, ViU. See also Donald G. Mathews, *Religion in the Old South* (Chicago: University of Chicago Press, 1977), 11.

16 See Rhys Isaac, "Evangelical Revolt: The Nature of the Baptists' Challenge to the Traditional Order in Virginia, 1765 to 1775," *WMQ*, 3rd ser., XXXI (1974), 345–68. Also suggestive is Harold Perkin, *The Origins of Modern English Society, 1780–1880* (London: Routledge & Kegan Paul, 1969), 33–7.

17 Gewehr, *Awakening*, 47–51; Isaac, *Transformation*, 146–54. For the definition of "evangelicalism," see Mathews, *Religion*, xvi.

18 James Gordon, June 8, 1760, in "Gordon Journal," *WMQ* XI (1903), 200; Gewehr, *Awakening*, 71, 80, 122, 120–1.

19 Gewehr, *Awakening*, 212–13, and also 203–12; Isaac, *Transformation*, chap. 12.

20 Richard Hofstadter, *America at 1750: A Social Portrait* (New York:

Knopf, 1971), 292. See also the very relevant comments of Joyce Appleby in "Commercial Farming and the 'Agrarian Myth' in the Early Republic," *JAH*, LXVIII (1982), 848; and Perry Miller, "From the Covenant to the Revival," in James Ward Smith and A. Leland Jamison, eds., *The Shaping of American Religion* (Princeton, N.J.: Princeton University Press, 1961), 322–68.

21 Berger, *Sacred Canopy*, 28. Francis Taylor's diary records the denominational peregrinations of a nominal, although not devout, Episcopalian; in the 1790s, he attended services at Episcopal, Presbyterian, Baptist, and Methodist churches. Francis Taylor Diary, typescript, SHC-NCU. See also the diary of Louisa Holmes Cocke, Cocke Deposit, ViU. After hearing three sermons in one day, Mrs. Cocke exulted, "Oh, how sweet it is to feel oneself free from illiberal & sectarian feelings . . . & to participate with our fellow christians of other denominations in all the rich provisions of the gospel" (May 18, 1828).

22 Patrick Parker to James Parker, September 29, 1789, Parker Family Papers, microfilm from Liverpool Record Office, at ViWC. See also May, *Enlightenment*, 327–8, for the decline of skepticism.

23 C. H. Harrison to Susan I. Harrison, February 12, 1826, Harrison-Meem Collection, ViU; Edmund Ruffin to John Cocke, April 29, 1827, Cocke Deposit.

24 The quotation is a paraphrase of George Whitefield by Josiah Smith, in Alan Heimert and Perry Miller, eds., *The Great Awakening* (Indianapolis: Bobbs-Merrill, 1967), 5.

25 "Preamble and Constitution for Color'd Persons," May 1, 1830, Cocke Deposit; Peggy Nicholas to Jane H. Randolph, February 18, 1823, Edgehill-Randolph Papers. Henry May believes that "conversion to evangelical Protestantism can be seen as part of the assimilation of the old Virginian aristocracy and its offshoots to the bourgeois mores of the whole section" (*Enlightenment*,328).

26 John Clopton to John Bacon Clopton, January 19, 1806; November 23, 1807; January 13, 1810; February 20, 1808; Sarah Clopton to John Bacon Clopton, January 21, 1813; John Clopton to John Bacon Clopton, January 16, 1806, John Clopton Papers, NCD.

27 [John Bacon Clopton], Resolution, January 9, 1821, ibid.

28 Louisiana Hubard Diary [before September 14, 1831]; September 14, 1831; September 29, 1831; October 13, 1831, Hubard Family Papers, SHC-NCU.

29 Mathews, *Religion*, 41–2, 60–4; Isaac, "Evangelical Revolt."

30 See especially Donald G. Mathews, *Slavery and Methodism: A Chapter in American Morality* (Princeton, N.J.: Princeton University Press), 1965; and John C. Dann, "Humanitarian Reform and Organized Benevolence in the Southern United States, 1780–1830" (Ph.D. diss., College of William and Mary, 1975).
31 See Cott, *Bonds*, 64–74.
32 Wilson J. Cary to Virginia Cary, July 21, 1821; January 6, 1823, Carr-Cary Papers, ViU. For Wilson J. Cary, see Fairfax Harrison, *The Virginia Carys: An Essay in Genealogy* (New York: Devinne Press, 1919), 111–13.
33 Peter Bowdoin to Joseph Prentis, December 12, 1808, Prentis Family Papers, ViU; Catherine Ambler to John Jacquelin Ambler, September 4, 1823, Elizabeth Barbour Ambler Papers, ViU; Susanna Bowdoin to Joseph Prentis, January 10, 1825, Prentis Family Papers; Thomas Jones to Thomas Jones, Jr., June 19, 1785, Papers of the Jones Family; Eliza Custis to David Warden, June 6, 1829, Custis Family Papers, DLC.
34 Jane H. Randolph to Sarah Nicholas, November 1828, Edgehill-Randolph Papers.
35 May, *Enlightenment*, 66–9, 133–49.
36 Mary Terrell to Louisa H. Cocke, October 18, 1830, Cocke Deposit. See also Karen Horney's discussion of "The Meaning of Neurotic Suffering," in *The Neurotic Personality of Our Time* (New York: Norton, 1937), 188–206. Although I do not wish to suggest that early nineteenth-century Virginia culture was necessarily pathological, Horney's insights into the dynamics of masochistic thought and feeling are useful for understanding some Virginians of that period. Also valuable is Philip Greven, *The Protestant Temperament: Patterns of Child-Rearing, Religious Experience, and the Self in Early America* (New York: Knopf, 1977), for its exploration of the psychological bases of religious experience.
37 Sarah Andrews Diary, February 8, 1827, Papers of the Willis Family, microfilm, ViU.
38 Peter Lyons to Lucy Hopkins, May 22, 1807, Peter Lyons Papers, SHC-NCU; Elizabeth Williamson to Polly Farquharson, December 8, 1803, Galt Family Papers, ViWC; Sally Faulcon to John Cocke, January 21, 1817, Cocke Deposit. It should be mentioned that, by and large, the well-to-do Virginians under consideration here were Arminians, loosely speaking; that is, most believed that God offered salva-

tion to all and that the crucial issue was whether one would accept that offer. Although each denomination took a different stance on the efficacy of the individual will in gaining salvation, few Virginians seemed to worry about matters of theology. In fact, in the letters and diaries that I have read, I have seen no discussion of doctrine, yet an intense interest in (nondoctrinal) religion.

39 Sally Faulcon to Louisa Cocke, July 2, 1822; E. B. Kennon to John Cocke, March 26, 1817, Cocke Deposit.

40 John T. Dabney to Elizabeth T. Dabney, February 23, 1818; Mildred Lewis, Statement, September 30, 1829, Charles William Dabney Collection, SHC-NCU.

41 F. H. Allison to Margaret Coalter, July 15, 1797, Brown, Coalter, and Tucker Papers, ViW.

42 Although well-to-do Virginians worshipped together as various denominations, their personal writings convey little sense of religious community; they more often discussed their personal trials than church or shared religious life. Religion for poorer whites and slaves, as well, may have been less individualized and more communal. See Mathews, *Religion.*

43 See p. 45.

44 Sally Lacy to William A. Graham, June 14, 1819, Graham Family Papers, NCD; John Woodson to John Cocke, February 16, 1828, Cocke Deposit.

45 B. Meriwether to Virginia Carr and Lucy Ann Terrell, June 25, 1815, Terrell-Carr Papers, ViU; Paulina Legrand to Louisa Holmes, March 8, 1817, Cocke Deposit; Louisa Holmes Diary, October 27, 1816, Cocke Deposit; see also Ahlstrom, *Religious History*, esp. 373, 438–9; Joseph Nourse to Charles Joseph Nourse, June 17, 1817, Nourse and Morris Family Papers, microfilm, ViU.

46 [?] to Sarah Jackson [c. 1830], Robert Anderson Papers, ViWC; B. Meriwether to Virginia Carr and Lucy Ann Terrell, June 25, 1818, Terrell-Carr Papers; Martha Tabb Watkins Dyer Diary, July 1, 1823, ViU.

47 Elizabeth Carr to Lucy Ann Terrell [n.d.], Terrell-Carr Papers; Paulina Legrand to Louisa Holmes, March 8, 1817, Cocke Deposit.

48 Mary Chandler to John Cocke, January 22, 1821, Cocke Deposit; Sarah Nicholas to Jane H. Randolph, June 2, 1827, Edgehill-Randolph Papers; Ann B. Cocke to Judy Applewhaite, February 18, 1816, Cocke Deposit.

49 Lucy Smith to Louisa Cocke, June 9, 1824, Cocke Deposit.

3. DEATH

1 Thomas Jefferson to John W. Eppes, June 24, 1813, in Bernard Mayo, ed., *Jefferson Himself* (Charlottesville: The University Press of Virginia, 1942), 299; Dumas Malone, *Jefferson and His Time,* vol. 1, *Jefferson the Virginian* (Boston: Little, Brown, 1948), 396–7; Merrill D. Peterson, *Thomas Jefferson and the New Nation* (New York: Oxford University Press, 1970), 246–7.

2 Malone, *Jefferson the Virginian,* 396; Thomas Jefferson to Major John Cartwright, June 5, 1824, in Adrienne Koch and William Peden, eds., *The Life and Selected Writings of Thomas Jefferson* (New York: Random House [Modern Library], 1944), 174. Jefferson made this statement just two years before his death, but he expressed the same thought in almost the same language as early as 1789. See his letter to James Madison, September 6, 1789, as well as those to Rev. Samuel Knox, February 12, 1810, and to Samuel Kercheval, August 1, 1816 (Koch and Peden, *Thomas Jefferson,* 488, 599, and 674–6). Jefferson believed that the laws and constitutions made by previous generations could not bind the present one. He made the statement so often and so emphatically, however, that it may be taken as a more general philosophical principle.

3 Anne Blair to Martha Braxton, August 21, 1769, "Letter of Anne Blair to Martha Braxton," *WMQ,* XVI (1908), 179; Frederick Jones to Thomas Jones, January 10, 1765, Papers of the Jones Family, DLC; Robert Wormeley Carter Diary, July 15, 1766, typescript, ViWC. See also his entries for February 22, 1766, and July 7, 1766. See also "Journal of Col. James Gordon, of Lancaster County, Va.," September 10, 1760, and August 1, 1762, *WMQ,* XI (1903), 202 and 232.

4 William Byrd II, June 3–14, 1710, in Louis B. Wright and Marion Tinling, eds., *The Secret Diary of William Byrd of Westover, 1709–1712* (Richmond, Va.: Dietz Press, 1941), 186–91.

5 William Byrd II, January 3–24, 1710, in ibid., 125–33. William Byrd I had died in 1704.

6 William Lambert to Elizabeth Galt, October 8, 1797, Galt Family Papers, ViWC; Theodorick Bland to Frances Randolph, August 1, 1777, and Martha Bland to Frances Randolph, August 12, 1777,

Tucker-Coleman Collection, ViW; Thomas Jones to [Frederick Jones], [c. 1762], Papers of the Jones Family.

7 A. Hansford to Molly Craig, September 14, 1782, Galt Family Papers.

8 William Ronald to James Parker, October 14, 1769, Parker Family Papers, microfilm from Liverpool Record Office, ViWC. For a different reading of this passage and, more broadly, eighteenth-century Virginians' attitudes about death, see Daniel Blake Smith, *Inside the Great House: Planter Family Life in Eighteenth-Century Chesapeake Society* (Ithaca, N.Y.: Cornell University Press, 1980), 267–73. Smith notes Ronald's "commiseration": "It was very difficult for a parent to accept such a loss, Ronald noted, 'when deprived of those whose infant prattle and dawning reason . . . has deeply impressed their image in our Breasts'" (269). In omitting Ronald's comparison, Smith makes him seem more unqualifiedly sentimental and compassionate than he in fact was. See also Walter Jones to Thomas Jones: "When I heard of the Death of your youngest child I . . . received some comfort, that Heaven had spared those who had already endeared themselves to me –" July 23, 1769, Papers of the Jones Family.

9 Peter Fontaine to Brother Moses, April 17, 1754, in Ann Maury, *Memoirs of a Huguenot Family* (New York: Putnam, 1853), 343.

10 S. Norton to Frances Randolph, June 27, 1777, Tucker Coleman Collection; Landon Carter, April 25, 1758, in Jack P. Greene, ed., *The Diary of Landon Carter of Sabine Hall, 1752–1778,* 2 vols. (Charlottesville: University Press of Virginia, 1965), vol. 1, 221.

11 Rebecca Aitchison to Margaret Parker, March 4, 1785, Parker Family Papers. See also Wilson Blount to Charles Pettigrew, April 25, 1786, Pettigrew Family Papers, SHC-NCU.

12 Anne Washington to Hannah Washington, October 23, 1774, American Philosophical Society Miscellaneous Manuscripts, microfilm, ViWC; Martha Carr to [Lucy Terrell], March 15, 1795, Terrell-Carr Papers, ViU; Landon Carter, April 25, 1758, in Greene, ed., *Diary of Carter,* vol. 1, 221–2. See also George Washington to Elizabeth Custis, September 13, 1789, typescript included in Custis Family Papers, DLC.

13 Judith H. Tomlin to Virgilia Savage, August [1824], Brown, Coalter, and Tucker Papers, ViW; see also Philip Barraud to St. George Tucker, September 30, 1823, Letters of Dr. Philip Barraud to St. George Tucker, ViWC; Joseph Nourse to Charles Joseph Nourse, September 28, 1805, Nourse-Morris Family Papers, microfilm, ViU.

For nineteenth-century Virginians, statements about the uncertainty of life were almost clichés. See also William Waller to George Blow, May 24, 1822, Blow Family Papers, ViW, and Susan Bowdoin to Joseph Prentis, August 22, 1832, Prentis Family Papers, ViU. Historians have recently established that the life expectancy for Virginians was low in the seventeenth century – perhaps the mid-forties for adult men and women – but that it increased significantly in the eighteenth century – to around the mid-fifties; these figures are summarized in Smith, *Great House*, 44–5, 106–7. Whether there was any further change into the nineteenth century is unknown, although it seems unlikely that there was any change in life expectancy for the gentry significant enough to account for their heightened awareness of death. It is perhaps most useful to consider seventeenth-century Virginia as an unhealthy environment that routinely made widows out of women and orphans out of children, whereas Virginia during Jefferson's lifetime saw most children grow to a respectable age, although death before that time – particularly for infants – was quite common.

14 Susan Bowdoin to Joseph Prentis, March 10, 1826, Prentis Family Papers; [Louisa Holmes Cocke], Address to the Sabbath School, November 4, 1827, Cocke Deposit, ViU.

15 John Cameron to Duncan Cameron, August 2, 1803, Cameron Family Papers, SHC-NCU; Ann Tazewell to Sarah Skipwith, August 28, 1820, microfilm from Virginia State Library, ViWC; W. H. Cabell to Louisa Carrington, November 20, 1831, Cabell-Carrington Papers, ViU; D. Cary Barraud to John Cocke, January 1, 1830, Cocke Deposit; Peter Bowdoin to Joseph Prentis, March 24, 1823, Prentis Family Papers. For the American Puritans' attitudes about death, see David E. Stannard, *The Puritan Way of Death: A Study in Religion, Culture, and Social Change* (New York: Oxford University Press, 1977), esp. chap. 3. Philippe Ariès has found that ". . . in the nineteenth century, people scarcely believe in hell anymore; except half-heartedly – and then only for strangers and enemies, those outside the narrow circle of affectivity." *The Hour of Our Death* (New York: Knopf, 1981), 473.

16 Louisa Mercer to Frances Coalter, June 25, [1810], Brown, Coalter, and Tucker Papers; Eliza Custis to David Warden, September 7, 1825, and Eleanor P. Lewis to Mary Pinckney, February 10, 1804, Custis Family Papers.

17 Agnes Cabell to Louisa Carrington, December 28, 1826, Cabell-

Carrington Papers; L[elia] T[ucker] to Rebecca Cary, February 1, 1822, Carr-Cary Papers, ViU. See also Joseph Nourse to Anthony Morris, June 21, 1825, Nourse-Morris Family Papers, and Thomas Jefferson Randolph to John Smith, February 9, 1827, Edgehill-Randolph Papers, ViU, on the death of his son: "On his account we should not grieve, we have both seen that the Cares and afflictions of life, by far outweigh its pleasure."

18 Virginia Terrell to Lucy Ann Terrell, February 27, [1815], Terrell-Carr Papers, ViU; L[elia] T[ucker] to Rebecca Cary, February 1, 1822, Carr-Cary Papers.

19 George Blow to Scervant Jones, September 29, 1827, Blow Family Papers, ViW; Peachy Gilmer to John Cocke, February 12, 1830, Cocke Deposit. See, similarly, Peter Bowdoin to Joseph Prentis, Jr., January 22, 1825, Prentis Family Papers; [Bernard] Carter to John Cocke, May 13, 1809, Cocke Deposit; and George Blow to Richard Blow, September 12, 1828, Blow Family Papers.

20 Ann Barraud to Nancy Barraud, October 18, [1801], Cocke Deposit; Lavinia Brown to Capt. Henry Brown, November 6, 1822, Brown, Coalter, and Tucker Papers; St. George Tucker to Philip Barraud, October 20, 1826, Barraud papers II, ViW; Sally Faulcon to John Cocke, January 21, 1817, and E. B. Kennon to John Cocke, January 20, 1817, Cocke Deposit.

21 See John Thom to Joseph J. Lewis, July 21, 1822, Lewis Family Papers, microfilm, ViU: A woman who had died in childbirth had gone "to join that circle of Relations who enjoy the reward to good & virtuous actions in the Regions of everlasting *Beatitude.*" The nineteenth-century conceptualization of heaven as an eternal family reunion has been noted by Ariès (*Hour of Our Death*, 611) and by Ann Douglas ("Heaven Our Home: Consolation Literature in the Northern United States, 1830–1880," in David E. Stannard, ed., *Death in America* [Philadelphia: University of Pennsylvania Press, 1975], 49–68, and *The Feminization of American Culture* [New York: Knopf, 1977], chap. 6). Thus, such an image of heaven was widely shared; it was specific to neither a region nor a nation. Although often brilliant, Douglas's analysis can be perverse. She argues that the authors of consolation literature were women and ministers, two groups who had lost influence in nineteenth-century America and who hence sought "indirect and compensatory social control": They "were intent on claiming death as their peculiar property, one conferring on them a

special professional mission and prerogative: necessarily they wished to inflate and complicate its importance" ("Heaven Our Home," 55). Douglas has read politics into theodicy and assumed that power relations in a society shape and take precedence over the understanding of the meaning of life and death. Such a view of human existence and history seems narrow and reductionist; it is difficult to see how the "importance" of death could be either "inflated" or "complicated." If anything, the general trend over the past several centuries has been the opposite. See Ernest Becker, *The Denial of Death* (New York: The Free Press, 1973).

22 John H. Cocke Diary, November 8, 1816, November 23, 1816, and November 26, 1816, Cocke Deposit.

23 Ibid., November 29, 1816. For Cocke, see M. Boyd Coyner, "John Hartwell Cocke of Bremo: Agriculture and Slavery in the Ante-Bellum South" (Ph.D. diss., University of Virginia, 1961).

24 John H. Cocke Diary, December 5, 1816, Cocke Deposit.

25 Ibid., December 9, 1816.

26 Ibid., December 1816.

27 Ibid.

28 For a broader discussion of the ways in which modern men and women have confronted the possibility that death is without meaning, see Becker, *Denial of Death.*

29 These new rituals would become quite elaborate in the decades prior to the Civil War in both the South and the North. See James Nelson Kenworthy, "Selfishness or Individualism? The Emotional Life of Antebellum Americans" (Ph.D. diss., The University of Michigan, 1978), chap. 7, and Russell Lindley Blake, "Ties of Intimacy: Social Values and Personal Relationships of Antebellum Slaveholders" (Ph.D. diss., The University of Michigan, 1978).

30 Sarah E. Nicholas to Jane H. Randolph, April 1827, Edgehill-Randolph Papers; Sallie Cocke Faulcon to Ann Cocke, June 23, 1813, Cocke Deposit.

31 Louisa Holmes Cocke Diary, October 12, 1829, and November 22, 1829, Cocke Deposit.

32 Martha J. Terrell to Dabney C. Terrell, May 5, 1817, Terrell-Carr Papers; Joseph Nourse to Reverend Jno. M. Mason, July 30, 1805, Nourse-Morris Family Papers; Agnes Cabell to Louisa Carrington, Cabell-Carrington Papers. See also Susan Bowdoin to Joseph Prentis, December 1, 1815, Prentis Family Papers.

33 Philip Barraud to St. George Tucker, March 25, 1814; August 3, 1818; March 1, 1820; April 7, 1820; and July 7, 1821, Letters of Dr. Philip Barraud to St. George Tucker.

34 See Ariès, *Hour of Our Death,* part IV, for a discussion of "the death of the other."

35 John Cocke Diary, April 12, 1817, Cocke Deposit. Cocke retained his acceptance of death throughout the remainder of what would be a long life. See also James Morrison to Henry Brown, October 11, 1824, Brown, Coalter, and Tucker Papers.

36 Eliza Prentis to Joseph Prentis, November 15, 1807, Prentis Family Papers. See also Anthony Morris to James Pemberton, February 29, 1808, Nourse-Morris Family Papers.

37 Eleanor Parke Lewis to Mary Pinckney, January 17, 1800, Custis Family Papers; Bathurst Jones to Thomas Jones, January 11, 1797, Papers of the Jones Family; Judith H. Tomlin to Virgilia Savage, July 26, 1824, Brown, Coalter, and Tucker Papers.

38 Virginia Terrell to Lucy Ann Terrell, February 27, [1815], Terrell-Carr Papers; Peggy Nicholas to Jane H. Randolph, March 14, 1822, Edgehill-Randolph Papers; John Faulcon to John Cocke, April 18, 1817, Cocke Deposit; L[elia] T[ucker] to Rebecca Cary, February 1, 1822, and M[ary] H[arrison] to Virginia Cary, April 1, 1816, Carr-Cary Papers.

39 Sally Clopton to John Clopton, February 1, 1807, John Clopton Papers, NCD; [Rebecca Nourse?], September 29, 1822, Nourse-Morris Family Papers.

40 Lucy Smith to Louisa Holmes, July 30, 1815, Cocke Deposit; Thomas Bolling to his Parents, June 19, 1833, William Bolling Papers and Letters, NCD. See also Lucy H. Oliver to Newm. Williamson Barnes, September 30, 1824, ViW.

41 Thomas Williamson to Mary Farquharson, September 23, 1803, Galt Family Papers; Joseph J. Lewis, October 3, 1822, Lewis Family Papers.

42 Jean Cameron to Duncan Cameron, July 17, 1799; Mary Anderson to Duncan Cameron, October 12, 1799; John Cameron to Duncan Cameron, June 12, 1800; Mr. R. Anderson to Duncan Cameron, July 20, 1800; July 31, 1800; August 2, 1800; and November 8, 1801, Cameron Family Papers.

43 Jean Cameron to Rebecca Cameron, September 24, 1803; M. R. Anderson to Duncan Cameron, October 16, 1803, ibid.

44 D[abney] Carr to Dabney C. Terrell, May 30, 1817, Terrell-Carr Papers; [Wilson J. Cary to Virginia Cary], February 3, 1813, Carr-Cary Papers.

45 Eliza Parke Custis to Mr. Barlow, [1811], Custis Family Papers; Betsy Ambler to Miss Cairnes, March 1795 and [n.d.] 1800, Carrington-Ambler Letters, ViWC.

46 Ebenezer Pettigrew to Mary Shepard, November 19, 1830, and [fragment], December 6, 1830, Pettigrew Family Papers, SHC-NCU.

4. SUCCESS

1 Peachy R. Gilmer to John Cocke, April 24, 1824, Cocke Deposit, ViU.

2 Peter Fontaine to Brothers John and Moses, April 15, 1754, in Ann Maury, *Memoirs of a Huguenot Family* (New York: Putnam, 1853), 340–1.

3 J. H. Coles to Duncan Cameron, August 22, 1802, Cameron Family Papers, SHC-NCU; John Lewis to James Minor, January 5, 1807, James Minor Papers, ViU; Bathurst Jones to Thomas Jones, March 1799, Papers of the Jones Family, DLC.

4 Maria Armistead to Jane Armistead, April 9, 1789, Armistead-Cocke Papers, ViW; R[ichard] K. Meade to Brother [Everard Meade], April 12, 1785, Meade Family Correspondence, ViU. See also William P. Graham to Edward Graham, July 7, 1813, Graham Family Papers, NCD.

5 For republican ideology and contemporary thought about political economy, see Gordon S. Wood, *The Creation of the American Republic, 1776–1787* (Chapel Hill: University of North Carolina Press for the Institute of Early American History and Culture, 1969), part one; J. G. A. Pocock, *The Machiavellian Moment: Florentine Political Thought and the Atlantic Republican Tradition* (Princeton, N.J.: Princeton University Press, 1975), chap. 14; Drew R. McCoy, *The Elusive Republic: Political Economy in Jeffersonian America* (Chapel Hill: University of North Carolina Press for the Institute of Early American History and Culture, 1980), chaps. 1 and 2.

6 See Emory G. Evans, "Planter Indebtedness and the Coming of the Revolution in Virginia," *WMQ*, 3rd. ser., XIX (1962), 517–25; Bernard Bailyn, "Politics and Social Structure in Virginia," in James Morton Smith, ed., *Seventeenth-Century America* (Chapel Hill: Universi-

ty of North Carolina Press for the Institute of Early American History and Culture, 1959), 90–115.

7 For Ambler, see Chap. 1, 6–8. For the source of planter wealth, see James A. Henretta, *The Evolution of American Society, 1700–1815: An Interdisciplinary Approach* (Lexington, Mass.: Heath, 1973), 76–7; Aubrey C. Land, "Economic Base and Social Structure: The Northern Chesapeake in the Eighteenth Century," *JEH* 25 (1965), 639–54. See also Bailyn, "Politics and Social Structure," and Louis Morton, *Robert Carter of Nomini Hall: A Virginia Tobacco Planter of the Eighteenth Century* (Charlottesville: Va.: Dominion Books, div. University Press of Virginia, 1941; repr. 1964), chap. 1.

8 William Fitzhugh to Henry Fitzhugh, January 30, 1686/7, in Richard Beale Davis, ed., *William Fitzhugh and His Chesapeake World, 1676–1701* (Chapel Hill, N.C.: University of North Carolina Press, 1963), 192; John Smith to Edward Ambler, June 2, 1751, Elizabeth Barbour Ambler Papers, ViU. See also McCoy, *Elusive Republic*, chap. 1.

9 For Ambler, see Chap. 1, 6–8.

10 John Taylor to Wilson C. Nicholas, April 13, 1805; Peter Carr to Lucy Terrell, February 10, 1803, Edgehill-Randolph Papers, ViU. The availability of land in pre-Revolutionary Virginia enabled gentry parents to provide an estate or bequest for each son and daughter, whereas in Britain usually only the eldest son inherited his father's estate. See Bailyn, "Politics and Social Structure," 109–10; Daniel Blake Smith, *Inside the Great House: Planter Family Life in Eighteenth-Century Chesapeake Society* (Ithaca, N.Y.: Cornell University Press, 1980), 242–8. For the expectation that daughters, and not just sons, should share in their fathers' estates, see William Lewis, Jr., to William Lewis, Esq., December 8, 1804, Cabell-Carrington Papers, ViU.

11 See especially Paul Boyer and Stephen Nissenbaum, *Salem Possessed: The Social Origins of Witchcraft* (Cambridge, Mass.: Harvard University Press, 1974); Marvin Meyers, *The Jacksonian Persuasion* (Stanford, Calif.: Stanford University Press, 1957).

12 McCoy, *Elusive Republic*.

13 John Lewis to Gabriel Lewis, February 24, 1806, Lewis Family Papers, microfilm from the University of Chicago, ViU.

14 James O. Carr to Dabney S. Carr, June 11, 1819; D[abney] Carr to Dabney S. Carr, July 23, 1819, Carr-Cary Papers, ViU.

15 William C. Galt to Alexander Galt, May 12, 1793, Galt Family Papers, ViWC; John Ambler to John Jacquelin Ambler, August 1, 1823, Elizabeth Barbour Ambler Papers.

16 Richard Ambler to Neddy and Johnny, May 20, 1749, Elizabeth Barbour Ambler Papers; St. George Tucker to Theodorick Randolph, June 9, 1788, Bryan Family Papers, microfilm from ViU, ViWC; Sarah Kolcock to Mary Nash, February 10, 1804, Cameron Family Papers.

17 Joseph Prentis, Sr., to Joseph Prentis, Jr., July 5, 1805; March 5, 1806; May 24, 1806, Prentis Family Papers, ViU.

18 Joseph Prentis, Jr., to Joseph Prentis, Sr., May 22, 1807, September 6, 1808, ibid.

19 Philip Barraud to St. George Tucker, January 25, 1816, Letters of Dr. Philip Barraud to St. George Tucker, ViWC; Agnes Cabell to Louisa Carrington, February 17, 1823, Cabell-Carrington papers; Thomas P. Hunt to John Cocke, July 22, 1822, and Thornton Rogers to John Cocke, April 1823, Cocke Deposit; Sidney Carr to Jane Randolph, October 28, 1828, and Peggy Nicholas to Jane Randolph, October 29, 1829, Edgehill-Randolph Papers.

20 Larkin Smith to Littleton Waller Tazewell, August 17, 1804, Tazewell Papers, microfilm from Virginia State Library, ViWC. Peter Carr's lack of energy was noted by his brother; see D[abney] Carr to Lucy Terrell, April 26, 1798, Terrell-Carr Papers.

21 Joseph Prentis, Sr., to Joseph Prentis, Jr., August 10, 1808; Eliza Prentis to Joseph Prentis, [Jr.], July 13, 1810; June 15, 1830, Prentis Family Papers.

22 McCoy, *Elusive Republic*, 77–80.

23 James Greenhow to [Alexander Galt], July 18, 1792, Galt Family Papers; David Meade to Joseph Prentis, September 9, 1825, Prentis Family Papers (his son was then forty); Margaret Parker to James Parker, Parker Family Papers, microfilm from Liverpool Record Office, ViWC; Martha McGill to John Cocke, July 3, 1820, Cocke Deposit.

24 Ellen Wayles Randolph to Martha Randolph, [March 30, 1814], Ellen Wayles Coolidge Correspondence, ViU.

25 George Nicholson to James Parker, May 10, 1785; Rebecca Aitchison to James Parker, November 7, 179[1], Parker Family Papers. The cultural ideal of giving children estates may also be examined from the perspective of childrearing practices and notions. Both Philip Greven, in *The Protestant Temperament: Patterns of Child-Rearing, Religious*

Experience, and the Self in Early America (New York: Knopf, 1977), esp. 269–81, and Daniel Blake Smith, in *Inside the Great House*, esp. 50–4, argue persuasively that, in the eighteenth century, at least, gentry children were greatly indulged both by their parents and by the slave mammies who brought them up.

26 P[eter] Minor to James Minor, July 13, 1805, James Minor Papers, ViU; James McPheeters to John Coalter, April 21, 1768, Bryan Family Papers; Ellen Wayles Randolph to Martha Randolph, January 28, 1818, Ellen Wayles Coolidge Correspondence.

27 Martha Randolph to Ellen W. Coolidge, October 13, 1825, and November 26, 1825, Ellen Wayles Coolidge Correspondence. See Fairfax Harrison, *The Virginia Carys: An Essay in Genealogy* (New York: DeVinne Press, 1919), 115. Wilson M. Cary to Virginia Cary, January 1, 1828, Carr-Cary Papers.

28 Peggy Nicholas to Jane Randolph, February 3, 1830, Edgehill-Randolph Papers. The couple were married in 1831; see Harrison, *Virginia Carys*, 115.

29 Peachy R. Gilmer to John Cocke, April 11, 1821, Cocke Deposit. See Drew Gilpin Faust, *A Sacred Circle: The Dilemma of the Intellectual in the Old South, 1840–1860* (Baltimore: Johns Hopkins University Press, 1977), 9, for a fine description of student life.

30 Wilson Miles Cary to Virginia Cary, October 28, 1823, Carr-Cary Papers; P[eter] Minor to James Minor, January 15, 1806, James Minor Papers; Robert T. Hubard to E. W. Hubard, March 22, 1825, and October 6, 1828, Hubard Papers, SHC-NCU.

31 Philip St. George Cocke to John Cocke, May 16, 1830, Cocke Deposit. Young Cocke was at West Point. See also John Cocke, Jr., to John Cocke, Sr., May 1, 1822.

32 George Blow to Richard Blow, March 20, 1804, Blow Family Papers, ViW. See, similarly, Theodorick Randolph's denial that he had been gambling at college: Theodorick Randolph to St. George Tucker, September 10, 1789, Brock Collection, ViU.

33 George Blow to Richard Blow, July 18, 1816, and December 5, 1826, Blow Family Papers. See, similarly, William Prentis to Joseph Prentis, Sr., December 20, 1805, Prentis Family Papers.

34 George Blow to Richard Blow, September 21, 1819, and October 2, 1821; Richard Blow to George Blow, August 19, 1827; Robert Blow to George Blow, September 27, 1827, and May 7, 1828; Richard Blow to George Blow, April 21, 1828; Richard Blow to George Blow, June 15,

1828; George Blow, Jr., to George Blow, Sr., October 17, 1827, and March 8, 1829, Blow Family Papers.

35 Eliza Custis to David Warden, February 28, 1814, Custis Family Papers, DLC; Ezl. Bull to Maria Nourse, August 3, 1784, Nourse Family Papers, ViU; William Nelson, Jr., to Henry Tazewell, Tazewell Papers, George P. Stevenson to Dabney S. Carr, March 2, 1818, Carr-Cary Papers; Martha Terrell to Virginia Terrell, October 22, 1812, Terrell-Carr Papers; Sarah Clopton to Sons, January 21, 1813, John Clopton Papers, NCD. For a somewhat different view, see Eugene D. Genovese, *The Political Economy of Slavery* (1965; repr., New York: Random House [Vintage Books], 1967), esp. chap. 1.

36 James Hubard to [?], April 20, 1795; James Hubard to Susanna Hubard, August 25, 1805; James Hubard to Susanna Wilcox, November 30, 1807, Hubard Family Papers.

37 M. M. Robinson to John Cocke, October 4, 1828, Cocke Deposit; John A. G. Davis to Dabney Terrell, April 18, 1824, Terrell-Carr Papers.

38 B[ernard] Carter to John Cocke, April 8, 1810, Cocke Deposit; Tobias S. Collins to Dabney S. Carr, June 4, 1819, Carr-Cary Papers; Gideon Fitz to Elizabeth Fitz, September 22, 1808, George Carr Manuscripts, ViU; Balsora Barnes to Williamson Barnes, October 3, 1825, Barnes Papers, ViW.

39 Jno. Lewis to James Minor, January 10, 1806, James Minor Papers.

40 Frances Bland to Frances Randolph, [c. 1770–1], Tucker-Coleman Collection, ViW; [Thomas Moore] to [John Baylor?], John Baylor Papers, microfilm from ViU, ViWC; Robert Wormeley Carter Diary, June 6, 1774, ViWC. See also Wood, *Creation of the Republic*, 75.

41 The last sentence is a paraphrase of Joyce Appleby, "Commercial Farming and the 'Agrarian Myth' in the Early Republic," *JAH*, LXVIII (1982), 842–3. For agricultural and economic change, see Henretta, *Evolution of American Society*, 60–76, 200–1; Paul W. Gates, *The Farmer's Age: Agriculture, 1815–1860* (New York: Holt, Rinehart and Winston, 1960; repr. Harper & Row [Harper Torchbooks], 1968), chaps. 5 and 8; Robert P. Sutton, "Nostalgia, Pessimism, and Malaise: The Doomed Aristocrat in Late Jeffersonian Virginia," *VMHB*, LXXVI (1968), 41–2; Faust, *Sacred Circle*, 11, 156–7. Although primarily about Maryland's eastern shore, Paul G. E. Clemens, *The Atlantic Economy and Colonial Maryland's Eastern Shore: From Tobacco to*

Grain (Ithaca, N.Y.: Cornell University Press, 1980), chap. 6, is very useful.

42 Peter Bowdoin to Joseph Prentis, February 21, 1824, Prentis Family Papers; Thomas Mann Randolph to Thomas and William Randolph, November 29, 1785, Edgehill-Randolph Papers; Andrew Johnston to Francis Walker, February 2, 1790, Thomas Walker Papers in the William C. Rives Collection, microfilm, DLC; Thomas Jones to Bathurst Jones, [c. 1800], Papers of the Jones Family.

43 Edward Graham to William A. Graham, March 31, 1819, and February 11, 1820, Graham Family Papers; George Blow to Richard Blow, February 21, 1819, and September 7, 1819, Blow Family Papers; Frances Booker to Robert Anderson, July 21, 1828, Robert Anderson Papers, ViWC.

44 Joseph Lewis to Susanna Lewis, October 29, 1815; Joseph Lewis to Warner Lewis, February 14, 1817, Lewis Family Papers, microfilm, ViU. Lewis vacillated for several years but never moved from his farm.

45 John Faulcon to John Cocke, December 5, 1828, and December 26, 1828, Cocke Deposit.

46 Ibid., December 26, 1828. The great importance of horses to the gentry has been beautifully shown by Rhys Isaac, "Evangelical Revolt: The Nature of the Baptists' Challenge to the Traditional Order in Virginia, 1765 to 1775," *WMQ*, 3rd. ser., XXXXI (1974), 348–9, and T. H. Breen, "Horses and Gentlemen: The Cultural Significance of Gambling among the Gentry of Virginia," *WMQ*, 3rd. ser., XXIV (1977) 239–57. So greatly did John Cocke esteem his favorite mount, Roebuck, that when the horse died, Cocke had him buried, standing in full harness, at the family estate. E. M. Barraud, *The Story of a Family* (London: Research Publishing, n.d.), 45.

47 John Faulcon to John Cocke, December 26, 1828, Cocke Deposit.

48 John Faulcon to John Cocke, April 29, 1829, ibid. Faith in new beginnings has often been cited as typically American. See, in particular, D. H. Lawrence, *Studies in Classic American Literature* (New York: Viking Press, repr., 1961), chap. 1. See also T. H. Breen, "Of Time and Nature: A Study of Persistent Values in Colonial Virginia," in *Puritans and Adventurers: Change and Persistence in Early America* (New York: Oxford University Press), 164–96.

49 My rough estimate is that a diarist would mention his slaves perhaps

once a month, and then not to comment upon the institution but rather to discuss their health or work. Discussions of slaves or slavery were similarly infrequent in correspondence. Men wrote more often about slaves than did women, which might be expected, as slaves were primarily part of the business side of the plantation rather than the home.

50 Quotation from John Cocke to "My dear friend," September 23, 1831. For the accommodation to slavery, see especially Donald G. Mathews, *Religion in the Old South* (Chicago: University of Chicago Press, 1977), chap. 4. Historians have long debated whether antebellum southerners were comfortable with or agonized over slavery. In a reworking of Charles Grier Sellers's classic "The Travail of Slavery," in his *The Southerner as American* (Chapel Hill: University of North Carolina Press, 1960), 40–71, James Oakes has argued that southerners were consumed by guilt for the sin of slaveholding, so much so that they were almost obsessed by the fear that they would face eternal punishment in hell. See *The Ruling Race: A History of American Slaveholders* (New York: Knopf, 1982), chap. 4. My reading of the evidence suggests that Virginians used their religion to help them accommodate to slavery rather than to condemn themselves. Reasons for their fear of death have been offered in the previous chapter.

51 Wilson J. Cary to Virginia Cary, January 9, 1822, and February 15, 1822, Carr-Cary Papers; Richard Blow to George Blow, February 5, 1819, Blow Family Papers. Other references to the selling of slaves can be found in Thomas Nelson, Jr., to Edmund Berkeley, May 18, 1817, Berkeley-Barn Elms Papers, microfilm, ViU, ViWC; Charles Cocke to William Cocke, March 26, [17]90, Armistead-Cocke Papers; George Blow to Richard Blow, November 26, 1822, Blow Family Papers. Debt-ridden Virginians disposed of their extra slaves with both frequency and lack of emotion.

52 Tobias S. Collins to Dabney S. Carr, June 4, 1819, Carr-Cary Papers; Gideon Fitz to Elizabeth Fitz, September 22, 1808, and Gideon Carr to Brother and Sister, May 15, 1824, George Carr Manuscripts; Mary Randolph to Ellen W. Coolidge, March 18, [18]27, Ellen Wayles Coolidge Correspondence.

53 Agnes Cabell to Louisa Carrington, December 28, 1826; William H. Cabell to Louisa Carrington, December 25, 1827; Agnes Cabell to Louisa Carrington, May 25, 1824, and February 18, 1825; William H.

Cabell to Henry Carrington, April 3, 1828, Cabell-Carrington Papers.

54 John Mack Faragher, *Women and Men on the Overland Trail* (New Haven, Conn.: Yale University Press, 1979), esp. 163–8. See also Mary Beth Norton, *Liberty's Daughters: The Revolutionary Experience of American Women, 1750–1800* (Boston: Little, Brown, 1980), 14–16.

55 Virginia Trist to Ellen W. Coolidge, February 11, 1827; March 23, 1827; and March 19, 1828, Ellen Wayles Coolidge Correspondence. Nicholas Trist, of course, became a diplomat and achieved some prominence (or notoriety, depending upon the historian) during James Polk's administration. For women's reluctance to pull up their roots, see also Nancy Graham to William A. Graham, June 14, 1819, Graham Family Papers; Francis Eppes to Jane Randolph, November 13, 1828; and Jane Randolph to Sarah Nicholas, November 25, 1828, Edgehill-Randolph Papers.

56 Peggy Nicholas to Jane Randolph, April 11, 1819, and May 20, 1819; Cary Anne Smith to Peggy Nicholas, September 1819; Dabney S. Carr to Jane Randolph, December 5, 1824; Margaret Nicholas to Jane Randolph, February 5, 1825; Cary Anne Smith to Jane Randolph, July 24, 1826; [Sarah Nicholas] to Jane Randolph, February 23, 1827; Peggy Nicholas to Jane Randolph, January 19, 1829, Edgehill-Randolph Papers.

57 For women who sold slaves, see Susan Bowdoin to Joseph Prentis, February 16, 1810, Prentis Family Papers; and E. B. Kennon to John Cocke, January 20, 1817, Cocke Deposit. For women who sold their estates, see Samuel Jones to Susanna Hubard, July 5, 1813, Hubard Papers; and H[etty] C[arr] to Dabney Carr, April 6, [1818], Carr-Cary Papers. For women who sold their needlework, see E. Kennon to John Cocke, June 17, 1817, Cocke Deposit; and Sarah Nicholas to Jane Randolph, December 21, 1830, Edgehill-Randolph Papers. For women who took boarders, see Archibald Alexander to Martha Graham, November 9, 1813, Graham Family Papers; M. Hubard to Susanna Hubard, March 23, 1814, Hubard Family Papers; and Martha Harrison to John Cocke, August 12, 1826, Cocke Deposit. For women who taught, see [?] to Ann Anderson Camp, [c. 1823–33], Robert Anderson Papers; Lucy Ann and Martha Terrell, orphans, were teaching in Virginia homes. See Terrell-Carr Papers, c. 1814.

58 Cornelia Randolph to Ellen W. Coolidge, November 24, 1825, Ellen Wayles Coolidge Correspondence.

59 Dr. Augustine Smith Papers, [c. 1791], ViWC; Richard Terrell to Patsy and Nancy Minor, May 9, 1785, Terrell-Carr Papers; Thomas Mann Randolph to Ann Cary Randolph, May 1, 1788, Nicholas P. Trist Papers, microfilm from SHC-NCU at ViU. Contemporary notions of the proper education for young men and young women are ably discussed by Nancy F. Cott, *The Bonds of Womanhood: "Woman's Sphere" in New England, 1780–1835* (New Haven, Conn.: Yale University Press, 1977), chap. 3; and Norton, *Liberty's Daughters*, chap. 9.

60 John Cocke Diary, December 9, 1816, Cocke Deposit; John Lewis to Gabriel Lewis, October 26, 1807, Lewis Family Papers (from the University of Chicago).

61 Peggy Nicholas to Jane Randolph, March 22, 1819; Cary Anne Smith to Jane Randolph, August 26, 1827, Edgehill-Randolph Papers.

62 Ellen W. Coolidge to Virginia Trist, May 3, [18]29; Ellen Wayles Coolidge Autobiographical Papers, June 15, 1828, and July 13, 1828, Ellen Wayles Coolidge Correspondence.

63 Ibid.

64 Alexis de Tocqueville, *Democracy in America*, 2 vols., Henry Reeve text, revised by Francis Bowen, ed. by Phillips Bradley (New York: Knopf, 1945), vol. 2, 99.

65 Martha Hinton to John Cocke, December 1, 1828, Cocke Deposit; James McDowell to Frances Preston, September 8, 1820, Papers of the Carrington and McDowell Families, DLC; St. George Tucker to Theodorick and John Randolph, June 29, 1788, Bryan Family Papers. See, similarly, David Graham to William Graham, April 8, 1815, Graham Family Papers.

66 Martha Randolph to Nicholas Trist, March 7, 1822, Nicholas P. Trist Papers; George Blow to Richard Blow, July 18, 1816, Blow Family Papers.

67 Daniel Anderson to Duncan Cameron, January 16, 1804, Cameron Family Papers; Edward Graham to William A. Graham, October 18, 1819, Graham Family Papers.

68 Mary J. Randolph to Septimia Randolph, June 18, 1827, Septimia Randolph Meikleham Papers, ViU; Peter Bowdoin to Joseph Prentis, July 4, 1805, Prentis Family Papers; Eliza Custis to David Warden, January 14, 1818, Custis Family Papers, DLC; James O. Carr to Dabney Carr, August 2, 1818, Carr-Cary Papers; Thomas J. Ran-

dolph to W. C. Nicholas, February 4, 1815, Edgehill-Randolph Papers.

69 Robert Hubard to Edmund Hubard, November 11, 1828, Hubard Papers; John B. Peachy to Robert Anderson, July 31, 1825, Robert Anderson Papers; Ann Barraud to Ann Cocke, [1811], Cocke Deposit.

70 George Blow to Richard Blow, May 4, 1805; December 15, 1809, and July 10, 1810; Richard Blow to George Blow, September 15, 1812, and January 16, 1816; George Blow to Richard Blow, August 3, 1819, Blow Family Papers.

71 Ibid., April 17, 1821.

72 Ibid., April 17, 1819. Tocqueville, *Democracy in America*, II, 98. For an elaboration and critique of this tendency, see Richard Sennett, *The Fall of Public Man* (New York: Knopf, 1977).

73 Richard Blow to George Blow, December 28, 1822; George Blow to Richard Blow, November 10, 1828, Blow Family Papers.

74 John Cocke to Mrs. [Ann] Barraud, October 7, 1805, Cocke Deposit; Philip Barraud to St. George Tucker, September 6, 1807, Letters of Dr. Philip Barraud to St. George Tucker; John Cocke Will, 1817, Cocke Deposit.

75 John Cocke, Jr., to John Cocke, Sr., August 29, 1828, Cocke Deposit; Ellen W. Coolidge to Virginia Trist, May 3, [18]29, Ellen Wayles Coolidge Correspondence.

76 Ellen W. Coolidge to Virginia Trist, October 5, 1830; Martha Randolph to George Wythe Randolph, June 30, 1828, Ellen Wayles Coolidge Correspondence.

77 The limits of Virginian abolitionism in the early national era are described and analyzed by Robert McColley, *Slavery and Jeffersonian Virginia*, 2nd ed. (Urbana: University of Illinois Press, 1973), esp. chaps. 6 and 7.

78 Pocock, *Machiavellian Moment*; McCoy, *Elusive Republic*.

79 For a brilliant exploration of the meaning and function of the concepts of *Cavalier* and *Yankee* in American culture in the years between the Revolution and the Civil War, see William R. Taylor, *Cavalier and Yankee: The Old South and American National Character* (1961; repr., New York: Harper & Row [Harper Torchbooks], 1969). Also interesting is Robert Shallhope, "Thomas Jefferson's Republicanism and Antebellum Southern Thought," *JSH*, XLIV (1976), 529–56.

80 Beverley Kennon to John Cocke, July 3, 1828, Cocke Deposit.

81 See Chap. 2, 54. Peggy Nicholas thought Cocke guilty of "illiberality," which was quite an insult for a southerner.

82 Peachy Gilmer to John Cocke, June 14, 1827, Cocke Deposit. For similar language from Jefferson, see Shallhope, "Jefferson's Republicanism," 539.

83 Charles Mosby to John Cocke, June 26, 1827, Cocke Deposit.

84 John F. Caruthers to William Graham, October 6, 1817, Graham Family Papers. See also Mrs. S. Carter Gray to John Cocke, December 20, 1826, Cocke Deposit.

85 Nancy Graham to William A. Graham, June 14, 1819; William P. Graham to Aunt, July 30, 1813; Edward Graham to William A. Graham, December 13, 1819, Graham Family Papers.

86 William Hardress Waller to George Blow, July 6, 1814; Richard Blow to George Blow, October 27, 1816; George Blow to William Hardress Waller, May 24, 1821, Blow Family Papers. See also George Blow to William Hardress Waller, May 17, 1823. For a similar story of failure, in this case an almost inescapable circle of debt, despondency, and drink, see the letters of George Tennent to John Cocke, 1803-20, Cocke Deposit.

87 John Warwick to George Blow, March 28, 1818, Blow Family Papers; Sidney Carr to Jane Randolph, February 1, 1831, Edgehill-Randolph Papers. See also William H. Cabell to Mrs. Legrand, March 15, 1827, Cabell-Carrington Papers.

5. LOVE

1 Martha J. Terrell to Virginia Terrell, September 16, 1814; Lucy Ann Terrell to Virginia Terrell, July 24, 1814, Terrell-Carr Papers, ViU.

2 Jack P. Greene, ed., *The Diary of Colonel Landon Carter of Sabine Hall, 1752-1778* (Charlottesville: University Press of Virginia, 1965), vol. 2, 941. I am greatly indebted to Professor Rhys Isaac for pointing out this passage in Carter's diary. He, no doubt, will show how this reflection of the pre-Revolutionary planter is crucial to an understanding of Carter and his times in his forthcoming work on that topic.

3 Mrs. S. A. Pool to Louisa Cocke, October 29, 1827, Cocke Deposit, ViU.

4 J. H. Coles to Duncan Cameron, August 22, 1802, Cameron Family Papers, SHC-NCU.

5 Richard Sennett, *The Fall of Public Man* (New York: Knopf, 1977), 89–99.

6 See Lawrence Stone, *The Family, Sex and Marriage in England, 1500–1800* (New York: Harper & Row, 1977), part four; Randolph Trumbach, *The Rise of the Egalitarian Family: Aristocratic Kinship and Domestic Relations in Eighteenth-Century England* (New York: Academic Press, 1978).

7 See Daniel Blake Smith, *Inside the Great House: Planter Family Life in Eighteenth-Century Chesapeake Society* (Ithaca, N.Y.: Cornell University Press, 1980). For an excellent exploration of family dynamics among eighteenth-century genteel families, see Philip Greven, *The Protestant Temperament: Patterns of Child-Rearing, Religious Experience, and the Self in Early America* (New York: Knopf, 1977), 265–331. For an interesting discussion of what Virginians read, see Garry Wills, *Inventing America: Jefferson's Declaration of Independence* (New York: Doubleday, 1978), esp. part four; for the reading tastes of Americans generally, see David Lundberg and Henry F. May, "The Enlightened Reader in America," *AQ*, XXVIII (1976), 262–93; and Jay Fliegelman, *Prodigals and Pilgrims: The American Revolution against Patriarchal Authority, 1750–1800* (New York: Cambridge University Press, 1982). The tendency of the Virginia gentry to imitate their English counterparts is described in Louis B. Wright, *The First Gentlemen of Virginia* (1940; repr., Charlottesville: University Press of Virginia [Dominion Press], 1964.) The "mimetic" impulse of the colonial gentry is analyzed and put into a historic context in Jack P. Greene, "Search for Identity: An Interpretation of the Meaning of Selected Patterns of Social Response in Eighteenth-Century America," *JSocH*, LXXV (1970), esp. 205–20.

8 See Michael Zuckerman, "William Byrd's Family," *Perspectives in American History*, XII (1979), 253–311. In fact, Zuckerman finds Byrd *more* devoted to his public life in Virginia than when he visited in London, for in the New World "community had to be consciously constructed and purposefully fostered or scarcely exist at all" (306). Virginia's conditions, it is argued, dictated a different kind of social and family life compared to the mother country. Almost alone among those who have recently turned their attention to the early American and particularly the southern family, Zuckerman finds the southern

family significantly different from its British counterpart. Of course, southern historians have generally liked to consider the southern family as different in a feudal, patriarchal way, a position with which Zuckerman takes issue (298–9).

9 Rhys Isaac, "Evangelical Revolt: The Nature of the Baptists' Challenge to the Traditional Order in Virginia, 1765–1775," *WMQ*, 3rd ser., XXXI (1974), 353–62.

10 See Henry F. May, *The Enlightenment in America* (New York: Oxford University Press, 1976), 327–8; Donald G. Mathews, *Religion in the Old South* (Chicago: University of Chicago Press, 1977), chap. 4. Of course, as Philip Greven has ably shown, evangelical religion did not necessarily promote affection within the family. See his *Protestant Temperament*, part two.

11 See Peter L. Berger, *The Sacred Canopy: Elements of a Sociological Theory of Religion* (New York: Doubleday, 1967), and Ernest Becker, *The Denial of Death* (New York: The Free Press, 1973).

12 Alexis de Tocqueville, *Democracy in America*, Henry Reeve text, revised by Francis Bowen, ed. Phillips Bradley, 2 vols. (New York: Knopf, 1945) vol. 2, 98, 99. Becker, *Denial of Death*, 160ff. See also Philippe Ariès, *Centuries of Childhood: A Social History of Family Life*, Robert Baldick, trans. (New York: Random House [Vintage Books], 1972), 402–7.

13 The intensification of family life is an accepted premise that has not yet been adequately discussed by historians. Two recent biographies, albeit on somewhat distinctive families in the mid-nineteenth century, demonstrate admirably the ways in which parents and children could be intimately and intensely involved in each others' lives. See Jean Strouse, *Alice James: A Biography* (Boston: Houghton Mifflin, 1980), and David McCullough, *Mornings on Horseback* (New York: Simon & Schuster, 1981). For the assumption that "emotional ties between parents and children grew more intense," see Christopher Lasch, *Haven in a Heartless World: The Family Besieged* (New York: Basic Books, 1977), 5.

14 Patrick Parker to James Parker, June 29, 1786, Parker Family Papers, microfilm from Liverpool Record Office, ViWC. Patrick Parker was then twenty-three years old; his mother had died.

15 Ibid., February 9, 1787; March 20, 1787; May 1787.

16 Ibid., May 4, 1787.

17 Ibid., February 21, 179[?]; November 4, 1791; July 16, 1795. See also Chap. 2, 52.

18 Ibid., August 1, 1787.

19 Walter Jones to Thomas Jones, April 4, 1767, Papers of the Jones Family, DLC. See Chapter 1, 29.

20 Thomas Bolling to William Bolling, May 1821; May 22, 1824; November 28, 1825; August 8, 1826; and August 24, 1832, William Bolling Papers and Letters, NCD. Thomas Bolling was born in 1807.

21 Ellen W. Randolph to Martha J. Randolph, [July–September 1825]; July 28, 1819; March 30, 1814; Ellen Wayles Coolidge Correspondence, ViU. See also T D. Bennehan to Mrs. Bennehan, December 14, 1799, Cameron Family Papers, NCD.

22 George C. Thompson to George Thompson, October 16, 1821, Thompson Papers, MiU-C; Joseph Prentis, Jr., to Joseph Prentis, Sr., December 11, 1805, Prentis Family Papers, ViU; O. B. Barraud to John H. Cocke, Jr., November 31, 1823, Cocke Deposit, ViU. The young man's father recognized his son's social awkwardness: "Otway . . . seems to want to couple himself with a better half, but does not seem to know how, half as well the way to succeed in such an Enterprise as his Father has done before him." (Philip Barraud to St. George Tucker, August 13, 1827, Letters of Dr. Philip Barraud to St. George Tucker, ViWC).

23 Louisa Cocke to John Cocke, January 19, 1828; John Cocke, Jr., to John Cocke, Sr., December 29, 1829; Sally Faulcon to Louisa Cocke, November 11, 1822, Cocke Deposit.

24 St. George Tucker to Frances Coalter, October 3, 1810, Brown, Coalter, and Tucker Papers, ViW.

25 [Frederick Nash] to Mary Witherspoon, June 11, 1798, Cameron Family Papers; Eliza Blow to George Blow, June 26, 1826, Blow Family Papers, ViW.

26 D. Bryan to John Randolph Bryan, December 13, 1824, Bryan Family Papers, ViU.

27 See Chap. 1, 30–31.

28 F. H. A[llison] to Margaret Coalter, July 15, 1797, Brown, Coalter, and Tucker Papers; Robert Taylor to John Cocke, May 8, 1809, Cocke Deposit.

29 See Ariès, *Centuries of Childhood*. See also J. H. Plumb, "The New World of Children in Eighteenth-Century England," *Past and Present*,

LXVII (1974), 64–93; Stone, *Family, Sex, and Marriage*, chap. 9.

30 John Thom to Warner Lewis, September 30, 1814, Lewis Family Papers, microfilm, ViU.

31 Ebenezer Pettigrew to his sons, September 8, 1830, Pettigrew Family Papers, SHC-NCU. See, similarly, Martha Randolph to Virginia Randolph, April 23, 1819, Nicholas P. Trist Papers, microfilm, ViU; and J. Randolph to John Randolph, April 12, 1803, Bryan Family Papers.

32 Robert Saunders to John Cocke, August 17, 1821, Cocke Deposit.

33 Hetty Carr to Dabney S. Carr, December 21, 1817, and January 3, 1818, Carr-Cary Papers, ViU.

34 Ibid., March [1819].

35 Sennett, *Public Man;* Lasch, *Haven* and *Culture of Narcissism* (New York: Norton, 1979).

36 For the importance to women of the ideal of domesticity, see Mary Beth Norton, "Eighteenth-Century American Women in Peace and War: The Case of the Loyalists," *WMQ*, 3rd ser., XXXIII (1976), 386–409; Nancy F. Cott, *The Bonds of Womanhood: "Woman's Sphere" in New England, 1780–1835* (New Haven, Conn.: Yale University Press, 1977).

37 Randolph Harrison to John Cocke, August 2, 1822; Louisa H. Cocke Diary, December 10, 1830, Cocke Deposit. Bertram Wyatt-Brown's assertion that in the South "the prestige and power of the family as well as the possibility of acquiring property" were more important considerations in marriage than "mutual love and moral respectability" does not seem accurate for Virginia, at least. "The Ideal Typology and Ante-Bellum Southern History: A Testing of a New Approach," *Societas*, I (1975), 9–11.

38 Agnes Cabell to Louisa Carrington, January 16, 1823, Cabell-Carrington Papers, ViU; Peter Bowdoin to Joseph Prentis, April 5, 1816, Prentis Family Papers. See, similarly, Sarah Nicholas to Jane Randolph, March 27, [1826], Edgehill-Randolph Papers, ViU.

39 John Coalter to Maria Rind, July 4, 1790, and August 12, 1790; John Coalter to Michael Coalter, May [1790]; and John Coalter to Maria Rind, June 3, 1791, Brown, Coalter, and Tucker Papers.

40 John Coalter to Michael Coalter, May [1790], ibid.; John Addison Carr to Dabney S. Carr, March 9, 1818, Carr-Cary Papers; Joseph S. Lewis to Warner Lewis, November 1815, Lewis Family Papers. For the nineteenth-century's ideals of womanhood, see Barbara Welter, "The Cult of True Womanhood: 1820–1860," *AQ*, XVIII (1966), 151–74;

Cott, *Bonds of Womanhood*, 70ff., and her wonderful "Passionlessness: An Interpretation of Victorian Sexual Ideology, 1790–1850," *Signs*, IV (1978), 210–36. Cott errs, however, in assuming that her work on New England cannot be extended to the South. For a recent study that does not distinguish between northern and southern ideals, but rather assumes that notions of domesticity prevailed in both regions, see Carl N. Degler, *At Odds: Women and the Family in America from the Revolution to the Present* (New York: Oxford University Press, 1980), chaps. 1–5.

41 George W. Tennent to John Cocke, November 7, 1803, and December 11, 1803; John Coalter to Margaret Coalter, January 17, 1796, Brown, Coalter, and Tucker Papers. (Margaret Coalter was John Coalter's second wife, Maria Rind Coalter having died shortly after her marriage.) See also Francis Dabney to Mildred Dabney, July 1, 1815, Charles William Dabney Collection, SHC-NCU.

42 Mead Carr to Bernard Carr, April 8, 1829, Cocke Deposit; Thomas B. W. Gray to James Minor, May 26, 1807, James Minor Papers, ViU.

43 Charles J. Nourse to Rebecca Morris, May 1, 1815, Nourse-Morris Family Papers, microfilm, ViU.

44 W[ilson] J. Cary to Virginia Cary, January 9, [1822], Carr-Cary Papers; Thomas J. Randolph to Jane Randolph, January 30, 1826, Edgehill-Randolph Papers; [?] to Mrs. Louisa C. Lee, October 12, 1808, Teagle-Lee Papers, ViWC.

45 Edmund Randolph, "Mrs. Edmund Randolph," March 25, 1810, Edgehill-Randolph Papers.

46 William Byrd to Dear Cous[i]n Taylor, July 28, 1728, William Byrd II Letter Book I, 24, copy from Virginia Historical Society at ViWC.

47 Eliza Custis to David Warden, July 1, 1814, Custis Family Papers, DLC.

48 M[argaret] C[oalter] to John Coalter, May 10, [1795], Brown, Coalter, and Tucker Papers; Sarah Anderson Diary, May 6, 1827, and May 10, 1827, Papers of the Willis Family, microfilm, ViU.

49 Elizabeth Williamson to Polly Farquharson, December 8, 1803, Galt Family Papers, ViWC. Nancy Cott has found in New England a similar "withdrawal of emotional intensity from the too-burdened marriage choice" (*Bonds*, 80–1).

50 M[argaret] C[oalter] to John Coalter, May 10, [1795], Brown, Coalter, and Tucker Papers.

51 For examples of such characterizations of male and female nature, see

Nancy F. Cott, ed., *Root of Bitterness* (New York: Dutton, 1972), 115–16, 157–70. See also John S. Haller and Robin M. Haller, *The Physician and Sexuality in Victorian America* (Urbana: University of Illinois Press, 1974), 24ff. Such characterizations come from prescriptive literature, the preponderance of it northern. For a southern view, quite similar, see Virginia Cary, *Letters on Female Character* (Hartford, Conn.: H. Benton, 1831), eg., 14–15, 83, 86.

52 [Sarah Nicholas] to Jane Randolph, January 5, 1829, Edgehill-Randolph Papers; David Meade to Joseph Prentis, [July 1807], Prentis Family Papers.

53 Diary of Jane Gay Robertson Bernard, entries for 1825 (undated), ViW. See also Sally Lacy to William A. Graham, August 30, 1819, Graham Family Papers, NCD.

54 Louisa H. Cocke Diary, April 14, 1828, Cocke Deposit.

55 This point has been made most recently by Catherine Clinton, *The Plantation Mistress: Woman's World in the Old South* (New York: Pantheon, 1982), esp. chap. 9.

56 Cott, *Bonds of Womanhood*, 70ff; Linda K. Kerber, *Women of the Republic: Intellect and Ideology in Revolutionary America* (Chapel Hill: University of North Carolina Press for the Institute of Early American History and Culture, 1980), esp. 199–200

57 See Carroll Smith-Rosenberg, "Beauty, the Beast, and the Militant Woman: A Case Study in Sex Roles and Social Stress in Jacksonian America," *AQ*, XXIII (1971), 562–84.

58 Ann Cocke to John Cocke, February 9, 1811, and September 25, 1814, Cocke Deposit. Cocke's first marriage seems much happier than his second.

59 M[aria] A[rmistead] to Jane Cocke, April 26, 1793, Armistead-Cocke Papers, ViW; Agnes Cabell to Louisa Carrington, July 9, 1820, Cabell-Carrington Papers. See also Martha Carr to Lucy Terrell, August 9, 1794, Terrell-Carr Papers.

60 Tocqueville, *Democracy*, vol. 2, 99.

61 Otway Barraud to John Cocke, July 14, 1824, Cocke Deposit; Richard Terrell to Lucy Terrell, April 27, 1793, Terrell-Carr Papers; John Coalter to Margaret Coalter, January 21, 1796, Brown, Coalter, and Tucker Papers; Philip St. George Cocke to John Cocke, April 19, 1829; and Ann B. Cocke to John Cocke, October 10, 1825, Cocke Deposit.

62 Nancy Turner to Agness Alexander, October 26, 1810, Graham Fami-

ly Papers; M. E. Randolph Eppes to Jane Randolph, June 18, 1824, Edgehill-Randolph Papers; Fairfax Washington to William Cocke, February 21 [c. 1790–1820], Armistead-Cocke Papers.

63 Jane Randolph to Sidney Carr, December 10, 1826, Edgehill-Randolph Papers. See also Robert Anderson to Joseph Prentis, July 9, 1819, Prentis Family Papers.

64 John Clopton to John Bacon Clopton, February 16, 1816, John Clopton Papers, NCD.

65 Ellen Coolidge, undated autobiographical fragment, Ellen Wayles Coolidge Correspondence. For the replacement of religion by love, see Ernest Becker's provocative analysis of the work of Otto Rank: "Modern man fulfills his urge to self-expansion in the love object just as it was once fulfilled in God. . . . No wonder Rank could conclude that the love relationship of modern man is a religious problem" (*Denial of Death*, 161).

6. CONCLUSION

1 Martha Randolph to Ellen W. Coolidge, April 31 [*sic*], 1829, Ellen Wayles Coolidge Correspondence, ViU; Peggy Nicholas to Jane Randolph, February 3, 1830, Edgehill Randolph Papers, ViU. See, similarly, John Cameron to Duncan Cameron, February 3, 1830, Cameron Family Papers, SHC-NCU; Randolph Harrison to John Cocke, November 15, 1823, and March 17, 1826, Cocke Deposit, ViU; and Sidney Carr to Jane Randolph, October 28, [1828], Edgehill-Randolph Papers, ViU.

2 The gentry tradition of public service and its apotheosis in the Revolution are ably described by Rhys Isaac in *The Transformation of Virginia, 1740–1790* (Chapel Hill: University of North Carolina Press for the Institute of Early American History and Culture, 1982).

3 See Nancy F. Cott, "Passionlessness: An Interpretation of Victorian Sexual Ideology, 1790–1850," *Signs*, IV (1978), 219–36.

4 For example, John Demos, *A Little Commonwealth: Family Life in Plymouth Colony* (New York: Oxford University Press, 1970), 182–8; Mary P. Ryan, *Cradle of the Middle Class: The Family in Oneida County, New York, 1790–1865* (New York: Cambridge University Press, 1981).

5 For example, Daniel Scott Smith, "Family Limitation, Sexual Control,

and Domestic Feminism in Victorian America," *Feminist Studies*, I (1973), 40–57; Nancy F. Cott, *The Bonds of Womanhood: "Woman's Sphere" in New England, 1780–1835* (New Haven, Conn.: Yale University Press, 1977).

6 Diary of Jane Gay Robertson Bernard, November [1825], ViW.

7 See Alan MacFarlane, *The Family Life of Ralph Josselin: A Seventeenth-Century Clergyman* (1970; repr., New York: Norton, 1970), chap. 1.

8 Reverend Robert Rose Diary and Account Book, January 21, 1746, microfilm, ViU.

9 See Chap. 2, 45.

10 Louis B. Wright and Marion Tinling, eds., *The Secret Diary of William Byrd of Westover, 1709–1712* (Richmond, Va.: Dietz Press, 1941); Sarah F. Nourse Diary, Nourse-Morris Family Papers, microfilm, ViU. See also Maria Carter Copy Book, Armistead-Cocke Papers, ViW; Robert Bolling Commonplace Book, microfilm, ViU; "Diary of M. Ambler," *Virginia Historical Magazine*, XLV (1939), 152–70.

11 William Byrd, February 23, 1710, and December 3, 1709; Wright and Tinling, eds., *Diary of Byrd*, 145, 113.

12 Louisiana Hubard, "A Diary . . .," Hubard Papers, SHC-NCU; Louisa Holmes Diary, September 6, 1816, Cocke Deposit.

13 Sarah Andrews Diary, February 16, 1824, and November [1823], Papers of the Willis Family, microfilm, ViU.

14 Peter Berger, Brigitte Berger, and Hansfried Kellner, *The Homeless Mind: Modernization and Consciousness* (New York: Random House [Vintage Books], 1973), quotations on 77–8. For an excellent discussion of modernization and historians' attempts to use it as an explanatory device, see Michael Zuckerman, "Dreams That Men Dare to Dream: The Role of Ideas in Western Modernization," *Social Science History*, II (1978), 332–45.

15 Lawrence Stone, *The Family, Sex and Marriage: In England, 1500–1800* (New York: Harper & Row, 1977), esp. 257–69; Jay Fliegelman, *Prodigals and Pilgrims: The American Revolution against Patriarchal Authority, 1750–1800* (New York: Cambridge University Press, 1982).

16 Isaac, *Transformation*, 305. See chap. 13 for an excellent discussion of change in Virginia at the close of the eighteenth century. For increasing rates of literacy, see Kenneth A. Lockridge, *Literacy in Colonial*

New England: An Enquiry Into the Social Context of Literacy in the Early Modern West (New York: Norton, 1974), chap. 2.

17 Rhys Isaac, "Evangelical Revolt: The Nature of the Baptists' Challenge to the Traditional Order in Virginia, 1765–1775," *WMQ*, 3rd ser., XXXI (1974), 345–68.

18 See Philip Greven, *The Protestant Temperament: Patterns of Child-Rearing, Religious Experience, and the Self in Early America* (New York: Knopf, 1977), part two.

19 See Bernard Bailyn, "Politics and Social Structure in Virginia," in James Morton Smith, ed., *Seventeenth-Century America* (Chapel Hill: University of North Carolina Press, 1959), 90–115; Edmund S. Morgan, *American Slavery, American Freedom: The Ordeal of Colonial Virginia* (New York: Norton, 1975); and Isaac, *Transformation*, for several explanations of the Revolutionary impulse in Virginia.

20 For the changing status of the gentry, see Isaac, *Transformation*, chap. 13; for the growing pessimism of the gentry, see Robert P. Sutton, "Nostalgia, Pessimism, and Malaise: The Doomed Aristocrat in Late-Jeffersonian Virginia," *VMHB*, LXXVI (1968), 41–55; see also William R. Taylor, *Cavalier and Yankee: The Old South and American National Character* (New York: Harper & Row [Harper Torchbooks], 1957).

21 See Donald G. Mathews, *Religion in the Old South* (Chicago: University of Chicago Press, 1977), chaps. 3 and 4, as well as his earlier *Slavery and Methodism: A Chapter in American Morality* (Princeton, N.J.: Princeton University Press, 1965).

22 Willie Lee Rose, *Slavery and Freedom*, ed. William W. Freehling (New York: Oxford University Press, 1982), chap. 2. See also Mathews, *Religion*, chaps. 3 and 4; Winthrop D. Jordan, *White over Black: American Attitudes toward the Negro, 1550–1812* (Chapel Hill: University of North Carolina Press, 1968), 365–72; Isaac, *Transformation*, 308–10, and his work-in-progress on Landon Carter.

23 See particularly Cott, *Bonds of Womanhood*, esp. 64ff. Cott restricts her analysis to New England, yet the same notions of domesticity were shared and shaped by Virginians. See especially Virginia Cary, *Letters on Female Character* (Hartford, Conn.: H. Benton, 1831), and *Christian Parent's Assistant, or Tales for the Moral and Religious Instruction of Youth* (Richmond, Va.: Ariel Works, 1829). So interchangeable are Mrs. Cary's ideas and style with those of northern women that Cott mistakenly (but understandably) treats her as a

northern writer (see 67 and 71). Mrs. Cary adapted prevailing national notions about woman's character and sphere for her southern audience; thus, she advised her readers how to "mitigate the grievances of slavery to the unfortunate beings themselves [and how] to prevent the deleterious influence of their example on the domestic circle" (*Letters*, 194). Willie Lee Rose and Rhys Isaac have pointed to the softening of patriarchalism into paternalism as crucial in the "domestication" of slavery (see n. 22); a fuller view should take note of contemporary concepts of maternal influence as well.

24 Maria Carter to Maria Carter [her cousin], March 25, 1756, Armistead-Cocke Papers, ViW. See also Maria Corbin to Henry Tazewell: ". . . let me have a long letter, but let it be a merry one." (June 10, 1786, microfilm from Virginia State Library, ViWC.)

25 L[ucy] B. Randolph to Virginia Cary, March 4, 1826, Carr-Cary Papers, ViU; Maria B. Randolph to Polly Cabell, Brock Collection, microfilm, from the Huntington Library, ViWC.

26 Joseph Prentis, Sr., to Joseph Prentis, Jr., November 27, 1805, Prentis Family Papers, ViU. Surely one can understand why Prentis, Jr., would reply that his father's "affectionate epistle" moved him to tears (Prentis, Jr., to Prentis, Sr., December 18, 1805). Ellen W. Randolph to Martha J. Randolph, [March 1816], Ellen Wayles Coolidge Correspondence.

27 M[argaret] D[avenport] to F. Currie, [1794]; Louisa Mercer to Frances Coalter, October 15, [1812], Brown, Coalter, and Tucker Papers.

28 S[arah] T[rebell] G[alt] to Mary Galt, October 31, 1806, Galt Family Papers, ViWC; Harriet Anderson to Ann Camp (her aunt), December 1, 1808, Robert Anderson Papers; Mary Parker to James Parker, April 29, 1797, Parker Family Papers, microfilm from Liverpool Record Office, ViWC. For the age's growing fear of deception and concern for sincerity, see Fliegelman, *Prodigals and Pilgrims*, 240–2; and Lewis Kern, *An Ordered Love: Sex Roles and Sexuality in Victorian Utopias – the Shakers, the Mormons, and the Oneida Community* (Chapel Hill: University of North Carolina Press, 1981), 35ff.

29 John A. Carr to Dabney Carr, May 16, 1819, Carr-Cary Papers, ViU; George Minor to James Minor, April 8, 1803, James Minor Papers, ViU; Thomas ap T. Jones, May 10, 1808, Papers of the Jones Family, DLC; Mary Witherspoon to Frederick Nash, December 27, 1798, Cameron Family Papers.

30 Mary Randolph to Ellen W. Coolidge, October 30, 1826, Ellen Wayles Coolidge Correspondence.

31 Joseph Nourse to Maria Bull, February 10, 1784; Joseph Nourse to Maria B. Nourse, September 13, 1796; Maria Nourse to Joseph Nourse, September 22, 1796, Nourse-Morris Family Papers. See also Thomas Jefferson instructing his daughter, "Take care that you never spell a word wrong. . . . It produces great praise to a lady to spell well. I have placed my happiness on seeing you good and accomplished. . . ." (T. J. to Martha Jefferson, November 28, 1783, in Edwin Morris Betts and James Adam Bear, Jr., *The Family Letters of Thomas Jefferson* [Columbia: University of Missouri Press, 1966], 20.) See also Greven, *Protestant Temperament*, 289–90.

32 See Chapter 3, 99.

33 See, for suggestions, Ernest Becker, *The Denial of Death* (New York: The Free Press, 1973). Or consider, perhaps, Emerson's doctrine of "compensation."

34 Ellen W. Coolidge to Virginia Trist, November 1, 1829, Ellen Wayles Coolidge Correspondence.

35 Ibid., February 8, 1831.

Bibliographical essay

THIS BOOK, like all works of history, has grown out of the sources created by others. Manuscript letters and diaries are listed at the end of this essay. My understanding of these documents has been shaped by several important secondary works. What follows, thus, is not a comprehensive bibliography but rather an acknowledgment of certain intellectual debts.

Thanks to several outstanding works, we now have a good understanding of the dynamics of eighteenth-century Virginia history. Bernard Bailyn, "Politics and Social Structure in Virginia," in James Morton Smith, ed., *Seventeenth-Century America* (Chapel Hill: University of North Carolina Press, 1959), 90–115; Edmund S. Morgan, *American Slavery, American Freedom: The Ordeal of Colonial Virginia* (New York: Norton, 1975); and Rhys Isaac, *The Transformation of Virginia, 1740–1790* (Chapel Hill: University of North Carolina Press for the Institute of Early American History and Culture, 1982) share the virtue of placing Virginia's early history in its colonial context; both its British past and its American future are borne in mind. Also useful is Allan Kulikoff's summary of recent demographic findings in "The Colonial Chesapeake: Seedbed of Antebellum Southern Culture?" *JSH*, XLV (1979), 513–40. The picture is rounded out by two very different studies of important diarists and their milieus: Jack P. Greene, *Landon Carter: An Inquiry into the Personal Values and Social Imperatives of the Eighteenth-Century Virginia Gentry* (Charlottesville: University Press of Virginia, 1967), and Michael Zuckerman, "William Byrd's Family," *Perspectives in American History*, XII (1979), 255–311.

My focus, however, has been not so much upon what Virginia as a province was as upon what, in a democratic nation, it would become. Here, in defining democracy and suggesting its source and implications, Alexis de Tocqueville, *Democracy in America*, 2 vols., Henry Reeve text, revised by Francis Bowen, ed. by Phillips Bradley (New York: Knopf, 1945), is indispensable. More recent works of sociology, such as Peter L. Berger, *The Sacred Canopy: Elements of a Sociological Theory of Religion* (New York: Doubleday, 1967); Peter Berger, Brigitte Berger, and Hansfried Kellner, *The Homeless Mind: Modernization and Consciousness* (New York: Random House [Vintage Books], 1973); and Richard Sennett, *The Fall of Public Man* (New York: Knopf, 1977), are quite valuable for their descriptions and analysis of the modern world as it emerged in the nineteenth century.

One of the aspects of this transformation was a change in both religious sensibility and practice. Berger's *Sacred Canopy* provides a framework. For eighteenth-century Virginia, Isaac's *Transformation of Virginia* is unparalleled, and for the nineteenth, Donald G. Mathews, *Religion in the Old South* (Chicago: University of Chicago Press, 1977), is excellent. Both are exemplary in their sympathy with the religious longings of a different age. Wesley M. Gewehr, *The Great Awakening in Virginia* (Durham, N.C.: Duke

University Press, 1930), remains valuable, although it is largely supplanted by Isaac's book. The most useful survey of the Great Awakening may well be Richard Hofstadter's very brief one in *America at 1750* (New York: Knopf, 1971).

Because the religious sensibility of earlier times was so unlike today's, historians have often encountered difficulty in recapturing it; instead, religion is often reduced to a facet of politics, a topic more congenial to the modern mind. Such is the case with two important books: Ann Douglas, *The Feminization of American Culture* (New York: Knopf, 1977) and James Oakes, *The Ruling Race: A History of American Slaveholders* (New York: Knopf, 1982). Both argue that antebellum Americans (or in Oakes's case, just southerners) were led to inflate the importance of death by oppressive power relationships in their societies – northern women and ministers in compensation for their lack of power, or according to Oakes, southern planters in atonement for the sin of slaveholding. More useful models for understanding changing feelings about and perceptions of death are provided by Ernest Becker, *The Denial of Death* (New York: The Free Press, 1973); Philippe Ariès, *The Hour of Our Death* (New York: Knopf, 1981); and for colonial New England, David E. Stannard, *The Puritan Way of Death; A Study in Religion, Culture, and Social Change* (New York: Oxford University Press, 1977).

Because political and economic thought were closely entwined in the Revolutionary and early national periods, any discussion of attitudes toward success must begin with an understanding of the age's political notions. Important are Gordon S. Wood, *The Creation of the American Republic, 1776–1787* (Chapel Hill: University of North Carolina Press for the Institute of Early American History and Culture, 1969); J. G. A. Pocock, *The Machiavellian Moment: Florentine Political Thought and the Atlantic Republican Tradition* (Princeton, N.J.: Princeton University Press, 1975); Drew R. McCoy, *The Elusive Republic: Political Economy in Jeffersonian America* (Chapel Hill: University of North Carolina Press for the Institute of Early American History and Culture, 1980); and Joyce Appleby, "Commercial Farming and the 'Agrarian Myth' in the Early Republic," *JAH*, LXVIII (1982), 833–49. A different perspective, also useful, comes from Garry Wills, *Inventing America: Jefferson's Declaration of Independence* (New York: Doubleday, 1978). Daniel J. Boorstin, *The Lost World of Thomas Jefferson* (Boston: Beacon Press, 1948), is still exciting. It might be noted that the connection between a backward-looking classical republicanism and a more optimistic nineteenth-century liberalism has not yet been clearly established; it is, however, currently one of the most vital areas of historical inquiry.

The political economy of the South in the nineteenth century can better be understood by reading forward from the Revolution, as does James Oakes in *The Ruling Race*, than backward from the Civil War, as does Eugene Genovese, the object of Oakes's critique. In his influential *The Political Economy of Slavery: Studies in the Economy and Society of the Slave South* (1965; repr., New York: Random House [Vintage Books], 1967), Genovese misreads a southern aversion to certain types of moneymaking as a preference for aristocracy in both thought and deed. (It is instructive to remember, as does Richard Hofstadter in *The American Political Tradition and the Men Who Made it* [New York:

Knopf, 1948; repr. 1973] that Andrew Jackson was a southerner.) Oakes draws much of his information from middling planters and from the boom regions of the Southwest; thus, his conclusions are not entirely applicable to the elite inhabitants of the declining upper South. Both Oakes and Drew Gilpin Faust, *A Sacred Circle: The Dilemma Of the Intellectual in the Old South, 1840–1860* (Baltimore: Johns Hopkins University Press, 1977) suggest, in different ways, that region and class were important determinants of southern thinking. Notions of southern and northern distinctiveness are placed in a national context in William R. Taylor's unsurpassed *Cavalier and Yankee: The Old South and American National Character* (1961; repr., New York: Harper & Row [Harper Torchbooks], 1969), another book that works forward from the Revolution.

The history of the family, likewise, is best understood by proceeding from its colonial origins. Several studies of the European family are necessary for an understanding of the Virginia family; Lawrence Stone, *The Family, Sex and Marriage in England, 1500–1800* (New York: Harper & Row, 1977); Philippe Ariès, *Centuries of Childhood: A Social History of Family Life,* Robert Baldick trans. (New York: Random House [Vintage Books], 1962); and Randolph Trumbach, *The Rise of the Egalitarian Family: Aristocratic Kinship and Domestic Relations in Eighteenth-Century England* (New York: Academic Press, 1978). The eighteenth-century Virginia gentry family has been described by Daniel Blake Smith, *Inside the Great House: Planter Family Life in Eighteenth-Century Chesapeake Society* (Ithaca, N.Y.: Cornell University Press, 1980), which replaces Edmund S. Morgan, *Virginians at Home:*

Family Life in the Eighteenth Century (Williamsburg, Va.: Colonial Williamsburg, 1952). Smith's research, however, is undermined by flawed periodization, although Philip Greven, *The Protestant Temperament: Patterns of Child-Rearing, Religious Experience, and the Self in Early America* (New York: Knopf, 1977), shows that a history book may even reject periodization outright and still be rich and valuable. Michael Zuckerman, "William Byrd's Family," is an important challenge to the prevailing portrait of the Chesapeake gentry family as either a British clone or committed to affection above all else.

Recent works on the nineteenth-century southern family have ignored the findings of these students of the European and colonial southern family and have, instead, emphasized its supposed patriarchalism – which Bertram Wyatt-Brown (*Southern Honor: Ethics and Behavior in the Old South* [New York: Oxford University Press, 1982]) sees as a persistence from ancient times and Catherine Clinton (*The Plantation Mistress: Woman's World in the Old South* [New York: Pantheon, 1982]) as a sine qua non for slaveholding. Yet, other important works show that patriarchalism was not in the South a timeless absolute, but rather a term whose meaning and practice were undergoing an important transformation in the era of the American Revolution: see Willie Lee Rose, *Slavery and Freedom*, ed. William W. Freehling (New York: Oxford University Press, 1982, chap. 2); Jay Fliegelman, *Prodigals and Pilgrims: The American Revolution against Patriarchal Authority, 1750–1800* (New York: Cambridge University Press, 1982); and Isaac, *Transformation of Virginia*, chap. 13. All suggest, as does Nancy F. Cott in *The Bonds of Womanhood:*

"Woman's Sphere" in New England 1780–1835 (New Haven, Conn.: Yale University Press, 1977), that changes in political ideology and family relationships, as well as religion, may have been much more intimately connected than we have previously recognized.

A note on the sources

I HAVE been asked often enough about my "sample" to believe that a few words about my methods may be useful. A scientific sample would not be possible, even if it were desirable, because history itself, in preserving some letters and diaries while destroying others, has already, so to speak, tampered with the evidence. Historians have been left with a finite number of documents – a manageable number for the pre-Revolutionary period, but considerably more than a conscientious historian could (or would need to) read for the post-Revolutionary decades. Designing a sample of these documents in the way one would for the census or Harvard graduates would be intellectually deceptive, offering a false impression of certitude; because we do not know what history has destroyed, we cannot recover the population from which history's sample has been taken. The best that can be done is, first, to acknowledge that a certain amount of imprecision is inescapable in drawing conclusions from an incomplete record, and, second, to compensate for what we might suppose history's bias to have been. Letters and diaries were written, obviously, by the literate; they were the product, further, of men and women with the training, leisure, and desire to commit their thoughts and feelings to paper. Thus, this study is necessarily restricted to the gentry. We may also presume that archivists and descendants have been more inclined to preserve the papers of public figures than of less prominent men and women. Yet public service was an accepted norm of behavior for the gentry, so that a bias toward political life among the surviving documents should not present a particular problem: If anything, it should make even more significant my suggestion that the post-Revolutionary gentry were less committed to public service than their ancestors.

One question remains: If we cannot read all the documents that ever existed or even all those that have been preserved to this day, and a scientific sample is impossible, how do we know that a conclusion, based upon an inescapably incomplete record, is valid? This study is based upon thousands of letters and diaries, written by hundreds of men and women, a small fraction of the Virginia gentry but a large enough group to yield distinct patterns. I knew my research was complete when I was no longer surprised by what I read, that is, when newly discovered letters or diary entries fell into the patterns already suggested by others. This project has been designed to discover the patterns of thought and feeling in the past of a particular social class. Hence, although I have tried to make particular voices sound through, they are, in truth, members of a chorus.

I have also been asked why I have relied almost exclusively upon personal documents. On the one hand, there is no better source for uncovering the feelings of the past. The primary difficulty with manuscript sources is the matter of convention, which I have addressed in the Preface. On the other hand, the other major type of relevant document, prescriptive literature (including advice books, sermons, public speeches, and other similar published works), is fraught with problems. Works that told people how they ought to feel or behave do not tell us whether people followed such advice, or even whether they wanted to or could. Further, it is often difficult to ascertain whether advice literature was designed to serve particular class, ideological, psychological, political, or institutional ends; the current debate about the purpose and significance of nineteenth-century sexual advice manuals is a case in point. To be sure, studying such documents can answer important questions, but they are not within the scope of this study.

Selected bibliography

MANUSCRIPT LETTERS AND DIARIES

Library of Congress
The Papers of the Carrington and McDowell Families of Virginia
Custis Family Papers
Papers of the Jones Family
Thomas Walker Papers, in William C. Rives Collection, microfilm

William L. Clements Library, The University of Michigan
Forman Papers
Thompson Papers
Diary of Angelina Grimke Weld

Southern Historical Collection, University of North Carolina Library, Chapel Hill
Cameron Family Papers
Harrison Henry Cocke Papers
Charles William Dabney Collection
Hubard Papers
James Lyons Papers
Peter Lyons Papers
Pettigrew Family Papers
Francis Taylor Diary, typescript

Perkins Library, Duke University
William Bolling Papers and Letters
Robert Carter Papers
John Clopton Papers
Henry Fitzhugh Papers
Graham Family Papers

Selected bibliography

Manuscripts Division, University of Virginia Library

Elizabeth Barbour Ambler Papers, #1921 (on deposit)

Bell Family Papers, microfilm, #6688 (on deposit)

Leneaus Bolling Journal, microfilm, #3006a (on deposit)

Robert Bolling Commonplace Book, microfilm, #8708b

Bryan Family Papers, #3400

William Cabell Diaries and Memoranda Books, microfilm, #3119 (on deposit; used by permission of John H. Guy)

Cabell-Carrington Papers, #2447 (on deposit)

George Carr Manuscripts, #4869 (on deposit)

Carr-Cary Papers, #1231

Carrington-Ambler Letters, microfilm #6723 (also at the Colonial Williamsburg Foundation, Research Archives, as the Eliza Jacquelin Ambler Letters)

Cocke Deposit, John Hartwell Cocke Papers, #640

Ellen Wayles Coolidge Correspondence, #9090

Rev. John Craig Diary, microfilm, #1054 (on deposit)

Edgehill-Randolph Papers, #1397

John Wayles Eppes Correspondence, #1630 microfilm from Duke University

Diary of Ferdinando Fairfax, #1385 (on deposit)

Harrison-Meem Collection, #7661

Lewis Family Papers, microfilm, #1525

Lewis Family Papers, #2345 microfilm from the University of Chicago

Meade Family Correspondence, #10126b

James Minor Papers, #1214 (on deposit)

Wilson Cary Nicholas Papers, microfilm from the Library of Congress

Nourse-Morris Family Papers, #3490-D microfilm (on deposit)

Thomas Mann Randoph Letter, #7616

Septimia Randolph Meikleham Papers, #4726a & b

Rev. Robert Rose Diary, microfilm from the Colonial Williamsburg Foundation, Research Archives

John Ross Letter, #1185, microfilm

Philip Slaughter Diary, #6556b, c microfilm

Spooner, Eppes, Thweatt, Wilson Family Papers, #6574 microfilm (on deposit)

Terrell-Carr Papers, #4757, 4757a, b, d, e, f; 5670

Nicholas P. Trist Papers, microfilm from the Southern Historical Collection, University of North Carolina Library, Chapel Hill

Martha Tabb Watkins Dyer Diary, #7776d
Webb-Prentis Family Papers, #4136 etc.
Papers of the Willis Family, #8304a microfilm

Earl Gregg Swem Library, College of William and Mary
Armistead-Cocke Papers
Barnes Papers
Barraud Papers, I and II
Diary of Jane Gay Robertson Bernard
Blow Family Papers
Brown, Coalter, and Tucker Papers
Diary of Pleasants Murphy
Tucker-Coleman Collection

The Colonial Williamsburg Foundation, Research Archives
Robert Anderson Papers
American Philosophical Society Miscellaneous Manuscripts, microfilm.
Letters of Dr. Philip Barraud to St. George Tucker
Baylor Family Papers
John Baylor Papers, microfilm from the Alderman Library, University of Virginia
Berkeley-Barn Papers, microfilm from the Alderman Library, University of Virginia
Theodorick Bland Letters, microfilm from the Alderman Library, University of Virginia
Brock Collection, microfilm from the Huntington Library
Robert Wormeley Carter Diary, typescript
Richard Corbin Papers
Fontaine-Maury Papers
Galt Family Papers
Norton Papers
Parker Family Papers, microfilm from the Liverpool Record Office
Dr. Augustine Smith Papers
Charles Steuart Collection, microfilm from the National Library of Scotland
Tazewell Papers, microfilm from Virginia State Library
Teagle-Lee Papers
Waller Collection

Index

Aitchison, Billie, 124
Aitchison, Rebecca, 76, 124
Allison, F. H., 184
Ambler, Betsy (Elizabeth), 103
Ambler, John Jacquelin, 116
Ambler, Richard, 6, 111, 116, 117
Amelia County, Virginia, 139
Anderson, Harriet, 225
Anderson, Mary, 100–3
Andrews, Sarah, 214–15, 224
anger, 235 n27
Anglican Church, religion (Episcopal Church), 43–6, 50, 58, 60, 64, 66, 212, 219
  disestablishment of, in Virginia, 43, 49–50, 220
Ariès, Philippe, 246 n15, 247 n21, 249 n34
aristocracy, 8, 117, 172, 174, 187
Arminianism, 242 n38
Armistead, Maria, 203

Ball, Adeline, 191
Baptists (*see also* evangelical religion; Great Awakening), 49, 173
Barksdale, Mr., 123, 124
Barraud, John, 94–5
Barraud, Philip, 94–5
Becker, Ernest, 174, 248 n21, n28, 267 n65, 271 n33
Berger, Peter L., xvi
Bernard, Jane, 200, 211–12
Bland, Theodorick, 23
Blow, Eliza, 183
Blow, George, 80, 128–30, 157–9, 163, 166
Blow, George, Jr., 130
Blow, Richard, 142
Blow, Richard, Jr., 129–30
Blow, Robert, 129
Bolling, Thomas, 179–80, 184
Bowdoin, James, 189, 190
Breen, T. H., 255 n46, n48
Britain, 21, 110, 216–17, 219
  idealization of, 106, 111, 114, 261 n7
  notions of gentility in, 149, 172, 218, 219
Buchanan, William, 167–8
Byrd, William II, 11–15, 20, 38, 71–2, 99, 102, 107, 172, 195, 213–14, 261 n8

Cabell, Abram, 144
Cabell, Agnes, 79, 143–4, 204
Camm, John, 167
Carr, Dabney Smith, 114–15
Carr, Elizabeth, 67
Carr, Frank, 103
Carr, Hetty, 185–6, 187
Carr, James, 114–15, 156
Carr, Jane-Margaret, 125–6
Carr, John, 191
Carr, Martha, 76
Carr, Peter, 112, 121
Carter, Landon, 23–4, 32–6, 37, 45, 65, 75, 76, 170, 176, 187, 213
Carter, Maria, 223

Index

Carter, Robert Wormeley, 23, 32–6, 71, 135
Caruthers, John, 165
Cary, Virginia, 58, 194, 269 n23
Cary, Wilson Jefferson, 58, 141–2, 193
Cary Wilson Miles, 125–6
childhood, notions of, 74, 184–5, 219–20
children
  death of, pre-Revolutionary, 74–5
  death of, post-Revolutionary, 94–102
  and obligations to parents, pre-Revolutionary, 30–6
  and obligations to parents, post-Revolutionary, 174–186
  and success, 116–30, 133, 144, 152–5
Clinton, Catherine, 266 n55
Clopton, John, 31, 54, 208
Clopton, John Bacon, 54–6, 63
Clopton, Sarah, 54, 131
Coalter, John, 190–1
Coalter, Margaret, 199
Cocke, Ann (Nancy), 82–9, 94, 99, 150, 202–3
Cocke, Catesby, 9
Cocke, John Hartwell, 53, 62, 82–92, 96, 97, 102, 132, 139, 159–60, 163, 188, 249 n35, 255 n46
Cocke, John Hartwell, Jr., 160, 181–2
Cocke, Louisa Holmes, 77, 78, 241 n21
Cocke, Philip St. George, 127
Cocke, William, 9, 38
Cocke, William (son of John Hartwell), 126
Coles, J. H., 108
Coolidge, Ellen Wayles Randolph, 2, 40–2, 123–4, 148–9, 152–3, 160, 180, 208, 224, 229–30
commerce, 111–16, 122, 143, 161–2, 220, 222
Cott, Nancy F., 258 n59, 264 n36, n40, 265 n49, n51, 269 n23
conventions, in writing, xv, 31, 219
  about death, 70–1, 78–80, 86–9
  in diaries, 211–15
  about family, 204–5
  in letters, 223–9
  about love, 28–30, 36–7, 186, 193
  shaped by evangelical religion, 52, 59, 61
Custis, Eliza Parke, 196–7

Dabney, John, 62, 63
Davies, John, 132
debt, 109–11, 126–7, 139–41, 145, 147, 165, 177
Degler, Carl N., 264 n40
Deism, 41, 43, 46–7, 52
democracy, 41, 50, 61, 113–4, 173, 202, 217, 220
diaries, xiv–xv, 32, 83–9, 211–15, 255 n49
Douglas, Ann, 247 n21

economy, *see* Virginia, economy of
education, 154
  of men, 126–30
  of women, 149–50
emotion
  and evangelical religion, 51, 68, 81–2, 173, 214, 219–23
  expression of, pre-Revolutionary, 28–31, 36–8, 212, 217–19
  expression of, post-Revolutionary, 99, 102–3, 180–1, 205–6, 212, 214–29
  manipulation of, 183–6
England, *see* Britain
Enlightenment, 37–8, 52, 102
Europe, 171–2, 216–17
evangelical religion (*see also* sen-

Index

timental religion), 48–54, 220–1
and community, 57, 219–21, 243 n42
and diaries, 214
and emotion, 51, 68, 81–2, 173, 214, 219–23
and family, 262 n10
and slavery, 57, 141, 210, 221–2

family
modern, 30, 36, 210, 237 n47, 262 n13
notions of, 30–1, 36, 171–3, 176, 204–8, 219–20, 222
southern, 36, 238 n57, 261 n8, 264 n37
traditional, 30, 261 n8
Faulcon, John, 139–41, 151
Faulcon, Louisiana Cocke, 93, 139
Faulcon, Sally Cocke, 61, 62, 93
Faust, Drew Gilpin, 253 n29
Fithian, Philip Vickers, 15, 16
Fitzhugh, Henry, 26
Fitzhugh, William, 30–1, 136
Florida, 143–4
Fontaine, Peter, 12–14, 20, 75

Genovese, Eugene, 238 n57, 254 n35
gentry, definition of, xv
Gilmer, Peachy, 106–7, 111, 114, 117, 134, 164
Graham, Edward, 137, 155
Graham, William A., 165
Gray, Thomas, 192
Great Awakening, 49–51, 53, 173
Greene, Jack P., 261 n7
Greenhow, James, 122
Greven, Philip, 235 n27, 237 n47, 252 n25, 261 n7, 262 n10

Hampden-Sydney Coillege, 125, 129
Hanover County, Virginia, 48
Harrison, C. H., 52
Harrison, Polly, 188
Harrison, Randolph, 188
Harrison, Susanna, 52
Horney, Karen, 242 n36
horses, 139–41, 255 n46
hospitality, 22–3
Hubard, Dr. James, 131–2
Hubard, Louisiana, 56–7, 63, 214
Hubard, Robert, 127
Hubard, Susan, 132

independence, ideal of economic, 5, 12–15, 17, 108–11, 113–14, 116–20, 124, 128, 131, 134, 144, 151–2, 155, 161–2, 178
individualism, 5–6, 154–8, 164, 174, 187, 202, 204, 217, 229
Isaac, Rhys, 240 n10, 255 n46, 260 n2, 267 n2, 268 n16, 269 n22, n23

James, Henry, 2
Jamison, Neil, 122
Jefferson, Peter, 1
Jefferson, Thomas, xiii–xiv, 1–2, 39, 40–1, 69–70, 145, 148–9, 209, 244 n2, 271 n31
Jones, Bathurst, 96, 108
Jones, Dr., 121
Jones, Frederick, 24–8, 29, 46
Jones, Thomas (pre-Revolutionary), 28, 29, 72
Jones, Thomas (nineteenth-century), 136
Jones, Walter, 29

Kennon, Beverley, 162
Kentucky, 143–4, 147
King, John, 18–19

Lambert, William, 72
Lasch, Christopher, 187, 262 n13
Lawrence, D. H., 255 n48

Index

Lee, Col. Francis Lightfoot, 23
letters, xiv–xv, 223–8, 256 n49
Lewis, Eleanor Parke, 96
Lewis, John, 114, 134, 150
Lewis, Joseph, 99, 137–9, 141
Lewis, Mildred, 63
literacy, xiv, 217, 232 n3, 268 n16
Locke, John, 21
Lockridge, Kenneth A., 232 n3, 268 n16
Louisiana, 143, 145, 146–7
Luther, Martin, 48

McColley, Robert, 259 n77
McCullough, David, 262 n13
marriage
 pre-Revolutionary, 24–8, 36–7
 post-Revolutionary, 125–6, 188–204
Massachusetts, 19–20
Mathews, Donald G., 256 n50
May, Henry F., 241, n25
Meade, David, 200
Meade, Richard, 109
melancholy, 45–6, 99, 102–3, 165–8, 201–2, 214–15, 224
men, notions of, 56, 199, 265 n51
merchants, 111, 114–15
Methodists (*see also* evangelical religion; Great awakening), 49
migration, 143–7
Minor, Peter, 124, 127
Missouri, 143
moderation, *see* restraint
modern presonality, 214–17
modernization, 268, n14
money lending, 111
Monticello, xiii, 148, 193
morality
 and piety, 55–7
 pre-Revolutionary, 18–21
Morris, Samuel, 48
mortality, 77, 246 n13

New England, 4, 43, 162, 212
Nicholas, Peggy, 145–7, 151
Nicholas, Robert, 146–7,
Nicholas, Sarah, 58, 89–92, 199
Nicholas, Wilson, 146–7
Nicholas, Wilson Cary, 145–7
Norfolk, Virginia, 175–6
north, northern United States, 43, 143, 160–4, 191, 222
Norton, Mary Beth, 258 n59, 264 n36
Nourse, Charles, 192–3
Nourse, Joseph, 94, 227
Nourse, Maria Bull, 227–8
Nourse, Sarah, 213

Oakes, James, 256 n50

Panic of 1819, 137, 157
parents
 and death of children, 98–102
 and love of children, 174–86
 and marriage of children, 188–9
 and obligations to children, pre-Revolutionary, 25–30, 251 n10
 and obligations to children, post-Revolutionary, 144, 152, 154–5
 and training of children, 116–24, 128–30, 133
Parker, James, 175–9, 189
Parker, Patrick, 175–9
Peachy, John, 156
Pettigrew, Ebenezer, 104–5
planting, idealization of, 114, 133, 135–6, 138
Prentis, Eliza, 96, 121–2
Prentis, John, 121–2
Prentis, Joseph, 119–21
Prentis, Joseph, Jr., 119–22, 181
Prentis, Mary Ann, 121–2
Presbyterians, (*see also* evangelical

Index

religion; Great Awakening), 48–9, 129
Protestantism, 170
public life and service, 31, 157–8, 171–3, 187, 188, 209–10, 267 n2
Puritanism, 4, 43, 78, 163

Randolph, Cornelia, 2, 148, 151
Randolph, Edmund, 36–7, 47, 52, 195, 196
Randolph, Ellen, *see* Coolidge, Ellen Wayles Randolph
Randolph, Frances Bland, 72, 73
Randolph, George, 148
Randolph, Jane, 206–7
Randolph, Maria, 224
Randolph, Martha Jefferson, 40, 154, 160–1, 209
Randolph, Mary, 2, 148
Randolph, Thomas Jefferson, xiii–xiv 2–3, 145, 156, 193, 209–10
Randolph, Thomas Mann, 2, 40, 136, 150, 152
reading, 172, 217, 261 n7
reciprocity, ideal of, 22–30
republicanism, republican ideology, 5, 11, 110, 112, 113, 116, 202, 210, 220–1
restraint of emotions, 10–11, 17, 19, 22, 36–8, 48, 65, 72–3, 102, 170–2, 181, 212–14, 218–20, 222–3, 226
Revolution, American, 43, 49, 161–2, 175, 210, 220–1, 269 n19
Rind, Maria, 190
Ronald, William, 74
Rose, Robert, 213
Rose, Willie Lee, 269 n22, n23
Ruffin, Edmund, 52–3

self-reliance, 63–4, 117–18, 155–6, 164, 166–7
Sellers, Charles Grier, 256 n50
Sennett, Richard, 171–2, 174, 187, 238 n52, 259 n72
sentiment, 30, 141, 216–29
sentimental religion (*see also* evangelical religion)
  and death, 77–81, 89, 96, 207, 223
  and emotion, 173, 214
  and work, 54–9
  and women, 56–8
sex roles, *see* women
Shallhope, Robert, 259 n79
Shorter, Edward, 237 n47
slaves, slavery, 135, 138, 216, 255 n49
  accommodation to, 113, 221–2, 256 n50,259 n77, 269 n23
  as dependents, 5, 12, 15, 17, 21, 110
  and religion, 53, 55, 221–2, 243 n42
  selling of, 140–3, 147, 256 n51
Smith, Daniel Blake, 237 n47, 245 n8, 247 n13, 253 n25, 261 n7
Smith, John, 112
Smith, Larkin, 121
Smith, Lucy, 98
south, southerners (*see also* family, southern), 36, 113, 141, 159–64, 191
speculation, land, 111
Stevens, Wallace, xvi
Stevenson, George, 131
Strouse, Jean, 262 n13
Suffolk, Virginia, 119
Swann, Jane, 24–7
Swann, Samuel, 24–7
sympathy, 169–70, 172, 207, 217, 219, 222, 226

Tayloe, Rebecca, 23
Taylor, Francis, 241 n21
Taylor, John, 112
Taylor, William R.,259 n79
Tennent, George, 191, 260 n86
Tennessee, 143

Index

Terrell, Lucy Ann, 169–72, 187
Terrell, Martha, 94, 131, 169
Terrell, Richard, 149
Terrell, Virginia, 169
Thompson, George, 181
Thornton, Francis, 26
tobacco, 5, 111–13, 132, 135
Tocqueville, Alexis de, 153–4, 158, 174, 187, 204, 210
Toleration, English Act of, 48–9
Trist, Nicholas, 144–6, 257 n55
Trist, Virginia Randolph, 2, 144–5
Tucker, Lelia, 79
Tucker, St. George, 117, 154, 182
Turner, Nat, rebellion, 56

University of Virginia, 125, 129

violence, 15–21
Virginia
  economy of, 134–7, 157, 175, 177, 216–22
  history of, 4–6, 47–51, 216–19
  population of, 235 n26
virtue, 11, 114, 119, 128, 153, 163, 202, 209–10

Waller, Hardress, 167–8
Washington, D.C., 145
Washington family, 206
Weber, Max, 216
Welter, Barbara, 264 n40
whites, poor, 5, 18, 21, 48–9, 138, 220, 235 n25, 243 n42
William and Mary, College of, 125, 128, 157
Williamsburg, Virginia, 119
Williamson, Elizabeth, 198
Williamson, Frederick, 100
Williamson, Thomas, 99
Wirt, Agnes, 94
women
  idealization of, 196, 264 n40
  notions of, 199, 265 n51
  and politics, 209–11
  and religion, 47, 50, 56–8, 201
  and sex roles, 41, 188, 201–2, 203–4, 222, 264 n36, 269 n23
  and work, 147–52
world, grim image of, 51, 58–9, 64–5, 78–81, 165, 173, 186, 196, 204, 207, 210
Wyatt-Brown, Bertram, 238 n57, 264 n37

Zuckerman, Michael, 261 n8, 268 n14